HORACE'S SCHOOL

Theodore R. Sizer

HORACE'S SCHOOL
Redesigning the
American High School

HOUGHTON MIFFLIN COMPANY
Boston   New York   London
1992

Copyright © 1992 by Theodore R. Sizer
All rights reserved

For information about permission to reproduce selections from
this book, write to Permissions, Houghton Mifflin Company,
215 Park Avenue South, New York, New York 10003.

Library of Congress Cataloging-in-Publication Data

Sizer, Theodore R.
  Horace's school : redesigning the American high school / Theodore
R. Sizer.
      p.   cm.
  Includes bibliographical references (p.   )
  ISBN 0-395-57230-4
  1. High schools — United States.   2. Education, Secondary —
United States — Aims and objectives.   I. Title.
  LA222.S544   1992   91-869
  373.73 — dc20   CIP

Printed in the United States of America

AGM 10 9 8 7 6 5 4 3 2 1

For my wife, Nancy;
and for our children, Tod and Rebecca, Judy, Hal and Lyde;
and especially for Susan and Jim,
and for Cally, Lyde, Teddy, Julie, and Nicholas —
members of our family new since
Horace Smith first joined us

Contents

Contents

Introduction

FOR CONTEMPORARY AMERICANS, the process of growing up and the act of "going to high school" are profoundly intertwined. Graduation is a major rite of passage, and other rituals of school, from attending senior prom to taking examinations for admission to college, have become totems within the cultures of most communities, many of which depend on their high schools to define them.

Some Americans, among them the politically influential, believe that the schools are inept, their students ill prepared for life. The nation will not successfully compete in the contemporary world, they argue, unless its citizenry is better educated. The schools must change, and substantially.

The early 1990s are witnessing the confrontation of two forces: the protection of the culturally important and remarkably stable form of secondary education that Americans have shared for almost a hundred years and the press for new and more efficient forms of schooling. Will we yield local authority to the state and national governments? Will we give up funding Friday night basketball in order to offer advanced calculus? Will we discard the notion that everyone deserves to graduate at the age of eighteen and insist that students demonstrate their learning in order to receive a diploma? Will we demand that all must learn, or will we accept that only those who want to learn or whom we expect to learn will in fact succeed?

Because the pitch for reform is high, and political reputations are tuned to it, we know that there will be changes. High schools serve all citizens, and the values and habits they are mandated to instill are of moment to us all.

Since the late 1970s my colleagues and I have studied and worked with American high schools; recently we assisted them in shaping a new design, one that respects the best traditions of secondary schooling, yet acknowledges that we must do better in readying adolescents, for their sake and ours. *Horace's School* presents this design.

As with my earlier book, *Horace's Compromise,* the story depends in some measure on the device of nonfiction fiction. Franklin High School, Horace Smith, and his committee members are fictitious, but I know them all. Franklin is a composite of many schools I have visited; I have heard the members of Horace's committee saying the substance of what is here, though not always in the precise words you will read. Likewise, several of the descriptive anecdotes are constructed from multiple experiences I have had. The device, I trust, carries its own sort of authenticity.

Of course Franklin is not every school. It is not set in what Americans call the ghetto, nor is it in a rural area. It is a public school. Unlike many suburban high schools, it has a relatively diverse population. Many of its students aspire to college, but not all. Its politics are dominated by white Americans, but issues of race and class and ethnicity are in the air. It is as close to a "typical" school as I could describe, a place with a good local reputation but newly infected with self-doubt. Franklin is the kind of school that does not make the newspapers; it is familiar, so full of conventional practices that it is not noteworthy. We drive past Franklin High School every day on the way to work and never notice it.

While Horace's committee arrived at a design for its school that is consistent with the ideas of the Coalition of Essential Schools, with which I am associated, the design is not presented as the only model for an Essential School. We in the coalition devoutly believe that there is no one best model, that each school must be shaped by its own people and must respect the community it serves. We share ideas rather than models; we believe that these convictions should be apparent in the functioning of our schools, even as the ways in which we choose to express these ideas differ from school to school and from year to year.

In telling Franklin's story and in examining the process that led to its new design, I hope to define the coalition's ideas of what better schools should be. I am in debt to many friends in the Essential School movement: their reforms have influenced me and their support has sustained me. This book is not a report on the coalition, nor is it a detailed research study. It is an argument, an exercise of informed opinion. I hope that the account of the happy struggles of Horace's committee will aid us in serving our adolescents, and ourselves, with better schools.

Theodore R. Sizer
Brown University
June 1991

Goals

By the year 2000, all children in America will start school ready to learn . . . The high school graduation rate will increase to at least ninety percent . . . Students will leave grades IV, VIII, and XII having demonstrated competence in challenging subject matter, including English, mathematics, science, history, and geography . . . They will be prepared for responsible citizenship, further learning, and productive employment . . . U.S. students will be first in the world in science and mathematics . . . Every school will be free of drugs and violence and will offer a disciplined environment conducive to learning.

— from the education goals established by the president and the governors at the Charlottesville summit meeting on education, 1990

I want my children to succeed in school, to know they succeeded, and to feel good about that. I want the school to like my children, to know them, and to appreciate them as I appreciate them, to help them and to believe in them as individuals. I want the school to be safe and to be fair, for my children and for other children. I want my children to be content with school, confident, and part of a nice group of friends. I want the school to ready my children for the future, to give them real options for what follows after graduation. I want the school to help my children grow up to be happy, prosperous, and decent citizens.

— a parent

I am somebody.

— a student

HORACE'S SCHOOL

1
Horace's Compromise

MEET HORACE SMITH, fifty-nine, a veteran English teacher at Franklin High. Among parents and graduates, he is widely considered a star faculty member of this inner suburban high school of 1350 pupils. Certainly he is respected by his colleagues; they find him the professional's professional, even to a fault. While many of the faculty who are his age are already considering retirement, thanks to the state's generous annuity plan, Horace is not. He believes — perversely, he often thinks — that Franklin High is not nearly what it could be. He wants to stay on and make it better.

The good light in which the community sees the school is not deserved, he feels. Franklin is a caring place, but the kids worry Horace. Many are lively, well intentioned, and adept at cranking out acceptable test scores, but they are without the habits of serious thought, respectful skepticism, and curiosity about much of what lies beyond their immediate lives. They lack assurance, skill, and interest in confronting the stuff of Franklin's curriculum and committing their God-given minds to strenuous use.

Sure, they rack up lists of "extracurriculars" to dazzle university admissions officers, but even when they show a dash of substance, too many of them lack style, that gossamer quality which separates the interesting person from the conventional one. They get top grades on the English Advanced Placement exams, but never read a serious piece of fiction outside or beyond school. They score high on the social studies tests, but later will vote for political candidates on impulse, if they vote at all.

The kids play a game with school, making deals with us, striking bargains. What will be on the test, Mr. Smith? Will this count in the grade, Mr. Smith? How many pages must this be, Mr. Smith? When do we have to read this by, Mr. Smith? If we do this, will you ease up on that? They all ought to be ambassadors, Horace thinks, wheeler-dealers striking bargains and making treaties. However, the treaties will be ones to lessen work, lessen the pain of thinking anew, lessen anything that may get into the way of having a happy time after school. Treaties to protect the Good Life. Horace snorts at himself: What a cynic I am. Aren't we adults that way too, excessively so? What are all of us coming to?[1]

Many of Horace's colleagues find his criticism harsh, but he persists. We do not know the half of what these kids can do, he contends. But, his friends retort, can one school turn them around? The whole society is soft. The kids' culture is defined by MTV and cravings created by national merchandisers. Even their parents do not want the school to change much. Get Susie into a good college, they say. And if we do, they love us. If we do not, they blame us. But *style*? Come on, Horace.

Horace understands the familiar lament. And he knows that Franklin hasn't many of the searing problems swamping the nearby city schools. For kids in those schools, there's not even a question of developing style; sheer survival is their task. He also remembers the exceptional kids he taught who did have fresh, inquiring, informed minds, and thoughtful hearts too. Why can't we have more kids like those, he wonders. Schools can help shape them, or at the least encourage those happy tendencies. Why must schooling, and its typical products, be so mindless? It need not be so. And though the culture out there may be inattentive, the school — even Franklin High School — can do something about it.

That, Horace knows, is a presumption. Who are teachers to

set standards? Who says that they have a corner on wisdom? Horace worries about this. The schools should reflect what the culture wants, and if the culture is careless, then the schools can be careless.

But, then, what is the role of the teacher? Merely to be the agent of the culture? No, Horace says, we must try to be better than that. And, contrary to conventional wisdom, most parents are our allies. What they want, at heart, is more than a ticket for their offspring to a prestigious college. They want that, yes, but they want more; and it is by an alliance of aware and demanding teachers, parents, and adolescents that a better school can be molded, a thoughtful place to teach thoughtful young citizens.

A thoughtful place. Horace hesitates on this, because he knows from decades of experience that Franklin is, if nothing else, unexamined. Like most high schools, it just rolls on, fettered by routines of long standing. The result is a cacophony of jumbled practices, orchestrated only by a complex computer-driven schedule whose instrument is a bell system and whose ushers are assistant principals.

The faculty itself, he muses, is hardly thoughtful about its own situation. The status quo is never challenged. We have curriculum committees that talk only about revising the accepted subjects, never pondering what the curriculum could be. We have committees on schedule changes that never ask the basic questions about the uses of time. We "restructure" while assuming that all the existing building materials and architectural commitments — physical and intellectual — will remain as they are.

Horace knows that the status quo *is* the problem. It forces him to compromise in ways that cripple his teaching, his ability to create thoughtful students. Compromises are always necessary in the real world, Horace admits; and the issue, then, is which compromises will serve the students best. Only by examining the existing compromises, however painful that may be, and moving beyond them to better compromises, can one form a more thoughtful school. And only in thoughtful schools can thoughtful students be hatched.

Horace's complaints are many and fundamental. It would be

3

easier if the system were basically sound, but the lamentable truth is that it is not, and that the complex routines of schools are all related. Question one, and you question all.

Take Horace's student load. Officially it should be 120, five classes of twenty-four students each, the "contract ratio" for English teachers. This year it is 132. Horace's courses are popular, and he has difficulty saying no to eager kids, particularly those who have studied with him before. Horace knows that he should insist on a writing assignment from every one of those youngsters every day, or at least every other day, and that he should promptly read, comment on, and return these papers. But with 120? Impossible. Spending just five out-of-class minutes per week looking at the work of each student and, at least once a month, talking privately with the youngster would total ten hours — ten hours of enervating work, two hours every evening, Monday through Friday, week after week. And this in addition to all the rest he has to do outside those contact hours in class with the kids, not to mention his evening work at the family's liquor store to help meet the household bills. So, like most English teachers, he does not do the careful reading and criticizing he knows is so valuable for students.

Accordingly, Horace recognizes that he does not know many of his kids well enough to understand really how their minds work, how and why they make mistakes, what motivates them, what stars they seek to reach or whether each hankers after a star at all. Yes, most are acquaintances; they hail him in the hallways. But does he know them well enough to teach them powerfully, know the ways of their minds and moods? No, not even close. Horace compromises. He gets to know a few students well, usually those who interest him especially or who press themselves to his attention. The kids in the middle remain a genial blur. Indeed, Horace wryly admits most of them cherish their anonymity. If Mr. Smith really knows me, then he'd find out that . . .

During the school day, the students come to Horace by "classes," ninth grade, tenth grade, and the rest. A student is in a particular class on the basis of her or his birthday. To be out of step, sixteen in the ninth grade or fourteen in the eleventh grade, is cause for comment, usually contemptuous. Dummy. Nerd. One of *those* kids. The assumption behind the system is that kids of the same age are essentially alike, more or less teachable in the same ways and properly held to similar standards. Franklin High School splits each grade into three lumps, honors, college prep, and regular, as well as special needs. But the prevailing, and overwhelming, characterization of students is by grade level. Teachers ask, *What's your name? What grade are you in?* The answers provide the two critical labels. Because all the kids in each grade have experienced, it is presumed, the same number of hours of schooling, they should, save at the extremes, all know the same things.

Horace knows better. Young people grow intellectually, physically, and socially at different rates, often with mysterious spurts and stops along the way. Both doting parents and cool-eyed researchers know that. Some kids excel at language and flounder in mathematics; the hotshot in one area is not necessarily great in another. Further, not all kids pay attention at school at any given moment, for benign or deplorable reasons. So by their high school years the youngsters' potential and actual school performance often diverge: "ninth grade" is an administratively useful concept, but one that tells a teacher far less about a student's intellectual and emotional development than the grouping would suggest.

One copes, however, largely by not being careful, by deliberately not attending to the record and specialness and stage of growth and disposition of each youngster. They are all *ninth-graders*. Treat them the same — same curriculum, same textbook, same pedagogy, same tests, same standards, same everything.

It defies common sense, Horace knows. Age grading hurts some kids, swelling the heads of those who appear, for whatever obvious or mysterious reasons, to be "swift" and humiliating the "slow." Pigeonholing honors, regular, and special needs students sets up the self-fulfilling prohecies. *Oh no, Mr. Smith, I couldn't take AP English. I'm not an honors student . . .* Every year Horace sees the swift kid who plugs hard, with the confidence of being perceived as honors quality, and the slow youngster who ignores his talents, giving up, acting up, not caring, finding school a place of unrelieved and anticipated failure.

Franklin High School uses plenty of public relations talk about "taking each child individually," but the school's practices belie the boast. For example, there is virtually no attempt, Horace ruefully recalls, to get thorough information to a student's new teacher about the youngster's history in school. Students do have files someplace, Horace knows. Teachers don't read them, though, and are not encouraged to do so. In any event, there are too many to absorb. May as well treat 'em all the same. Or accept someone else's judgment about how swift a kid is, and go with it. Expect more, or expect less. Compromise with your common sense: the kids are different, but we can't admit it, even to ourselves.

The curriculum does not help. Franklin High School has a statement of goals, but it is as vague as it is hortatory and conventional. The goals connect only rhetorically with the formal Course of Study. The latter is laid out by course and grade and is usually cast as a list of ideas, classics to be read, facts, skills, procedures, and qualities of character to be admired, opportunities to stock one's mind. Simply, the curriculum, however artfully described, is a listing of what the *teachers* will do, what "things" the kids will be "exposed" to. The students remain invisible, lumped in their age-graded cohorts, ready to watch the teachers' parade of things.

Horace knows this is backward. What counts is what the students do, as Horace has learned from the Theater Club plays he directs. The members know what the "target" is. Others find targets in some of the more imaginative Advanced Placement courses. But there are few such compelling ends in view in the core curriculum; the destinations are clearly cast in terms of what the students should be able to do. Except for aiming to help students pass the tests, the formal Course of Study Guide says little about what the material *means*. We teachers are "to cover" the Lake poets, and the students should then be able to answer questions about them. How the students are to *use* the experience is not addressed. This is as depressing as it is confusing, but Horace continues to compromise. We will all read *Hamlet* during the spring term, and there will be one test for all eleventh-graders . . .

Franklin's "goal statement" talks of graduates able to "function in society and the economy as useful citizens." Horace would put that as "making sense of the world." Either way, it assumes that Franklin alumni will see which issues are of consequence to themselves and others, will be competent to analyze these situations, to sort them out, and will be both able and disposed to do something about them. Some would say that this means that graduates should be interested in learning and practiced in teaching themselves, able to figure out their world and motivated to do something about it.

Fine, Horace thinks. But how is the school's curriculum organized? By subjects, most of which are poorly defined and each of which is planned in almost total isolation from the others. The stuff of these subjects is offered up to students in fifty-two-minute slivers of time, rapid fire.

Horace wonders whether this gives kids practice in making sense of the world. Even the teachers in the English Department can't agree on what their subject really is; the mathematics sequence has no planned connection with science courses; and the teachers of literature, art, music, and drama pay attention only to each art separately. Making sense is tough even for adults; despite its goal statement, Franklin gives students little practice in the craft. Indeed, the high school's presentation of the curriculum guarantees superficiality.

These realities sting Horace, but he goes along. He compromises. The faculty doesn't like to hear any sort of fundamental criticism. We're tired of being the butt of all the griping, they say. Furthermore, this list of subjects is what the colleges want. A likely story, Horace thinks. Do the colleges want kids schooled in intellectual chaos?

Give a little, get along, compromise. Yes, sometimes there is electricity in the classrooms, but not often enough. The kids compromise too, taking what is offered, observing that to which they are exposed, more or less cranking out the tests, and then forgetting most of it. Feeling good is important, not only about oneself but also about the school. Franklin Pride.

HORACE'S SCHOOL

Horace remembers a devilish experiment that a visiting consultant recently suggested: give students a test they took twelve to fifteen months earlier, and see how they perform. What had they retained? Horace winces at the thought. Kids forget so much so quickly. It is better that school accentuate the immediate, the stuff of the last unit, rather than instill intellectual habits. Horace plays the game too. Last year's English is expected to be gone, and if we hold a student responsible for it, we are "unfair." And so we stress the immediate.[2]

All this is agonizing for Horace. He resents his compromises, and derides himself for making them. Some respected colleagues share his frustration, but they know that an honest evaluation of the school's compromises will open a Pandora's box. Everything in the school affects everything else. That finely tuned complexity which is the daily schedule cannot withstand more than trivial adjustments, and more than trivial adjustments are needed to improve Franklin High. The ultimate frustration for Horace is that even if a corps of like-minded, risk-taking colleagues evolved an ambitious, sensible new plan for Franklin, they would not have the authority to act on it. The major elements of schooling are controlled outside the teachers' world. The state, or its contractor firms, writes the tests. The state mandates when each subject is to be taught; it and the district control that key coinage of school, the time of teachers and students. Evaluations of school and teachers, the union contract, the departmental divisions, all run according to traditional formulas.

Horace knows that he has limited control over his own destiny. Others would have to affirm his intention to teach with better compromises, to organize his and the students' work along more sensible lines. Obviously, they don't trust us, Horace thinks. The folk higher up are sure they know better. We always have to ask permission. Teachers with hall passes not to the bathroom but to better schools, he snorts to himself. Of all Horace's feelings about his work, this is the most bitter.[3]

2

Putting It Right

ALTHOUGH AMERICANS in the 1980s were aware of a well-publicized resurgence of political interest in school reform, one spiced with warnings detailed in scores of studies and commission reports, Horace's compromises were little affected. He still had over 120 students, and their test scores had changed little from those of their predecessors eight or ten years earlier. The kids were no less prone to distraction from their school work as earlier — probably more so. About the same number stayed away from school, truants or dropouts. About the same percentage graduated.[1]

The source of Horace's compromises, primarily the routines of school and the assumptions that informed those routines, persisted. Bells continued to signal the progression of fifty-two-minute periods. The metaphors of schoolkeeping endured: school is what we teachers expose kids to. The tests came at the students much as they always had, although they were now given in greater profusion and more was made of them. The teachers' responsibilities remained as before, and the contracts negotiated on their behalf were familiar. Visitors could detect little change in the feel or intensity or purposefulness or culture of Franklin High School over the decade. It was as though most of those well-intentioned calls to "reform" had never really been trumpeted, or at best had been heard faintly.

However, mocking school reform efforts is an easy sport. Our schools, especially our high schools, serve important symbolic purposes — providing the expected rituals of growing up and helping young people learn how to be on their own — and they legitimate the social class sorting of Americans. Accordingly, part of their cultural value is their formal stability, so reform unsettles much more than just school practices. Expecting quick and easy change would be extravagant.

Some have said that the primary purpose of schooling, beyond teaching the rudiments, is to pass along the inherited wisdom of the American people. Make the kids be like us. We were schooled in a certain way; they should be too. If you challenge the effectiveness of the status quo, you challenge us. Am I not well educated? Of course I am. So make the kids do what I did. The burden of persuasion on those who would change schools is heavy.

Individual schools respond poorly to detailed commands for reform by distant authorities. Educational authority in America is largely dispersed, usually to local school boards, and many of these are fiercely jealous of their autonomy. Further, American communities are remarkably diverse, and regulations delivered from on high strike different communities in significantly different ways. Those offended buck. Finally, most decisions about children's learning are made at the bottom of the organizational pyramid, by specific teachers; it is they who decide what will happen and what will not. The heart of the system — the schools and the individual classrooms within them — is difficult to reach. Not surprisingly, change has been slight.

The fact that much of what passes for schooling fails even to meet the test of simple common sense counts for little. Critics can argue that few of us at any age do serious intellectual or imaginative work in isolated bits of time no longer than fifty-two minutes, or that mere exposure to a body of knowledge enhances a pupil's knowledge. They can easily explain that even a veteran teacher cannot get to know well 120 or 150 or 180 students at once, at least well enough to teach each efficiently. They can, in sum, explain the roots of Horace's compromises. However, their criticism, even when offered lovingly, is often greeted paradoxically: responsible people agree with it, but also agree to do little to address the failings. The analysis is met with embarrassed paralysis or, at best, inertia. Reform is for someone else's school. We're happy with the one we have, and we are skeptical of any effort to alter it. It is no wonder that there has been so little change.

What is especially interesting about the 1980s reform movement is what it did *not* attempt. First, it did not spawn a fresh and ambitious research effort, an inquiry into why American young people appeared to fall behind their international peers in academic performance. The assumption, usually tacit, was that we already knew enough to make the needed reforms.

Second, with few (if noisy) exceptions, the movement rarely attempted to attack the demonstrably inefficient bureaucracies that dominate public education. Other than indulging in rhetoric about the need for "decentralization" and issuing vague promises to allow more "choice" for parents — thus providing for competition for pupils — the protesters did little. Educational reform was to be forwarded, it was implied, by its current stakeholders, with a minimum of pain and dislocation. Power would remain with those presently in control — the school boards, the administrators, the unions — and they would bring about the changes that critics felt were essential.

Finally, the reform movement largely avoided the real world found inside the schools, thereby ignoring Horace's compromises. Indeed, the movement forced Horace to compromise even more grievously. "Tougher" courses often simply meant "more" to cover, maintaining the "exposure" metaphor and further trivializing a grotesquely overloaded curriculum. "More homework" usually meant more mindless busy work. A longer school year or school day translated into more of the existing regimen. There was no stomach to accept the hard reality that the ways Americans kept their schools were sadly misdirected.

However, the 1990s opened with more encouraging signs, as political leaders, particularly the governors, recognized that modest adjustments — more testing and "toughening up" —

were not enough, were not working, and will not work. Business leaders concurred in this sober assessment. President Bush joined in; his 1991 education message called for new kinds of schools, ones that "broke the mold." A new catchword — restructuring — was added to policy conversation.

Like most slogans, restructuring has taken on a variety of meanings. Most common is that the system has to be reconstructed, by means of "choice" plans, decentralization of authority, or the shifting of political power. Consistent among virtually all of these restructuring efforts is the assumption that top-down hierarchical control has to yield.

Less common is the sense that the school itself must be rethought and redesigned, that Horace's compromises must be addressed and remedied; yet the impulse to move on questions about the very nature of keeping school is sensed by a growing number of well-informed leaders. Many understand that one cannot redesign the system without having a clear sense of a better and more powerful school. The definition of the character of thoughtful and informed graduates should shape such a school, and that school should shape the system that nourishes it.

The pieces of the school reform puzzle are known; they are few, and they interconnect. Each must be addressed in order, but, given their interaction, must also be considered in combination. They are best cast as essential questions:

First, what is it that admirable high school graduates must display to deserve our respect and appreciation as well as their high school diploma?

Second, how can schools function so that all adolescents have a fair chance to display these accomplishments? How can schools see to it that the maximum number of youngsters in fact achieves them?

Third, what sort of political, administrative, and community context is required for schools that graduate such admirable young people.

Fourth, how can the distinctive concerns of individual students, their families, the communities in which they reside, and the larger state be respectfully accommodated and yet still nurture schools and a schooling system that serve all adolescents?

Most important is the emphasis on the students. Until we understand clearly just what they should do with their minds and hearts, and what standards they should meet, it is difficult to design a sensible school. Indeed, it is also difficult to *go* to school without such clarity: What should I achieve in order to merit the diploma? High school students are familiar with this sort of "ultimate thinking" from their extracurricular activities: as the sport is to be played or the concert given, they are aware of a standard to be met, they can envision what attractions open on its achievement, and they sense what they must do to reach that standard. Having a target is a crucial incentive. Knowing your destination helps you find your way. And knowing the adolescents' destination helps a school shape its priorities.

As Horace ruefully appreciates, the "destinations" in conventional schools are rarely cast in this way. What the students should know and be able to do is usually couched in generalized statements and measured by sharply limited tests that are created by outsiders and that have no connection with the world of the particular school within which the students live. Passing the tests becomes an end in itself. The detailed stuff of schooling is covered in lists of topics to which the students are to be exposed and in courses to be passed. What the kids are to do with all this material is left vague. How they are actively to use it in their lives is left even vaguer.

Delineating these matters is difficult and unfamiliar business. Relating the goals of schooling in terms of the powers that students gain from their education raises a host of troubling questions, both pedagogical and philosophical. Further, few school people have any experience in defining their work by specific ends rather than detailed means. Indeed, the very universities that trained them describe their academic functions almost entirely in terms of means. For most teachers, figuring out just what it is that provokes our respect for the youngster about to be given a diploma is a novel exercise.

If the question of ends is fairly answered, the one on means can be handled. When ends are reasonably clear, the means may become so. Of course, as Horace knows, kids differ, and there must be multiple means just as there are multiple ways that students can display their achievements.

The third question likewise follows on the second. Like students, communities differ. Schools differ. However, the state has its own proper standards, as do the individual students, their families, and the schools, and these must be met even while sensible diversity is respected. Balancing these imperatives is an unfamiliar exercise for most school administrators and policymakers. For them, rules have traditionally been the favored tool; the task of the system's functionaries is to superintend those rules and hold people to them.

The result is standardization, with teachers and schools and even kids (for example, "tenth-graders") being virtually interchangable parts. But designing a system that garners the strengths of the inevitable and rich diversity and of the reasonable claims of the larger community represented by the state is a stunningly new and challenging task.

The broad and deep support necessary for consequential school reform is at present far from being attained. Even after all the reform talk of the 1980s and the fresh zeal of the early 1990s, the numbers of those converted to the need for serious educational reform is still small. One reason may be the very case that the 1980s leaders adopted for their crusade, a case that basically was an argument for America rather than one for individual Americans. The leaders worried aloud about the quality of the labor force, the competitiveness of this country in a global economy, the quality of our civic culture. However important these issues are, they do little to allay the concerns encountered in the daily life of schools, concerns such as those of a typical parent: Will my children be safe at school? Does anyone know my children well and care for them? Will there be a future for my children, and is the school helping them to achieve it? These personal concerns are proper, untrivial, and not to be swept aside, especially in a democracy, even as they sound selfish: what *must* be done in school for *my* child.

Ambitious school reform will come about not only because

presidents and governors and Fortune 500 executives want it to, but because parents and local communities and teachers and principals want reform that addresses their appropriate concerns as well as broader ones. Certainly, the policy world needs the voters to be engaged. However, policymakers have usually restricted the agenda to their own concern: a *nation* at risk. The parent's overriding concern — *my child* at risk — implicitly has not been heeded any more than have Horace's compromises. That neglect, however unintentional, has been costly.

Policymakers must patiently address the real and local world of Horace, his students, his colleagues, his community's school boards, and the community itself. Happily, the legitimate needs found at this level are seldom in conflict with the national goals that have driven the 1980s and 1990s reform movement. Rather, they represent the absolutely necessary and critical condition for the success of a national effort. Given the powerful hold that the rituals of going to school have on Americans, only a broad-based reform effort will work.

This effort may be getting under way in many American communities where a coalition of interests to reconsider the nature and quality of the schools is quietly forming. Often the effort arises almost serendipitously from different quarters of each community: from teachers and principals, from parents, from the superintendent and the school board, from local employers, from community and church leaders, from high school students. It is truly grassroots, and it could well connect with the state and national effort — if that effort gives it status and credence and, ultimately, appropriate power over both the ends and means of education.

It was such a coalition that led to the appointment by the school board of a committee to review the purposes and practices of Franklin High School. The board appointed as its chair the respected English teacher Horace Smith, who had been vocal and persuasive about the need to re-evaluate his school. The committee had eighteen months for its deliberations. It met intensively first at the start of the academic year.

3

Horace's Committee

"IF IT'S NOT BROKE, DON'T FIX IT."

"Come on," someone said.

"No, I mean it. I do mean it." Patches, comfortably twisted in his tablet armchair and garbed in the familiar elbow-patched tweed coat that gave rise to his nickname, persisted. Yes, he meant it. "What is this committee all about? Are we a bad school? Are the parents raising hell with us? What's the problem?"

Horace knew this would happen. Better now than later. He wanted Patches on the high school's restructuring committee because the history teacher was smart and influential, though exasperating. Horace felt he could handle him, even if Patches mocked Horace's elevation to the chair of this committee, which Horace himself had suggested. The two had joined the Franklin High School faculty at the same time, a considerable number of years earlier. There was as much competition as friendship between them.

"If we're so good, we shouldn't be afraid to question ourselves."

"Who said we are all that good?"

"What is 'good' anyway?"

"Why 'restructure'? What's wrong with our present structure that a little money and commitment couldn't fix?"

"Come off it. Restructuring is the next new thing. We have to have it. The superintendent has to tell the school committee that Franklin is 'restructuring.' "

"Whatever that means . . ." Laughter. Horace's anger rose. He hoped it didn't show.

The conversation among the eleven committee members present that day wandered, full of stress, mostly owing to the vagueness of the charge to the group, and of wonderment about just what people felt was wrong with the school now. Confusion, hurt, defensiveness, a sense of something new, possibly good — all resonated. Yet they knew that the school board was serious about change, about whatever "restructuring" might be.

The board's members and the superintendent honestly believed that Franklin was not all that it could be. Further, they wanted the school to be seen in the vanguard of what to them was a new — and this time serious — reform movement. But they were as ambivalent as the members of Horace's committee: they were proud of the present system yet were sure it could serve its students better. That ambivalence led to the fuzziness of the charge given to Horace's group: we don't really know what we want, but we want it and we want you to give it to us and it should be bold. Horace knew that some board members had been impressed by President Bush's recent education message, in which he had urged Americans to design new schools. Horace thought the board wanted this community to lead in the breaking of the mold. And so here was the wide-open charge, one that clearly implied that fiddling with the status quo would not be enough.

Horace wondered whether to cut off the strained chatter. Fourteen teachers had been elected to the committee, with the new principal ex officio. She came to few of the early meetings, not that she'd squash the frankness of this bunch, Horace thought. They'll always speak their minds. Perhaps she doesn't realize this. Or maybe she's just bending over backward to allow candor. On the other hand, Horace knew that the three parent members to be appointed, one of whom would be a school board member, might well dampen straight talk. He was happy that the PTO hadn't gotten its act together yet to name the representatives. Maybe the committee needed some student members as well, at the least to provide a bridge between the teachers and the mothers and fathers.

Horace interposed: "Our problem is that many kids don't make it here, don't do as well as they might. The honors kids, they do fine, the apples of our eyes. It's that noisy, heedless bunch in the middle that we miss."

"Yeah, the food fighters." Laughter, and mutual acknowledgment of cafeteria chaos the week before.

"They don't want to learn. You can bring a horse to water . . ." Patches kept the floor. "A lot of these kids shouldn't be in school anyway. Let them work for a while and come back when they're ready to do something here. They're wasting our time and slowing down the kids who want an education." He paused. Others looked away. Were they angry or embarrassed, Horace wondered.

Horace was counting on two faculty stalwarts, but they remained quiet. The French teacher whom Patches had approvingly dubbed Margaret Chase Smith because she resembled the former senator from Maine — tall, silver-haired, a woman stuffed with good sense and principle — had a small smile on her face, but her eyes were focused on the vast crochet project that spilled around her feet. And Coach — the tall, balding, genial symbol of Franklin's athletic successes and a widely respected health teacher — seemed at this point unready to tangle with his history colleague.

Patches went on. "Let's not kid ourselves. What we care about isn't for everyone, or at least many kids don't act as though they wanted it."

Horace looked at the visitor, hoping that she'd step in — and hoping she'd stay quiet. The visitor twirled the coffee in her polystyrene cup. Was she smirking? Should the committee have agreed to let this retired teacher, now a part-time education professor, sit in on its deliberations? Her consultancy to Franklin High School was paid for by the state; she was to be what the state bureaucrats called the school's "critical friend." Was she the commissioner's spy? While she clearly was an experienced school person — a veteran English teacher — she was also now a member of the outside establishment, the people who wanted change but dared not define it.

"What *do* we care about? That's the question we ought to be considering." Here was the voice of an intense thirty-five-ish science teacher well known in the corridors of the high school for a Boston Celtics warm-up jacket she persistently wore with her jeans. The kids called her Green, even to her face. They liked her. She looked down as she spoke. Horace knew that the older talkative faculty, particularly the males, threatened her. Her worry was justified, he knew. The old guard found displeasing what they decided was her penchant for aggressive sloppiness, and they let her know it. Her unease in speaking both reinforced their dismissal of her and her own unwillingness to step forward. Horace was happy she tried now.

No one responded to her question. The visitor filled the awkward silence. "Look at the Course of Study Guide you give the kids at the opening of school. Read the course descriptions. They're all written from your point of view, what *you* will do. There's nothing there about what the kids have to do. But you do care about what the kids can do, ultimately." She turned to Green: "That last question was a good one. Can you express this school's program in terms of what the kids do rather than in terms of what you do?"

Horace flared. Won't this visitor let us do it our way? She should listen and watch. And keep her mouth shut. Or at least until we ask her opinion. Happily, he sensed that the visitor had picked up that message. Obviously both he and the visitor were working together, gingerly, confused, competing in a silly way even as they were like-minded on matters of schooling.

Fortunately, Green kept going. "I know what I want my kids to be able to do: to do science, to be able to figure things out on their own, to have opinions about scientific things in their lives, not to be afraid of science . . ." She ran on, speaking ever faster as she heard herself talking. "I know that they'll forget most of the details, most of the nomenclature. Some of them won't; they'll need it in college. It's a way of thinking science that I'm after, a certain kind of skepticism . . ."

"Scientific process?"

"Sure, that's some of it. The process alone isn't enough. You have to know some things to 'process.'"

"What are those things? Aren't they just what the Course of Study Guide outlines?"

"Yes," Green replied. "But the guide mentions only them, those things for the kids to cover. I want them to use those things, to do something with them. The guide should stress that, explain that, show everyone that that's the goal."

"You mean," Horace interjected, "the doing is the ultimate achievement?"

"Yes. The doing is the ultimate achievement. Just knowing stuff isn't enough. Not for me, anyway. It's not real science."

Horace pressed. "Can you give us an example of what the kid who's met your standard would in fact do, what he'd show you that you'd really respect?"

"Sure."

"If you can do this, why not tell the kids what it is, instead of just listing all the stuff you and they are going to cover."

"I could."

"Wouldn't that be better?"

"Sure. But it would be risky!"

"Why?"

"That's not the way the College Board treats science. That's not the way we now 'do' science. Many of the things we cover don't come up for 'doing' by the kids."

Patches broke in, uncharacteristically interested in this exchange between Horace and Green. "If the kids don't have to use it, why teach it?"

"Good point," Green agreed.

Silence descended. A new voice, sarcastic, that of a young English teacher, new to the school, intense, and seeming to flaunt assurance. "Must everything be *used*?"

"No, of course not."

The young English teacher persisted. "Just what do you mean by 'using'? I mean, people shouldn't be expected to do experiments all the time or become scientists . . ." Green flushed.

Horace intervened. "Use shouldn't be too narrowly defined, the mere doing of things, solving today's limited problems." He paused. This was a fine line to draw. "Wise use requires not only problem-solving skills but a context from which the solver draws. One uses one's habits of imagination, one's *understanding*, one's taste . . ." It sounded limp, but no one challenged it.

Patches again, this time with a whiff of exasperation: "But how *do* you decide what to teach and what not to teach?"

Horace couldn't resist responding, "You mean, how do we decide what the kids will learn or not learn." Patches ignored him. Most of the others got the point, though. They liked Horace to poke his old friend — or so he believed. It showed he was in control.

Green: "That's right. How *do* we decide? Or do we just do what we've always done?"

Horace: "Let's turn the whole process around. Let's start backward, by describing what we admire in our best graduates. Let's be clear about what it is that the best kids do, how they use what we give them. If we can't describe this, how can we set priorities? If we *can* describe it, we'll be on the way to improve this school."

A hiss of exasperation. "Oh, God, not more of this sort of airy-fairy stuff. We'll just gab away and string together more words. Get practical, Horace!" An aside really, a whisper from somewhere. Horace decided to acknowledge it.

"Maybe the best way to get started is to figure out what kind of questions we'd like to be able to ask our seniors in June, questions that should get us intelligent, informed responses. So let's be practical, specific. What is it precisely that a kid — any kid — should be able to show off to us?"

"Do you mean test scores? The SATs?"

"No, more than that, deeper than that. Our stuff, not what comes from the Educational Testing Service. Stuff the kids will have to show us, hang in display for us, argue about with us publicly, at the end." He paused. "What do we care about in our older kids?"

There were stares, silence, some embarrassment. Green started: "I give the kids a problem, say to take water samples . . ."

A mathematics teacher, formal, respected, the pens and pencils in their appointed row in the plastic case in his shirt pocket, known to be scrupulously fair: "I give them problem sets. They get word problems. I know what they're supposed to be able to do in mathematics. I don't see where you're taking us, Horace."

Margaret, finally: "The coach knows best of all, when his team plays a game well and wins." Coach gave it back: "And the French play lets the kids show their stuff too."

Horace tried again. "Let's try to get beyond our specific subjects. Sure, we give a handful of the kids, like some of the honors track and voc ed kids, plenty to do, to show off, in our classes. But what about all those other kids? Is Franklin High the sum of our departmental parts? If we care about more than that, and we do, what questions would we ask these kids about how they think and act in some general, broader way? That's what's on my mind."

More silence. Clearly the committee was on unfamiliar ground.

"Give us an example, Horace. You've obviously been thinking about this."

"OK. Like any of us, I'm a creature of my subject. But let me try an idea that goes well beyond English, to the arts generally and the typical graduate's ability to use them, both to appreciate and employ them. The kids ought to be able to Exhibit to us, talk with us about, and debate with us, some mastery of the use of the arts and humanities. I have some examples. They sound easy, but aren't . . . Let me try one on you . . . Now don't jump all over me before you reflect on what such an exercise would entail. Think what it would take for all of us here to prepare the kids to do this, and think how *we'd* have to change. Think whether this sort of skill and knowledge is needed and respected out there in the big, wide world . . .

"Let me try on you an example from the arts and humanities in general, about emotions . . ."[1]

An Exhibition: Emotions

Select one of the following familiar human emotions: fear, envy, courage, hunger, longing, joy, anger, greed, jealousy.

In an essay, define the emotion you choose, drawing on your own and others' experience. Then render a similar definition using in turn at least three of the following forms of expression: a written language other than English; a piece of drawing, painting, or sculpture; photographs, a video, or film; a musical composition; a short story or play; pantomime; a dance.

Select examples from literature, journalism, the arts, and history of other people's definitions or representations of the emotion you have chosen. These should strike you as important and arresting, even if they do not correspond with your own definition.

Be ready in four months to present this work and to answer questions about it. The Exhibition — a portfolio collected by you over the next months — will be judged on the basis of its vitality and overall coherence as well as the quality of its individual components.

Here is an educational target.

This Exhibition is a valid one. We ourselves are creatures of our emotions, and we make judgments about others' emotions every day. Actions follow from such judgments. All students realize that.

It is important. Being reflective and self-conscious about fundamental human characteristics is a mark of a thoughtful and civil individual. People who are known to *understand* the emotions of others, and the actions that may follow on them, are universally admired. The ability to recognize emotions is a requisite for such understanding.

It raises issues that are at once highly personal and universal. While there is no one crisp all-purpose definition of, say, anger, every one of us, without exception, employs one, consciously or unconsciously. Thoughtful people from all walks and conditions of life ponder not only their own practical definitions but those of others, in the present and from the past. We hope that people will act in principled ways on the basis of their considered, practical definitions.

It cuts across traditional scholarly disciplines in a respectful way while it demonstrates practice in the use of knowledge in a palpably "real" sense. Further, it puts matters raised independently in a variety of subjects into a sensible context, powerfully affirming the work in each discipline.

It asks each student to speak in several voices, through several media. While all students are expected to display clear written English, beyond that each can present herself in the ways she personally finds most persuasive.

It gives the student a reasonable choice of topic — the specific emotion selected — thus allowing him to plumb an area of particular interest.

It requires reflection. Idle guessing will not work. The student must inform himself and be precise in transmitting what he means.

It requires persistence and organization.

It provokes the student to think about the *use* of her definition by means of "speaking the same message" through different media and searching out arresting examples from others' expressions.

It allows the student to display his ability to unearth examples from a variety of sources, his skills of description and communication, his mastery of a range of information, and his ingenuity and imagination.

It reinforces the modern habit of using in combination a variety of forms of expression to give power to meaning.

It allows time for serious work to be accomplished. Although all of some comprehensive list of emotions (if one ever could be created) are not "covered," the student will practice the complex thought that is required to get a fair handle on the meaning of any emotion. That is, she will have the happy experience of pressing a critical definition with the thoroughness it deserves.

It promises that the student's work will be taken seriously and respected: it will be viewed and heard publicly and subjected to questions.

For most students, such an Exhibition on emotions is an interesting exercise and for many, indeed, fun.

For teachers, it is a demanding exercise, requiring scholarly breadth, ingenuity (how to help a student connect various forms of expression around a common idea), and judgment (how to assay the time required for a particular student to complete the work; how to instill some self-confidence in a youngster hellbent on avoiding anything new).

For the school, it requires a rich library, or student access to a nearby and cooperative public library, with patient and knowledgeable librarians.

Why an *Exhibition*? The word clearly states its purpose: the student must Exhibit the products of his learning. If he does that well, he can convince himself that he can use knowledge and he can so convince others. It is the academic equivalent of being able to sink free throws in basketball. You may not ring all of them, but if you consistently hit a good percentage, you gain confidence in yourself, and the coach will have the confidence to play you.

To shoot baskets well one needs to practice. To think well one needs to practice. Going to school is practicing to use one's mind well. One does not exercise one's mind in a vacuum; one rarely learns to "think" well with nothing but tricky brainteasers or questions embedded in a context that is neither realistic nor memorable. One needs to stimulate its exercise with engaging ideas in an equally engaging setting. Such ideas require the grasp of fundamental information.

However, the heart of it is in the play. Merely "knowing" ideas is as inert as knowing that one has to sink the free throw from the foul line. One has actually to sink the shot, has to *use* the ideas, has be in the *habit* of using them, and *use* is always far more complicated than simple recall of propositions or rules or even an analysis of them. Fortunately, the use of ideas is the best vehicle for fixing their underlying information and skills into an individual's mind.

The Exhibition, then, is not only the target. It is also a representation of the way one prepares to reach the target. That is, school is about practicing to wrap one's mind around real and complex ideas, those of fundamental consequence for oneself and for the culture. It is not merely about "coverage," or being informed, or displaying skills. It is the demonstration of the employment of all of these toward important and legitimate ends.

The final Exhibition is a "test," yes; but it is really an affirmation for the student herself and for her larger community that what she has long practiced in school, what skills and habits she has developed, have paid off.

Exhibitions can be powerful incentives for students. Knowing where the destination is always helps in getting there, and if that destination is cast in an interesting way, one is more likely to care about reaching it.

Truly genuine Exhibitions may be difficult to "grade"; that is, it may be hard to render a precise assessment of the achievement of the student. This Exhibition on emotions will likely have to be judged by a team of adults, somewhat like that empaneled to judge a diving event at a swimming meet. For example, approval could be given for the clarity of written, oral, and other forms of presentation; for sophistication, the subtlety and perceptiveness of the student's definition, and his use of other people's definitions; for coherence and orderliness; and for appropriateness, the fitting of the definition to the examples the student puts forward. Grading will thus be time- and people-intensive. However, the effort will feed back into the school's habit of tuning its standards and assessing its own effectiveness. Grading must be careful, but it can never be icily objective. It will rely on distributed judgment, but it will always be colored — and appropriately — by particular circumstances.

Exhibitions give focus to a school's program. Unless a faculty is clear about what a student must present in order to deserve the high school diploma, it is difficult to state what the curriculum, its pedagogy, the routines of school, and its standards should be. That is, it is difficult to prepare the players if one does not know what playing the game entails. The nature of the play must be presented in terms of the action of the players — and not of the coach, whose activities are only a means to the players' ends. A school's program presented essentially as what the teachers do is misdirected.

A mindful school is clear about what it expects of a student and about how he can exhibit these qualities, just as a mindful student is one who knows where he is going, is disposed to get there, and is gathering the resources, the knowledge, and the skills to make the journey.

4

Kids Differ

IT WAS early December. The restructuring committee was well along with its discussion when Patches erupted with his version of Franklin High's Dirty Little Secret. Amid some serious but inconclusive talk about tracking, about how one shouldn't stereotype kids and at the same time one couldn't teach students of widely varying achievement in the same classroom, Patches spoke:

"Why aren't there more black kids on the Honor Roll? Why do the black kids take over basketball? Why is it that so many black kids end up on suspension? Why do the black kids always eat together in the cafeteria? If we're talking about kids being apart, the black kids are."

Protests followed an embarrassed silence. African-American and Hispanic kids made up about 30 percent of Franklin's students. Most were from working-class or low-income households. Asian-Americans constituted about 4 percent of the enrollment, and most of these young people came from middle-income or more affluent homes.

"I've got great black kids in my honors English class."

"Remember last year's senior class officers, how several were black?"

"These are good kids . . . Why shouldn't they lunch together? All the jocks lunch together, and you don't object to that."

Patches: "I'm not objecting. I'm just reporting."

"Things are much better than they used to be. Remember the strain of the seventies. It's peaceful here now."

"It's peaceful if you're white," retorted the mathemetics teacher, one of the three black members of the committee. He gave no example. The white faculty, who had not believed their colleague to be what some of them would call "militant," stared at him, astonished. He stared back.

The young English teacher: "What about our Hispanic kids. They do even worse." More silence.

Someone said, "You can't expect kids to do well when they show up at high school semiliterate. They segregate themselves by their poor achievement." These particular words, uttered guilelessly, stunned their hearers. Green protested: "We're not for segregation. We can't be for segregation. We must treat all kids alike . . ."

Patches: "But they aren't all alike."

"But you can't blame the victim, the victim of lousy schooling and careless homes."

"Who says that black homes are careless?" Another of the black teachers. Again, an electric shock through the group.

One of the white teachers: "The problem is racist teachers, a racist school, a racist society . . ."

Patches: "Are you calling me racist?" Tense silence.

The principal, who happened in her ex officio role to be attending this committee session, intervened. "No one of us here is racist and we are all racist." The remark, predictable, helped little. The discomfort was palpable; the two parent members, one of whom was Hispanic, were visibly distraught.

A social studies teacher: "It's a matter of class, not race. Show me a middle-class kid, and I'll show you a candidate for our Honor Roll. Show me a poor kid, and I'll show you an academic loser."

The mathematics teacher: "So, what's the lesson, then? Just accept the curse of class? And don't you find it revealing that so many of the Chapter One kids here at Franklin are minorities? Does that make them dumber, somehow?"

"Maybe the problem is the school, not the kids."

An exasperated voice: "Can we expect Franklin High to solve *all* the social problems of the world? Racial discrimination, those girls who don't take physics and cuddle up to football heroes, the rich, the poor, insipid television, pregnancy, Just Say No, violence . . . It's a mess. What can *we* be expected to do about it? We always get the shitty end of society's stick." The vulgarism, curiously, broke the spell.

"Well, we can't just sit and do nothing." The voice, quavering, low, belonged to one of the two students who had been added to the committee at Horace's suggestion.

The second student: "What about special programs, Martin Luther King Day, Awareness Weeks?" No one picked up on this.

The principal tried again. "The fact of the matter is that no two kids are ever really the same at all. Not even twins. Sure, one's race and gender and class give some definition." She kept going. "Kids do pattern, with the overlaps probably more important than the differences. Kids are kids. The trick is in getting to know each one well enough to provide for each." Her voice swelled as she stressed *each one*.

"How in hell do you expect me to do that with 130 kids?" Horace exploded. The principal blanched, apparently unfamiliar with Horace's passion on this topic. Horace went on: "Until we have a realistic chance of knowing each kid well, we'll be stuck with our nasty stereotypes, and the kids will fall in right behind us, little self-fulfilling prophecies."

Green picked up the theme. "Just knowing the kids, black or white or Hispanic or Asian or shy or clever or chubby or nerdy, is only the beginning. It doesn't make an awful lot of difference if I merely know them and can't act on the knowledge. If we're so set in our rigid ways of doing things, we can't accommodate kids who don't fit into our traditional patterns."

"Procrustes' bed," muttered the young English teacher. Whether or not they got the allusion, the committee members paid him little heed, but they knew he was right. The strain was still very much there; resentment. Yet Horace knew that his committee was getting somewhere: the hard truths were getting out in the open.

Parents know how kids differ, kids of all kinds, one from another and each one over time, often it seems almost day to day. One need only listen to the parents' voices, echoing each other about the specialnesses of their offspring. Let me tell you about Phyllis . . . Jorge is different, you've got to understand that . . . Amelia is really ahead of the class, she's bored . . . You must remember that Joe's granny just died . . .

To this chorus, predictable, defensive, and self-congratulatory banality, we school and college teachers sometimes say: The kids are eleventh-graders. Let them get on with it. The SATs are given on April twelfth. The doting mums and dads have cramped views, are blind to their children's calculability and to the march of the calendar. These kids are growing up, and they've got to learn to fit in.

And surely they must, at least into a system worthy of the fit. But the parents are nonetheless more correct than are the protectors of the traditional high school, that generous but highly routinized product of early twentieth-century American Progressivism. There are patterns to adolescent development, but the individual variations within these patterns are as important as the patterns themselves. Parents see this even among their own offspring, young people who share the same gene pool, household, family rituals, neighborhood, and TV programs. While the sixteen-year-olds who walk into that eleventh-grade class are conditioned to be a coherent crowd — the Junior Prom is ours this year — they are inevitably a highly differentiated crowd, and not just by the obviousnesses of race and gender. They, of all people, know it, to some degree. They hate to be stereotyped. Treat me as me, they tell us, teachers and parents. I'm not my brother. I am different. I am special. *I am somebody.*

The nature of these differences is familiar and patent. People of all ages vary by gender, race, ethnicity, geographic origin. Some are richer and some are poorer, in the financial as well as other meanings of those words. Young people mature at different rates, in spurts and starts. Johnny didn't make the basketball team last year, but this year he's the starting center — five inches taller and twenty-five pounds heavier. Some get the point quickly in physics class, some don't. Some have benefited from early rich nutrition, biological and spiritual, others have not. Some care about making it, some do not, some have not thought about the matter at all, living each moment as it comes. Some reside in a community that values schooling, others with uninterested elders. Some live essentially alone.

Parents, like children, vary too, and the ambiences of home life, or even the existence of a home life worthy of the name, diverge. So too do neighborhoods, the pack of kids with which each happens to run, the events of their particular time, the fads of the moment, Elvis or Prince, Marilyn or Madonna, even Mahler or Mozart.

Other differences run much deeper. People do not learn in precisely similar ways. There are patterns, but these are merely guideposts for teachers and students. Where and how and why and at what rate a particular learner "gets it," or is interested in getting it in the first place, vary widely, certainly far more so than is implied by traditional school syllabi. The class will "study" Gauguin this morning. All will learn about Gauguin from a slide-tape lecture. Following that, all will read an excerpt from the text. All will be expected to have got it by Tuesday, when the test will be given. Why is Gauguin a celebrated painter? When was he born? Where did he live? Who were his contemporaries? The assumption is that most, if not all, the students are ready for this topic, all are disposed to try to learn it, all will learn it best in a similar way and at a similar rate, and all can be fairly "tested" with the same "instrument" in the same timed session. Assumptions go even further: if any student was treated differently, if the material was presented in any but a universal way for all youngsters, the teaching would be unfair. Treat all alike. Anything else is discriminatory, undemocratic.

But people do not learn alike, and to run a school on the basis of One Best Curriculum and One Best Pedagogy and One Best Pace of Learning and One Best Test and March the Kids Through by Their Chronological Ages is itself profoundly discriminatory. Those who fit these One Best routines, and only these, get a special benefit. A wealth of recent research, in some respects still speculative, reinforces the observations of thoughtful teachers and parents. There is among individuals a variety of learning styles, a variety of sources of abstract reasoning and sensing powers. There may also be different "intelligences," as it were. Some learn better through hearing than seeing, and vice versa. Some can tell us well, others show us better. Some grasp complexity by sequential analysis, some by a more inductive process. And so on.[1]

A thoughtful school will accept these differences and use them constructively. Doing so is not only an act of respect for each young person's individuality but also an act of simple efficiency. Trying to force a child to learn in a way that does not suit that child is like trying to run a Ford Escort on kerosene. If the aim of schooling is to help each child move from ignorance to understanding, then using the proper fuel for that child's particular intellectual engine makes obvious sense.

A familiar argument shoved at those who would teach students in a variety of ways is that standards will be compromised. However one learns it, $5 \times 12 = 60$. An incoherent sentence is incoherent, whatever the sources of its expression. Wise schools do not vary the standards of acomplishment when they are clear. What they vary is the means to the ends, in ways that respect the particular differences of particular children. Such is not a compromise of academic standards. Indeed, it is a modeling of good scholarship, an example of the use of knowledge in practice: it takes serious account of what we know about human learning, about the variability of ways of learning, of making sense of the world.

American schools have long asserted that they respond to the needs of the individual child, and in many remarkable ways they do. In most high schools, three policies reflect this intent — if not common sense.

First is the familiar practice of grading by age, September's fourteen-year-olds being ninth-graders and so forth. There is some break from this practice at the extremes: the youngster who "skipped" second grade or the one who was "held back." However, "ninth grade" means something; it is designed for the "needs" of fourteen-year-olds or those who act like fourteen-year-olds. Within that ninth-grade plan there is almost no accommodation to differences other than age, no deference to matters of gender, race, ethnic origin, and the rest. Indeed, such adjustment would usually bring down furious charges of discrimination, of sexism or racism. All ninth-graders must be "treated the same." So the schools discriminate primarily and only on one dimension, that of birth date. Ageism, it seems, is incontestably allowable.[2]

Second are the exceptions, the "special," the kids at the "obvious" extremes. The physically "handicapped." The emotionally hobbled. The children with exaggerated learning "disabilities," usually meaning demonstrable inability to accommodate to the One Best Pedagogy or One Best Pace of Learning. The actors-out, the kids so difficult to handle that "special" arrangements are needed for them. The "gifted and talented," the kids who appear to flourish bountifully under stern academic or athletic or artistic regimens. The arrangements made for many of these youngsters often break their age classification. Frequently the cost of a special program exceeds the funding available for the regular program. This discrimination is rationalized either by the severity of the "disability" the child suffers or by the presumed worth to society of the special schooling of a child of large talent.

Third is the policy of "tracking." There will be ninth-grade English, but it will be taught to the fourteen-year-olds in sections, perhaps honors, college prep, and regular. A student is placed in one of these categories on the basis of test scores or recommendations of teachers from the previous year or a combination of both. Parental pressure sometimes influences the placement. Tracks vary in expectation and intensity: the higher the first, the greater the second.

In some tracking situations, the student in honors English finds himself also in honors social studies and so forth. The school thereby comprises more or less coherent tracks, the honors, the regulars, and the rest, really several schools within a school. These de facto units often result in circumscribed social groupings, friendships; except sometimes in athletics and the performing arts, kids rarely cross the lines.

A device that implicitly tracks is the system of student choice of subject. A cornucopia of courses is offered, and students are allowed, within some limits — usually those set by the state — to choose among them. The school's descriptions implicitly label some courses for the swifter, some for the strugglers, more for the lackadaisical and the rest. Among the array of courses there is rigor and fluff. If students want the former, it is there for them. If they want only to get through, they can do that. Getting through means passing courses, having their titles and credits on their transcripts, little more. Fluff, doing the minimum, will suffice.

The school accommodates the variety among students by offering different courses, but not by using strikingly different teaching styles. "The course" stands: it is a piece of time — say, five periods a week — and it is taught by a single teacher with the purpose of covering some subject matter. School is made up of such courses. The time spent in class is the coinage of school. The kids are to fit in to it.

There is much here that is pernicious. Students get the idea that serious work is not for all, that only some can do it. Of course, serious work is expected of all when they hit the real world after high school. Those who are simply passed along in school without realistic challenge end up in serious jeopardy. Accordingly, if a school is to justify its existence as well as to keep its soul, it has to push all kids to do such "serious work." Again, this does not mean that every student is taught in the same way, that there is One Best Curriculum. Nor does it mean that everyone will learn at the same rate or in the same way. Nor does it mean that everyone will strive steadily all the time. It means that the same meaningful standard is set for all, that the kids know it, and that the school will help them to achieve it, whatever the cost and however long it takes.[3]

Tracking — the assigning of students to groups that represent their supposed academic ability and interest — appears to be another self-fulfilling prohecy. To a substantial degree, we all are what we believe we are. And we believe, more often than not, what the teachers or the test scores or our immediate community tells us.

The effects of tracking stare us in the face. Students in schools where the expectations for all are high and the program geared to help youngsters rise to those expectations do so in dramatically greater numbers than in tracked schools. As one Texas middle-schooler put it to her principal, "We did what we were unsupposed to do."[4] In a northeastern senior high school, a student teacher found two "misassigned" students in his Curriculum Two junior English class; they "should have been" in a "lower, slower" Curriculum Four group. His mentor teacher, a maverick, told him just to let it be: the two kids wanted to stay and the guidance office computer would take longer than the term's length to figure out that an "error" had been made. How did the students do? One did fine, a B. The other struggled and passed, though barely. Both seemed to gain much. The youngster with the B had the exquisite pleasure of knowing that he had beaten the system. Both had been treated to the expectation of serious work, which each now knew that he could do, one way or another.

Tracking draws lines by race, class, and sometimes gender, though there is not a shred of evidence that sex or race or economic status prescribes once and for all time one's powers of intellect, imagination, or determination. The stereotypes abound: girls are no good at math. That black kid in Michael Jordan sneakers couldn't be interested in physics or "do" serious science even if he wanted to. Poor kids are shiftless; they lack ambition; they're going nowhere. Asian-American kids achieve. Hispanic kids don't care. Blond kids are cheerleaders and will go to college . . . The litany is familiar. We decide about children by how they appear and what we have been expected to believe about their appearances. Unwittingly, usually, schools draw the lines, signaling to particular students what they are good for. There are tracks for everyone and anyone.

All too often, the tracking is set early and is made permanent. What a kid can do is decided on, say, when she or he is thirteen, and the youngster is slotted in accordingly. While most American schools allow shifting from track to track, this is usually difficult to do, because the "top" tracks are organized into sequences of courses, each with prerequisites that a student not in the track from the beginning is unlikely to have. More telling, however, is the level of mastery: a student who is not challenged for a period of years, or even months, finds it difficult to catch up with students who have been stretched during the same period. Indeed, the very struggle of trying to catch up often tells the student that she *is* inferior, just as the school said she was. As the academic timetable moves inexorably along — we must get to quadratics by February — no catch-up time allowed. The kid is trapped. The late bloomer flourishes all too rarely. The waste to that student — and to society at large — is prodigious.

Few schools realize the unfair practices they subscribe to, just as few of us teachers are aware enough of the rigidities we foster in our classrooms. It usually takes outsiders' evidence to confront us with the discrimination, and we do not like hearing it, nor are we prepared to accept it. It is too painful.

When seeing schools as a visitor, I often ask to take a class. Sometimes teachers let me, though rarely with the brisk assent I received in a northeastern city high school when, on a moment's notice, I was handed a ninth-grade humanities group for a period of an hour and a half. I inherited the topic under study — crafting an essay — and plunged into questioning the kids on their topics. Each essay was to center on an incident involving a close family member and was to include, in one graceful way or another, a portrait of that person, the narrative of the incident, and a description of the writer's deeper or differing sense of his relative on the basis of that incident. It was a demanding topic for fourteen-year-olds.

However, not every kid presented the essence of fourteenness. Of the twenty or so youngsters eyeing me doubtfully, there were little and big ones, the bearded man and the childish boy, the women-girls looking like mothers or children, sometimes both. They were surely a tough lot, on the whole; they had probably seen much of life, much that was foreign to my own experience. The class was predominantly black and brown; there were no Asian-Americans or Asians.

Some talked easily about their work; most did not. Two large girls stumbled badly in English; their whispers to each other were in rapid, easy Portuguese. The most vocal student was a stringy, slouched boy wearing a black T-shirt emblazoned with the face of a recent film character and a Chicago Bulls cap with the visor turned to the back. He had a quick retort for everything, usually spoken into thin air, not to me or even to his classmates. These comments were usually apt, always funny, clever, bordering on but never crossing the line of insolence. He was utterly unignorable. He was intensely watched by a virtually mute bigger boy, a particular friend, obviously, who grinned and nodded assent from time to time.

In one corner, leaning against the wall, the tablet of her desk teetering, was a slight white girl, apart from the rest of the group but attending with care. She wore studiously unkempt clothes, jeans well ripped at the knees. She took her time to talk, but when she did her language was standard English, her references from a different part of town. Her language separated her even more than her race, but the others ignored her. She seemed oblivious of her isolation. By contrast, the group's central figure was an older-looking tall boy, whose talk was carefully phrased, melodious with Caribbean intonations, and as precise as it was predictable. He seemed the class's leader, an Eagle Scout in deportment, an ad for a college admissions brochure.

My impressions of these kids and my conversation with them immediately evoked stereotypes. I guessed from their appearances alone who they were. I knew that this mental sorting-out was happening; it happens to us all: we try to make sense of strangers, the quicker the better. Although one tries to rein in one's judgments, one still makes them.

After a time, the students set to work on their essays. I traveled among them, peering over shoulders, reading the starts of their work. Different people — different stereotypes — emerged. Some could barely write simple prose but could whisper to me rich ideas they were struggling to put to paper. Others, like the isolated white girl, could write easily but could not tell me clearly what they wanted to express. This student of the kneeless jeans presented a tangle of notions. Whatever her technical writing skills, she lacked a coherent story to tell. She was childish, not so much naïve as living in a world of flat simplicities.

Some had no idea of what a narrative was. Others created tales about their brothers that would have dazzled Steven Spielberg. Some loved writing, seemingly losing themselves in concentration. Chicago Bulls whipped off a pageant of paragraphs, his bon mots of the earlier discussion now finding their way to paper. His work was sloppy but wonderful. Others slouched, pencils relentlessly tapping, gazing around, a few words put down, not even a sentence, utterly unengaged. Only the Caribbean-American proved true to form. He whispered and wrote as he had talked publicly. He exuded assurance.

As their attention waned, I shifted the activity to a discussion of a historical incident that once raised and still raises some enduring issues of fundamental justice. As I go among schools, I like to use this particular exercise, because it gives consistency to my class watching. The merchant vessel *Emily,* out of Salem, Massachusetts, in 1819, dropped anchor in the harbor of Canton, China, to sell and buy goods. While the captain carried out the major transactions, several Chinese entrepreneurs tied their junks up to the ship and noisily hawked their wares to the men on board. One of the seamen, named Terranova, was swabbing the deck near the tethered boat of an especially persistent woman peddler. Somehow a large pottery jug on deck was loosened and fell onto the hawker's junk. The peddler fell overboard and drowned. The Cantonese authorities demanded that the captain turn Terranova over for trial by a Chinese magistrate. The justice of Canton harbor was balanced, the captain knew, on different scales from those of Massachusetts. The question to the students: If you were the captain, would you turn Terranova over?[5]

The case can elicit all sorts of responses: fact gathering, weighing of alternatives, separation of the immediate situation from principle, empathy for a different cultural position, the need to understand trade, Salem, and Canton in the first part of the nineteenth century. And more. The kids jumped in, at first tentatively, then more vociferously. I served as a human encyclopedia, a fact giver; I expressed no opinion. The Cape Verdean girls took positions of principle; Chicago Bulls looked for a quick way out. Just pull anchor and sail away, he argued. Others protested. What about the *Emily*'s trade next year? What about the rights of the family of the drowned woman? And more. Some refused to make a decision, paralyzed. Again, patterns of response were different; now different stereotypes emerged. The quick portraits I had twice formed disappeared again. Eagle Scout, for example, was silent. He could not make a decision. What might be right for him was not only unclear but unfathomable. I was unfair to push for a decision. He and a few others angrily resented my final call for each student to put on a slip of paper his or her "answer" to the authorities about Terranova's release to Cantonese law.

The complexity of young people was displayed in a ninety-minute spread in the restricted world of a high school classroom, even to a stranger who had had no briefing about these kids and who had his hands full simply maintaining order, no less being amateur ethnographer. My impressions changed several times. One "cut" at establishing what each youngster could or could not do, even with a test, carefully crafted, was not the answer. What kind of day was each student having? Where was his mind this morning? Could she understand what I was saying? Did a word I used mean something different to him from what I intended? Did my "style" smother one but provoke another to do what he was "unsupposed" to do? Beautifully complicated these students were, and to pretend otherwise would be to deny humanity.

How can teachers know the students, know them well enough to understand how their minds work, know where they come from, what pressures buffet them, what they are and are not disposed to do? A teacher cannot stimulate a child to learn without knowing that child's mind any more than a physician can guide an ill patient to health without knowing that patient's physical condition. Tendencies, patterns, likelihoods exist, but the course of action necessary for an individual requires an understanding of the particulars.

And so, what to do? Remedies are actually obvious. They promise, however, to challenge a clutch of traditional educational practices.

First, the number of students per teacher must be limited. Teachers, even the most experienced, can know well only a finite number of individual students, surely not more than eighty and in many situations probably fewer. The typical secondary school teacher today is assigned anywhere from 100 to over 180, coming at him, rapid fire, in groups of twenty to forty. Horace Smith daily sees five groups of some twenty-four students each for three quarters of an hour. Can he really know well how each youngster thinks, how each one is progressing and why, what each one cares about?

People, adolescents included, are complicated and changeable, and knowing them well is not something one can easily attain or hold on to forever. Kids seem different to different adults; they respond in different ways to different situations or when studying different disciplines. Few students open up to older people they do not know or trust; to know a youngster in order to teach her well means knowing her first as a person. Moreover, there are no perfect tests one can administer to get a permanent fix on a child, no matter how educators struggle to create such devices and to believe in them. Current research on learning and adolescent development is full of speculation, of conflicting findings and incomplete results, and it gives no simple answer to the nature of learning or growing up. In sum, teachers (like parents) are very much on their own, drawing on a mixture of signals from research, from experience, and from common sense as the basis for their decisions.

Accordingly, and reflecting the ambiguous nature of each student's progress or lack thereof, wise teachers, knowing that they must be diagnosticians of the youngster's progress, take counsel regularly with their colleagues about the student, sharing impressions, hunches, and suggestions. Teachers confer with parents. And teachers make time to confer with the student himself, privately — formally or more likely informally — not only in the rush of class time.

Just fine, skeptics say, usually with more sarcasm than incredulity. No more than eighty students per teacher. Time to chat regularly about each student with that student's other teachers. Time for contact with parents. Quiet time with each pupil. It is utterly unrealistic. Taxpayers won't pay for all those extra professionals required to close the gap.

However, continuing with a system that leaves the majority of the students essentially anonymous, at the mercy of crude stereotyping, is what is unrealistic. Efficient learning in our current system is simply impossible, to any rewarding and demanding degree. Evidence for this is overwhelming. Moving kids along in cohorts by their ages, labeling them and putting them into tracks that fix their academic futures permanently, are sad practices for a school system that takes learning seriously.[6]

The matter is really one of priorities. If knowing each student well is a necessity, other things will yield to it. The typical public high school today has an overall professional-student ratio of 1 to 14, even as the typical teacher, in his five classes per day, may encounter 150. Careful studies of a growing number of typical schools demonstrate that the existing complement of professionals — teachers, administrators, counselors, and others, over a hundred in a school of fifteen hundred — readily and imaginatively can be deployed to ease the current classroom loads dramatically.[7] Combine this redistribution with other steps (taken for other sound reasons) to simplify and focus the school's work, and the result for a teacher can be a total student load in his several classes of no more than eighty, this without changing the school's operating budget much if at all.

Critics still scoff. Who will do this? Impossible, they say. Granted, the barriers are real. Some are technical, relating to teacher certification and state requirements. Others, such as the sharp distinctions between teachers and administrators, are erected by the traditions of collective bargaining. Yet others are structural, because any serious change in one important part of a school will inevitably affect the other important parts. Given the synergistic quality of school routines, reform by tiptoe, or by little steps at a time, is not possible.

Most barriers are more personal, poignant. Teachers would have to teach differently, and — even if they could imagine the prospect — they fear doing so. They are ill trained to shift the way they work, having been studiously prepared in the universities for the school world as it is, by which was unwittingly meant an unchangeable world. To get the load of students down to an acceptable level, most would have to collaborate with colleagues, an unsettling business. Working alone in the castle of one's classroom is preferable to exposing to peers what one thinks of individual students and how one would teach them. Some "specialists" would have to carry out more broadly defined jobs, ones that would challenge them and challenge the mystery of their specialty.

The frustration is powerful. At a meeting at a city high school a cherubic-looking white-haired chemistry teacher kept nodding and agreeing with the argument I made in my presentation to the faculty that the number of students assigned to each teacher had to be radically reduced. She balked, however, at any compromise on her wish to teach nothing but chemistry, at least as she defined chemistry. I reasoned with her: this is too poor a school to more than double the teaching force. Couldn't she teach some mathematics to kids who were her chemistry students? *I'm not a mathematics teacher,* she replied. I countered, I'm not suggesting that you teach advanced math, just algebra. *I'm not a math teacher.* Can you teach chemistry to any standard without math? *That's different.* How? She broke into tears. *I would rather teach two hundred students chemistry than teach anything else.* But you can't know that many kids at all . . . *I know, I know, I know.*

A second remedy to the problem of costly and inefficient student anonymity is to vary ways of teaching, manners of testing, and assumptions about the rate of an individual student's progress.

The necessary condition here is clarity about goals. Teachers and students must know what is to be expected and at what standard. The goals that are set must respect the integrity of the destination — say, the ability to understand human emotions and to make constructive use of that understanding — and that of an individual, allowing her to present her grasp in the way most powerful for her. When this destination is clear, many roads to its achievement can be mapped.

Some of this is simple for thoughtful teachers. They never explain anything in just one way: they describe orally; they diagram or sketch; they assign reading; they push forward examples; they suggest analogies; they set different sorts of problems, some based on familiar ground, others in unfamiliar contexts. These teachers poke along the dawdling student, but they make allowances for different rates of the march to understanding. All students will reach the destination but not in the same ways or at the same rates. The program will be flexible; there will be checkpoints that allow student and teacher to see how progress is being made, and the rate of progress will be tailored to the student's capacity. The destination is bounded by exercises — Exhibitions — which yield the richest possible evidence of each student's arrival or delay. The school will tolerate — ideally, honor — the individual styles and routes to mastery. It will also reward a student who stretches beyond mastery, with performance of high merit.

Is this in effect a kind of tracking? Are students within a particular classroom "organized" along the lines of their level of skill and accomplishment? Yes, often; but in a flexible, tentative way, without a public label ("honors") that categorizes them for a particular sort of adult expectation. Paradoxically, the most reasonable form of tracking is the most extreme: every student is "grouped" as she or he needs at any time.

All this personalization can be taken too far, or worse yet can be bureaucratized with solemn Meetings called on a Schedule to examine Each Student's Brain and Navel. Compromises and common sense and flexibility are always needed in schools, just as they are in good families. Adjustments must be made quickly and thoughtfully. The key ingredients here are time during the school day for people to meet, schedules that allow the teachers of particular youngsters to gather together, teachers committed to such gatherings, and a school program flexible enough to respond to adjustments recommended for each student. Schools should do no less for students than effective hospitals do for patients. Good hospitals allow time for staff consultations. They expect collaboration in the diagnosis of problems and the selection of remedies. Good hospitals consult patients carefully.

Schools are not hospitals and school kids are not "sick," yet the analogies in this case hold.

Finally, the mores of the school — the ways it goes about its business — must implicitly show respect for individual students, for the expectation that each can succeed, and for the belief that each deserves success. It is in this context that schools' "dirty little secrets," incendiary issues like race, can be addressed. A school faculty that knows its students has taken each beyond his or her race, has accepted each as a person. This is not to say that race or gender or ethnicity is not of consequence; it means only that other matters, such as a kid's personality, his hopes, his friends, his passions, his family, his idiosyncrasies, count more. It is one thing to say, "Those three black kids and those two white kids over there are . . ."; it is better to say, "Bill, Amanda, Susan, Roger, and Ernest . . ." The person emerging from the caricature can help to dissolve the stereotype. A stereotype is one of the roots of prejudice, one readily confronted in good schools. The "dirty little secrets" will never be eliminated or go away: America's prejudices run too deep for that. The tensions and wranglings they incite will always be with us, and schools must accept them — but always in the context of the reality that no two people, young or old, are ever quite alike, nor should they ever be treated precisely alike.

A thoughtful school "culture" cannot be readily codified or structured. An advisory period merely offers the possibility of "advice" given and taken. What happens within that opportunity is the nub of it. Fuzzy but fundamental qualities of caring and honesty, attentiveness both to the immediate and to a young person's future, empathy, patience, knowing when to draw the line, the expression of disappointment or anger or forgiveness when such is deserved — indeed, those qualities which characterize us as humans rather than programmed robots — mark the essence of a school that is at once compassionate, respectful, and efficient.

How do such schools come to be? Through the leadership of their adults, people who set and reset the standards, people who stay around a school long enough to give it a heart as well as a program, people who are ready to build a community that extends beyond any one classroom, people who know the potentials and limitations of technical expertise and of humane judgment. One does not "design" such schools.

Such schools, rather, grow, usually slowly and almost always painfully, as tough issues are met.

Horace's committee seemed stumped about how to respect the differences among students and yet meet the need for some absolute academic standards. Comparisons to athletics were tried, but what kept cropping up was tracking — with academic varsities, junior varsities, and the rest.

The problem, committee members knew, was that the game of life was all played at the varsity level. In the use of their minds, if not their passing arms and kicking feet, all the young people had to be made as competitive as possible.

"Take your taxes," Margaret suggested. "Everybody has to do his taxes. Taxophobes are not let off. Everyone must be able to play that game."

There was laughter. "The Form 1040 is the test we all must pass . . ." More embarrassed laughter.

"Not everyone will be able to make sense of all that IRS gobbledygook."

"Why not?" Margaret persisted. "It isn't all that hard. It takes time, persistence, careful reading, good records, patience galore. Why can't we set those ends as a standard for any Franklin graduate?"

"In the real world, lots of people do their taxes with others. In our house it's a collective late March hassle. And if we don't understand, we ask for help."

"So, isn't that OK?" Margaret again. "We can't teach every student the tax code forever and ever, but we should be able to expect every one of them to do some sort of tax return. If in collaboration, so much the better. It will give each young person the confidence that with help as needed he can complete the 1040."

"Can we expect the same of the faculty?" More laughter. The committee was learning to like itself.

Green: "The 1040 is the Real World. Why isn't that a good Exhibition?"

Again someone protested: "It will be too hard for some of the kids!"

Coach: "It can't be. They have to be able to do it."

An Exhibition: Form 1040

Your group of five classmates is to complete accurately the federal Internal Revenue Service Form 1040 for each of five families. Each member of your group will prepare the 1040 for one of the families. You may work in concert, helping one another. "Your" particular family's form must be completed by you personally, however.

Attached are complete financial records for the family assigned to you, including the return filed by that family last year. In addition, you will find a blank copy of the current 1040, including related schedules, and explanatory material provided by the Internal Revenue Service.

You will have a month to complete this work. Your result will be "audited" by an outside expert and one of your classmates after you turn it in. You will have to explain the financial situation of "your" family and to defend the 1040 return for it which you have presented.

Each of you will serve as a "co-auditor" on the return filed by a student from another group. You will be asked to comment on that return.

Good luck. Getting your tax amount wrong — or the tax for any of the five families in your group — could end you in legal soup!

* * *

Here is another educational target.

It is authentic, painfully so. The importance of the 1040 is self-evident. Knowing how not to be intimidated by the process of filing is obviously worthwhile.

It will appeal to students. It deals with two issues paramount in most of their lives: money and fairness (the latter particularly if the families selected come from radically different walks of life).

Taught intelligently, it opens the door wide, and for many students in a compelling way, to a cluster of important disciplines such as microeconomics, politics, ethics, and political history. It can thereby be the springboard for sustained serious study in several directions. For example, it raises provocative questions about equality, about what "tax breaks" are and who gets them and why. It is an example of government at work, with its use of financial incentives. In all these respects, it spurs teaching, animates it — this is a quality of a good Exhibition.

It teaches the importance of accurate, consistent records, the necessity to read closely, the nature of the tax system, and who and what it favors. It also calls for a demonstration of arithmetic, logical, and analytic skills.

It is organized so that students can work together, helping one another. Some may promptly race out and consult a tax expert or call the IRS, asking for help. While this is not recommended, it is tolerable: the costs of such outside help are minimized by the necessity to withstand and explain an audit. Indeed, the act of getting such help may serve as a powerful teacher. Further, the necessity to be another person's co-auditor requires the display of useful knowledge.

It allows a teacher to vary the difficulty of material among the students involved, giving a financially simpler family to a struggling student and a more complex set of issues to the class tax whiz. The students will, of course, help one another, and they all must stand behind all five returns.

5

Places Matter

"I'LL BET no one in the White House has kids."

One of the parents made this dubious wager. The committee had been reviewing recent articles about school reform, several of which had come out of Washington. Most of them used an economic argument for an educational revolution: what the country urgently needed was an adept workforce to be able to compete in the global economy. The common term for students was "products." Good schools were to yield "good products."

"My kid isn't a 'product.' And I'll bet none of the president's kids was ever treated as a product."

"Come on," someone said. "It's just a way of talking. It says that schools are important to the economy."

"The economy isn't everything."

"How one talks is how one thinks. So much of this stuff we read leaves kids out. It's argument from on high. Bloodless. Big Brother. Scary."

Patches: "And oh so full of self-righteousness."

"A kid without the prospect of a job is a kid who won't concentrate in school," Horace intruded, fearful that Patches would start in on "the critics" again.

The parent persisted: "The people of this community aren't going to tie themselves in knots changing their schools just to compete with Toyota. They just won't. Maybe they should, but they won't. Parents look for different things. They care about kids as people and not as parts of business's engine."

"That's short-sighted."

"Maybe so. But it's true. At least it's true of this community."

Green exploded. "It wasn't the *schools* that made Americans buy Japanese cars. The schools taught the kids to think about spending their money wisely. It was the American *companies* that underestimated Americans' wish for good cars . . . Business ought to lay off us and start looking in the mirror."

This outburst, however irrelevant, stirred the meeting nicely. Patches took it further: "Maybe we should have a national exam for graduation from business school." The teachers chortled, one adding, "And a teachers' alliance to reform the S and L industry . . ." Laughter.

Horace tried to bring the meeting back. "So who's to decide about the schools? Parents? Our community? Or policy moguls who see our kids as products?"

"And who says that what this community wants is what other communities want?" There was a pause, not because anyone disagreed with the notion of differences among communities but because no one knew what to do with the apparent consensus about the fundamental importance of local control.

Horace: "So, what to do? Aren't there any common standards?"

The school board member: "We've got to have the right to choose the schools we want for our own children. If White House staff members want their kids in schools where they're treated as potential products, they should have that right. If some Texas town wants to go big with Friday night football, that's OK for them. We need *our* schools, ones that fit *our* way of living. No one should tell us what's right for this community."

A protest from one of the students: "Who says that this is one community? Do we all agree here?" The school board member flushed.

Horace, again: "Aren't there nationally common standards?"

The young English teacher finally addressed Horace's question: "Yes, there are, there must be, some common standards.

People move around. Kids in school won't stay in this place forever. The larger community has its claim on them."

The school board member: "But what about *our* rights, what's special about *this* place? America's strength comes from its towns, not from Washington bureaucrats."

"Nor should people who decide what's right for them in Mercer Island, Washington, or Little Silver, New Jersey, tell us what to do. Our kids are our kids . . ."

The student again: "Who says that there's a community, that we all agree on what our school should be? I don't see all that much agreement here . . . Maybe community's a fiction . . ."

The debate continued, aimlessly. Even as he admired the student's persistent wisdom, Horace knew that the committee could not deal with his issue. It was, perhaps, appropriate for some other kind of forum. All Horace knew was that when the debate was done and a plan for a redesigned Franklin High School was readied, it had to mesh with the ethos of its community. All the rhetoric in the press and in committee reports about the dire state of American education would count for little when compared with the pressure for local imperatives. Horace remembered the Tip O'Neill saying: "All politics is local." All education is local too, Horace believed. That was the price of democracy, the price of trusting the people. And if the people were not trusted, their resentment would eventually pull everything awry. Even state mandates would be sabotaged if they conflicted too much with local mores.

Horace wondered whether his committee would have an easier time in another place, another kind of community. Was there any place, he puzzled, where education really mattered? Who was willing to fight for the freedom and rigor of young people's minds? Just phrasing the thought that way made it seem extreme or sentimental. That it could sound that way spoke volumes. Horace remembered a bumper sticker he'd recently seen on a car parked in front of his family's liquor store: "Do we fear our enemies more than we love our children?"[1]

Take a small, homogeneous community with a stable population. The school superintendent has been in office for seventeen years, and he knows almost everyone in town. A trip to a local coffee shop with him fixes this impression; he is met with the friendly joshing that signals respect. He gets what he wants most of the time from his board — as long as Friday night high school basketball is competitive, peppy, and orderly. Wednesday night is church night in this small city, and the superintendent and the other school administrators deliberately move among the activities, sensing the mood of the community while taking part in its rituals. They are "of" this town, as are its teachers. Many grew up here. Over the years they've gained a sense of what goes and what does not go, how hard to push and for what. There is balance, order, and a sense of what people call "their" community. Intrusions of state law, much less federal law, are suspect. Since Supreme Court orders relating to school desegregation came down — over thirty-five years ago — suspicion of outsiders has prevailed.

Here is another community, rapidly growing. Its schools are organized within a county structure, and this is a large county. It will build six new schools during the next five years. The superintendent comes from out of state; he presides over a substantial administration; the professionals in it are experts in their fields. The school board is itself as changeable as the county's population; of the nine members who appointed the superintendent, now in only his fourth year, two remain in office. There is no town center: this is a county of discrete communities. Many of its residents work in a nearby large city, a place whose newspapers and television stations set the agenda for the region. Many of the newcomers are from minority groups; there is tension in the schools, not yet overt but surely there. The teachers know it, and their union representatives have alerted the administrators. The school board will not discuss the matter publicly. "We don't want to start something with this," its chairman says. The superintendent reports that he can't keep up with the currents in this large system; there is "something new every day," he tells us. Some semblance of order and forward motion is maintained by the use of an elaborate strategic planning mechanism within the school administration, one into which "my principals are plugged," says the superintendent. He feels under great pressure and appears exhausted. He and his family choose to live in another county. "They attack us at parties here," he says sadly.

Here is a city with several high schools. One dates from the 1840s; it was one of the first secondary schools in the state and has a modern reputation for sending most of its graduates to college. A student is admitted on the basis of a set of examinations — not standardized multiple-choice tests but serious exercises requiring extensive essay writing. The school's program has changed little since 1920 (when the sciences were finally given prominence), and some of the rituals, such as Prize Assembly, go back far beyond that. The ambience of the place is serious; the students gripe and josh about the routines but fiercely defend them when quizzed by outsiders. The faculty is older, veteran; one rises within the city school system eventually to earn a place here. The parents are restless; they gripe about the busy work required of the students — reports on this, exercises for that. They complain about the school's emphasis on college admissions, but when their own children are involved they hassle the counselors endlessly. The students and their families are a tight group. Most are white, middle class. The handful of black and Hispanic students are befriended at school, but ignored by the white majority in afterschool social activities. A few of the teachers are well known to parents and are perceived to be the school's academic superstars, the "professors." Several of them live in the upper-income section of town. Most of the teachers, though, live in the suburbs and see little of their students' families.

Another of the district's high schools enrolls adolescents from its western, working-class attendance zone as well as some youngsters from a lower-income enclave within an upper-income part of the city. Like the first school, this one is relatively old; it dates from the early 1900s. Physically, it resembles the first school, but the students are very different; they are largely from minority groups, many with home languages other than English, some 60 percent on "free or reduced lunch" (meaning that their families live at or below the poverty line). The turnover of students is heavy; about six students are admitted as newcomers each week during the year, and a somewhat larger number depart during the same period. Daily attendance runs about 80 percent on Tuesday, Wednesday, and Thursday; attendance is lower on Monday and Friday. Fifty percent go on to some sort of higher education. The teachers are veterans and sound cynical; the work expected of them appears endless, and the transience of the students saps energy. "You just get going with a kid and he's gone . . ." Few parents come to Student-Parent-Teacher Association events, even though the elected officers of the organization, most of them middle income, struggle to attract interest. The school has a bad reputation. "It isn't what it used to be," city old-timers say. The principal notes ruefully, "I spend most of my time being a cop."

A third high school, the "alternative program" of the city's schools, was started in the mid-1960s to serve adolescents who "did not fit in" to the other seven high schools. At any one time it enrolls no more than two hundred students and occupies the first floor of a renovated factory building near the city's center. The students, who come from all over the community, are mostly older kids who had dropped out by tenth or eleventh grade. The races are evenly balanced here. The atmosphere is warm: first name only, frank, raw, demonstrative. Many of the students are parents, and the place runs a small day care center for their infants. The turnover is very high; some in and out over a period of years. The daily group meetings are for discussing community concerns; they are intense, confrontational, and sometimes therapeutic. The students' problems, only some of which surface at school, are often severe; teachers ease up on academic assignments in order to help the kids deal with them. "A kid with a problem isn't going to learn much algebra until he copes with the problem. That's where we begin," says one of the teachers who founded the school and is still there over twenty-five years later. Some students have been formally identified as having "special needs," and the extra public funding allocated for them permits a richer faculty-student ratio here than at either of the two other schools. Students' parents are almost completely absent; many of the kids are on the run from their homes as well as from traditional schools. Few go to college. Most of those who persist in this school are fiercely attached to it: "This place cares." "We're a sanctuary," says the principal.

The superintendent responsible for these three schools and others is expected to set a standard for all of them, a single schedule, calendar, curriculum, and staffing program. The teachers' contract makes no distinctions among secondary schools. There is One City, and therefore, it is posited, One Community. "I have schools so different . . . I can't get them together . . . The board doesn't understand . . . They always blame us and then the kids . . ." He has been in office two years and is the third superintendent in six years. He is forty-eight and has had a heart attack. He laughs about that. "That's what I'm supposed to get in this job."

Much of learning depends on a student's disposition. He will try hard if it seems worthwhile to try hard, if the people whom he respects believe that trying hard is a good thing, if the community supports that kind of effort, and if something inside himself impels him to try hard. It is easy for him not to try hard. The opportunities for procrastination and for diversion are legion. He knows — as do his teachers — that the decision to use his mind is entirely up to him. It is easy to shut out new ideas, or any ideas.

The community — the community the school serves, not necessarily its political jurisdiction — is crucial. Its values, the "treaties" it lives by, set the tone in which a student is asked to learn. If a school lacks a community, it must build one. If a community distrusts a school, the school must change to regain trust. If teachers or parents or students see that they have no contract on behalf of the students, such a contract must be forged.

No two communities are alike. All have blemishes, all have strengths. The latter, the genius of a particular community, must be tapped. Its distinction must be respected; there is no common genius to be expected in all quarters. There are no shortcuts. All this commonsense lore about good schoolkeeping has been around for generations. Unfortunately, the hierarchical bureaucracies that have been erected to run the schools frequently ignore it.

How both to recognize and to capitalize on this reality? First, we must acknowledge the importance of a school's surroundings, not just for political reasons ("The parents should have a say in the running of a school") but for educational reasons. A heedless community will breed heedless adolescents. A community that supports learning will encourage each learner.

Second, we must respect the community served by each school and take the time to understand it. The arrogance and patronizing airs — "we know better than they could ever know" — so often exhibited by policymakers and pundits must be abandoned. It is not that the community always knows best or knows everything; it is that no one has any corner on wisdom, and what seems in a locality trivial or unconstructive may be in fact quite the reverse.

Third, each school must be free to adapt a program to its own immediate community, whether stable or transient. There can be no one approved system, no codicil to regulations about who should be involved and to what extent. Such impositions strain the special fabric of a particular community and connote official disrespect. And such disrespect corrodes the trust students must feel if they are to take their schooling seriously. This is "school site management" and much more; it is community organization and collective advocacy on the behalf of learning. There must be accountability, to the parents and to the state, but for the latter, the more general the better.

Fourth, to the maximum feasible extent parents and their children and teachers must be able to choose their school, in effect to choose their community. A policy of choice must not be a cover for segregation, as the countless critics of the "choice" policy fear it may be. But within a policy of openness, being able to choose one's school provides a powerful incentive for families, students, and teachers. "This is our place. We chose it. We can shape it. We have a stake in it."

Fifth, the stability of each school should be a high priority. Trust within a community cannot be built by leaders who are here today and gone tomorrow. There should be incentive for school people to dig in to their school, to shape it, to stay with it. It is people who are trusted, not some amorphous reputation of a school. Likewise, the stability of the community leaders is critical. They cannot be this year's parents. They must be the neighborhood's most revered leaders, and their politics respected.

Sixth, those with central responsibility for education should always be guided by the aphorism "The least imposition is the best imposition." A search for standards must not lead to standardization. Control must not become a fetish ("We need to have the data on what's going on"). Imposition is *by definition* suspect. It weakens the sense of responsibility and obligation of the school's community, including its teachers: "They don't trust us, so they make us do this. If they're so smart and know so much, why don't they run the whole thing?" A community that believes it has little real control of its schools is likely to be a community that little supports them. An unsupportive community will not goad and cajole and encourage and take pride in its students. Unencouraged students are unlikely to work hard or to believe that school is important.

One returns, then, to students' dispositions, their willingness and even excitement to learn. All of us learn what we want to learn. We learn when we feel that we are able to learn, when we believe there is a happy end to the struggle to learn. We learn when we understand the dead end that awaits us if we do not learn. We learn when we are convinced that we eventually will have the power to act on that learning to take ourselves someplace we want to go that is in reality there. If school is about preparing people for a world that for whatever reason is not theirs to seize, it is a living lie.

It is here that educational policy and practice rest on economic and social policy and practice. A place where adolescents have nowhere to go economically, and where some racial or ethnic groups are treated as unwelcome castes by the power structure, is a place whose schools will never operate well. Schooling is investing in the future. You must learn this, the teacher says, so that you can get ahead. If there is nothing ahead, why learn? The quickest way in which a community can improve its schools is to

want and to need its graduates. School reform in many communities once again depends on — indeed, is even hostage to —
social and economic reform.

Even if there is a real and legitimate future for each student in
the community, we still must work to engage her. She has to see
it, understand it, want it, be prepared to work toward it. It is here
that the school has its proper task. How can the school help each
student see a worthy future and gain the self-confidence to strive
for it? How can the school nourish each student's resources and
sense of purpose?

At least two practices make obvious sense. First, every effort
must be made to reinforce the student when he deserves it. Lying
to a kid — "That was a fine essay, Sam," when it was in fact a
mess — is quickly spotted as hypocrisy and usually deepens the
student's lack of self-worth by signaling the teacher's despair.

The second practice is less familiar, because it posits that
adolescents should be assumed to be responsible. Most schools
infantilize and pamper their students. They are not be trusted: all
will need hall passes to go somewhere when classes are session.
Adults attend to their creature comforts — operate their libraries, cook their meals, guard their premises, sweep their halls,
coach their teams, cut their schools' lawns. Such practice is
generous ("The students are here to study their algebra, not to
cook luncheon") but thwarts opportunities for young people to
take responsibility, to develop the habit of delivering on that
responsibility. What is most corrupting, it indicates to them that
they need not care — someone else will clean up — and are not
to be trusted with the obligations of caring.

If you expect kids to be irresponsible, they won't let you
down. Yet even those adults who are cynical about students have
marveled when adolescents take responsibility during a crisis —
digging out after a paralyzing snowstorm, quickly ministering to
a kid suffering a seizure in class, taking on duties during a custodians' strike. And we often observe adolescents holding very
responsible jobs after school. The person who needs a list of
rules about when to use the school library assists us at the public
library or superintends our luncheon at Friendly's restaurant or
raises her own child. Then she's not a kid; she's a young adult.

We must not romanticize. Many of us of all ages do not welcome responsibility. When we first seize it, we often foul things up and, as a consequence, take a thorough dislike to it. Taking responsibility often means shouldering the scutwork of life or doing the unpopular thing, even if all agree that it is necessary. Taking the lead can provoke jealousy or scorn. Fouling up a duty holds us up to criticism. Being a follower, a drone, has apparent merits.

Yet if school is about learning to use one's mind well, about resourceful thinking on important matters, about the inculcation of thoughtful habits, it must give the students opportunities to practice those habits. If being unnecessarily dependent — irresponsible — is a thoughless habit, then the school should press the alternative. Do nothing for students that they can do just as well for themselves, whether in algebra class or the cafeteria. A good school asks much of its students all the time, makes them do the work if they can, gets them into the habit of taking responsibility for their lives. In so doing it expresses respect for them, a respect that can elicit responsibility.

Being needed is a tonic for any one of us at any age, a spur to activity, virtually the most powerful incentive of all. Being wanted is a boon to our confidence; it is evidence of others' recognition of our worth. Acting on that need — helping a younger person, fixing something broken, getting out the school newspaper — gives us faith in ourselves, a conviction that lets us struggle with difficulties when they arise. I can "get" this math eventually, because I can do other things people admire; I know I am respected, so I can live with the current failures. This power to do things is the sense of agency; successful adolescents are invested with it. It can be fostered.[1]

A good school makes sure its students are legitimately needed. It can do this through formal programs of community service but must take care not to foster patronizing airs, an attitude of noblesse oblige. Sound community service should start with young students and take place within their own community. It is not simply another program, an option alternative, say, to physical education. It fills the center of the school's operation; it is a habit for that school.

The school that makes this habit an absolute expectation teaches well. The habit can flourish, however, only in a larger community that shares those values and practices them.

Unfortunately, these are not happy years for localities and branches of local government, including school boards. State and national policymakers may voice the right sentiments, but they seem not to trust the locals. They fear a lack of control, and believe that only they know what the people really need. Some authority will be paid out gingerly to "school sites." Then these communities will be largely forgotten or will be patronized by "consultation" with a few "representative" citizens or hemmed in by regulations and expectations for "neighborhood involvement." As a result of this patronizing centralism, many serious citizens shrug off local involvement. Why be involved, they say, if the people "up above" insist on making all the important decisions?

Local leaders watch as their communities' values are more and more affected by national and international influences, overwhelmingly those of commerce. The local deli is likely now to be part of a chain, selling its own version of a good meal. The local department stores push goods that are seen in Düsseldorf as well as Denver. The television is largely national. Even the evangelical preachers come over TV. What local parson can compete with the myriad successors of Jerry Falwell? Ideas come from without, not from within. In such nationalized conversation, local mores are ignored.

Yet communities matter, especially in education; not all of those national, largely commercial messages serve adolescents well. Without the advocacy of their own communities, committed to serious learning, adolescents will not become involved.

Paradoxically, the nation in its own service, in its search for more effective schooling, needs to rediscover immediate communities, respect their diversity, and profit from their strengths.

Horace asks for "common standards," an academic coinage that will well serve a peripatetic population and a national economy and polity. The school board member asks for local or community standards, ones that reflect the values of particular families in particular neighborhoods in particular places. Both sets of criteria have merit, and neither can be met without the other. For national standards to have any practical meaning, they must be accepted and supported by the locality. And unless the nation honors generous localism, the community is likely to wither or resist.

Today the power of the nation is increasing at the expense of the community. Americans must ponder whether that is wholly in the culture's best interest. Unfortunately, it is seductive to believe it is.

Places differ. Kids differ. Good schools differ. In the teeth of an insistent national culture, the characteristics of individual schools gain additional meaning. Perhaps we no longer need common schools. Perhaps our future will be better served by uncommon schools.

Horace's committee had been laughing over an account of a prank confessed to by one of the students. Good feeling reigned. The members had their differences but seemed able to compromise, or at least to identify where the areas of honest difference lay. The visitor had been helpful here; it often took an outsider to tell the committee what it had in fact been saying.

The visitor had never really been accepted into the group. She did not come to all the meetings; she came only when Horace asked her to. And she seemed addicted to pointed questions, never opinions. Our Lady Socrates, Coach once named her, and the moniker stuck. That made her blush. But perhaps in response to this prodding, the committee was beginning to make up a list of key issues, themselves cast largely as questions. *What should students be able to demonstrate in order to deserve the diploma? How can the school's program be shaped to help the students prepare for their Exhibitions? How can Franklin assert common standards and show respect for individual student differences? How can the school's human resources be distributed so that no teacher has responsibility for more than eighty students? How can the character of this particular community be respected, nurtured, honored?*

Questions wouldn't test the willingness of people to change

the school. Only answers would. It was the school board member who first expressed concern about the good feeling that had been forged. "Are we having fun because we're too stuck in our own community? Are we now too easy among ourselves, and thus with ourselves? Will we be as congenial when we have to bite some bullets?" These questions hushed the laughter. The fact that they came from a political leader gave them added weight.

The visitor interjected, deflecting the discussion. "Why not visit some other places, a good distance from here?" The committee had made several brief calls at nearby respected schools and had listened to the administrators' show-and-tell, with no great enthusiasm.

"Why not visit some really different schools and invite their staffs to visit here?"

"There's no point in studying schools whose kids are unlike ours," countered the mathematics teacher.

Horace demurred. "We're not going to *copy* anybody. We should travel not to pick up tricks but to open our minds. It could force us to think less parochially." The school board member nodded, and the mathematics teacher shook his head. There goes the end of the Era of Good Feeling, thought Horace.

Later there was more talk of parochialism, started by the school board member. She had been the one earlier pushing for local control — these are *our* schools. Now she wanted the committee to travel far afield.

She explained: "Unless we sample widely, no one will take us seriously." Her worries, it seemed, had less to do with local pride than with political tactics. "We'll soon have to invite to our discussions more members of the school board. We should have someone from the state meet with us . . . they have to know what we're up to. We may need regulatory waivers." She paused. "This committee is heading toward what might be a bold proposal, and though we're the ones charged with preparing it, nobody of importance should be surprised by it, and as many as possible should be in our corner when the report is issued."

"The faculty have to buy in, too," Green observed.

"Most of them," Margaret added. "We've got quite a job

ahead. The more we seem to be making progress, even on questions, the more it 'shows' in us. Our progress is making some teachers nervous."

"Maybe it's because we're having fun." Coach was ever upbeat. The prospect of bringing along their colleagues, however, was a concern. It was enough to spend the hours talking within the committee. Taking on the rest of the staff was daunting.

"Parochialism isn't all bad." Margaret brought the warmth back. "Young people should know this place well. They should know its idiosyncracies, its foibles."

The conversation drifted toward what it meant to "know" a community, and talk of recalling the local past led to the value of memory. The old folks remember. Let's get a Foxfire program started here. Let's get the kids to value the little, important things in their lives, the stories, the poems, the songs, the rituals, the people.[2]

Inevitably such talk led to the craft of memorizing: How does one recall the past?

"If we value memory, we'd better teach it."

"Our talk so far has been about general habits of mind. We've sloughed off specifics."

"But the skill of memory work is what remains." Margaret again. "And the way one hones that skill is by practice . . ."

"You mean kids should memorize things?"

"Absolutely. Not too much. But what's done should be first class. And it should be the sort of thing that will stick with each boy or girl forever."

An Exhibition: Performance from Memory

As a part of your final Exhibitions, you must show yourself and us that you can do the following, from memory:

1. Recite a poem or song or story that is special to your family or community.

2. Draw a map of the world, freehand (conventional Mercator projection), and be prepared to place properly on your map at least twelve of fifteen members of the United Nations that we shall randomly select for you.

3. Draw a map of the United States, freehand, and accurately position on your map at least twelve of fifteen states that we will select for you at random.

4. Identify and answer questions about the current United States president and vice president, this state's two United States senators, the representative from your district, your state representative and senator, and the mayor of this city.

5. Recite for us from memory a speech from history or literature that you find compelling and that we agree is appropriate for this exercise.

6. Present a time line since 1750 that you have assembled over the last several years and be prepared to answer questions about any event that appears on it.

7. Be prepared to identify five birds, insects, trees, mammals, flowers, and plants from our immediate local environment.

8. At a time mutually agreed on, we shall give you a text or an analogous "problem" (such as a machine to disassemble and reassemble) and three days in which to memorize or master it. We will ask you then to show us how well you have done this exercise.

9. Be prepared to reflect with us on how you completed this memory task — that is, how you best "learned" to memorize.

This Exhibition demonstrates that the student has skill in memorizing and that she is aware of basic facts that will serve her well.

It allows for a time trial, which implies that the student is sufficiently prepared in memory work to meet a reasonable deadline.

In several areas, it allows for student and faculty choice, thus providing opportunities for the faculty to match the exercises with a student's interests and capabilities.

It provides — if the teacher wisely chooses to use it — a springboard to the discussion of important matters — the politics or physical geography of southern Africa illuminated by national boundaries, or the meaning of "family" as expressed in a poem.

It indicates the importance of knowing some things well enough to commit them to memory, and the joy of reciting them.

It provides students with the confidence that arises from memorizing something of consequence.

6

Habits

"THIS PLACE doesn't really value academic excellence. At least the kids don't. Serious students here are given a hard time. Kids don't respect them. They call them nerds, geeks," the young English teacher complained.

The first student smirked. "They deserve it." The fact that this student was herself on the Honor Roll made the comment ripe.

"Why?" Horace asked.

"They're so into themselves. They have all the answers . . ."

"Grade grubbers," added the second student.

The first student: "They're full of facts. They think they know everything. They stay to themselves."

Horace protested, "Come on. *You* don't stay to yourself, and you don't put kids down in class with your knowledge. Aren't you drawing a stereotype here?" Horace was quietly acknowledging that she knew what a stereotype was. She did not respond, but was hardly cowed.

"We don't value the scholars here enough because we ourselves are uncertain of what scholarship is," the mathematics teacher chimed in. "We reward students for their grades and test scores, class rank, and that sort of thing. Yet we know these are only part of real scholarship. We all know Honor Roll kids who are just test chasers, Trivial Pursuit and Scrabble types, and we all know kids who don't get the scores but who are deep people. The students who are called nerds are often the self-absorbed, fact-filled ones. Their peers find them helpless, backward, inept, unconnected . . ."

"That's my point," the first student persisted. "Geeks are geeks because they're so . . . just full of facts. They're not real people . . ." She groped.

"Let's not criticize people just because *we* don't understand that what they're studying may be useful," the mathematics teacher continued. "New ideas sometimes do seem useless, even silly. We have to be careful to give people the benefit of the doubt . . ." He was looking at the first student, lecturing. She respected him, returned his gaze, stayed still.

"The main word there was 'use,'" said Green. "People don't use the bits of knowledge that make up Trivial Pursuit. Using knowledge is the heart of it." The science teacher wouldn't let go of the point, one that she had stressed since October.

"I agree," said the mathematics teacher.

"So do I," said Margaret. "We all must push our students to use knowledge . . ." She paused. "That will take time. It's easy to tell things to our classes and much harder to get them to use what we've told them."

"But the Honor Society is about grades, and grades are about knowing the facts," protested the second student.

"It's not as simple as that. Too often we don't Honor what we really need to honor," said the mathematics teacher, his voice capitalizing the word. Green nodded vigorously. "We should honor students who know how to use knowledge, who have the knowledge to use, and who use it unfailingly."

"After they graduate, too."

"Yes, after they graduate. That's what school is for, isn't it?"

Good schools are places where one gets the stuff of knowledge — that is, crudely, "the facts" — where one learns to use that stuff, and where one gets into the habit of such use.

A student learns the Bill of Rights, what those constitutional amendments say, precisely, and what they meant at the time of their framing. He learns then to use the Bill of Rights to under-

stand past, present, and even possible situations. Is the requirement to register a privately owned firearm a violation of the
Second Amendment? When does wiretapping a home telephone
violate the Fourth Amendment? An American, he must learn to
examine social and civic life in this way, through the lens of
personal rights; that is, he must develop the habit of routinely
addressing such situations.

Learning is not this neat, of course. Few of us learn the facts
very well unless we see their utility for us as individuals and
unless we practice their use. We need to want to learn them;
practicing will cement our grasp of the essential detail. Habit
grows from a mixture of conviction ("This is good for me; it is
persuasive; I can use this to good advantage"), of practice ("I
can do this stuff in my sleep"), and of reinforcement from the
community ("The place where I live and study is a place that
values this").

Ultimately, it is people's habits we most value and respect.
Schools must embrace this commonplace, and organize themselves to nurture good habits. Certainly schools are not cradles
of all virtuous habits. Their focus, to the extent that it can be
isolated, is on the intellect. It is the habit of thoughtfulness, of
bringing an informed, balanced, and responsibly skeptical approach to life, that schooling addresses. School, simply, is about
the habit of thoughtfulness.[1]

When put so baldly, the goal startles. It should not, as is
apparent when we reflect on which adults in a community are
often the most respected. The person who inevitably attracts our
admiration is the one on whom we can always depend: a person
who appears almost effortlessly able to keep a true perspective
on life, who gets important things done right, and who seems
always to have a good reason for deciding what is important. A
person who sees things coming and who perceives their most
likely consequences.

We admire the person who can be counted on to think before
acting, to weigh matters before dealing with them. He is known
not to be a gossip. We sense that he is aware of others and their
concerns. He hears us out and gets things sorted. We listen
especially to him at a public hearing on, say, property taxes: we

know that he is informed. He wouldn't talk if he weren't. We know he will stay with the issue as long as necessary: he is not a quitter. We can count on him not only to show up when he is needed but to maintain a sensible attitude and position. Before we vote, we often check with him.

We value the individual who can cope with something new, who, though not a CPA, can help us with our income tax returns. The friend who, though not in the insurance business, can explain our household policy. The person who, though not a mechanic, can deal with our stalled automobile. The person who, though not a chef, can produce a grade A meal. The acquaintance who, though not an artist, can sensitively draw us a design, take our picture, and convincingly explain to us why the new slipcovers in our living room are a visual disaster. We value people who, though neither nurses nor physicians, can get the straight story on our child's injury and explain it to us. We trust the person who, though not a philosopher, attends to the meaning and the fairness of things.

We admire the person who does not panic or disappear when something new or threatening comes into the community, who gets angry at what later turn out to be the right things to get angry about, but who stays cool the rest of the time. We respect the individual who regularly finds something new even in the familiar, who looks for reasons to laugh at the absurdities in life, and who enjoys sharing that laughter. We depend on the person whose predictions about what may soon happen are correct most of the time.

Such people, mercifully, are not rare. They are among our own friends. They are all kinds: the shy and loquacious, the young and the old, men and women. We do not at first think that they have much in common, but on reflection we perceive many traits they share. Annoyingly, however, when we are asked to define just what these are and why these people attract respect, our reasons drift into generalities or trivialities. He *thinks*, is able to keep his balance, and not let life get the better of him. She figured out how to get my new computer to display spreadsheets. These people are frustratingly difficult to characterize. However, we know them when we see them.

How did they get that way? Oh, most of us say, they are born with this difficult-to-define "it." Surely that is part of an explanation; nature works in some mysterious ways. But the "it" can be nurtured too. That is the purpose of education.

One reason that it is so difficult precisely to portray the person we respect is that what stimulates our admiration often arises from new situations, from activities that were impossible to predict. That is, these events could not be prepared for; we could therefore not fully describe what a person would do when faced with them. The automotive engineer is confronted with a new tough plastic that has the strength of sheet metal but can and must be fashioned in different ways. The stenographer faces new office technologies. The couple finds that their adopted infant has AIDS. The city manager discovers that there are no more landfills for garbage and that the EPA will, in any case, not let her city continue disposing of refuse as before. In many ways the world is perpetually new, and it is on those who effectively deal with challenges that the community confers respect.

Of course, the confidence to grasp the new depends on mastery of the old. Adults tend to forget that much of what is familiar to older people is totally new to students in school. One teacher I especially admire says she prefers to teach Chinese history to adolescents rather than to college students because she'll "be the one to watch them meet Confucius for the first time." Learning how to make sense of our most important "old" abstractions and issues — new to them but familiar to us — gives the young the experience and skill they require to cope well in the future. That is, they get into the habit of using their minds to figure out how to think and act in unpredictable situations.

Old matter is full of detail, specifics necessary to grasp if one is to understand. While the facts relating to the old matter are important for mastery, they may never be used again. That is, the details are a means to the end of understanding, not ends in themselves. Knowing that John Milton was blind when he wrote *Paradise Lost* gives us a special appreciation of the work, a slant on it that readies us to attend to the author as well as to the poem. However, remembering the seventeenth-century English writer's infirmity is of itself not important for most people, save perhaps in the playing of Trivial Pursuit. Knowing once how logarithms can be used to solve problems teaches a mathematical logic, but no one sensibly today uses logarithms anymore. Knowing the size and distribution of the United States population in 1860 affects an analysis of our Civil War, but those particular numbers have little merit in and of themselves. Forcing students to note the data is to give them practice in considering matters that must be accounted for in the assessment of a situation.

The residue of serious learning is a mixture of awareness and logic. One exercises these qualities of mind with specifics, but the qualities themselves are the end to be pursued, rather than the memorization of data. Such qualities are more difficult to posit than the details that characterize them. As a result, all too often Americans substitute as a measure of educational excellence the display of details instead of the abilities for which they are the fuel. Students who are apt with the details but inept with their thoughtful use are all too often pilloried as nerds and geeks. Adolescents, however cruelly and clumsily, correctly sense the profound limitations of such peers and object to the unrestrained honor the schools often accord them and, as well, the pomposity with which some kids accept that honor.

Awareness and logic are pretentious abstractions to describe the qualities of students and of neighbors we properly respect, members of a deeply legitimate Honor Roll. Nonetheless these two qualities are both valuable and serviceable. They arise from habit, from an exercise of the reflection and thoughtful consideration that characterize the person. These qualities lead to, in people we respect, "the settled disposition or tendency to act in a certain way," as the dictionary puts it. John Dewey labored over a richer definition: "The essence of habit is an acquired predisposition to *ways* or modes of response . . . Habit means special sensitiveness or accessibility to certain classes of stimuli, standing predilections and aversions, rather than the bare recurrence of specific acts. It means will."[2] Simply, a person exercises her habits by being sensitive to a range of issues and predisposed to think and to act in the full light of that sensitivity.

How does she get that way? Apart from nature, by observation and by practice. The first is fostered by a community's quality: the younger watch the older. If adults value thoughtfulness, the young are usually disposed to do likewise. If teachers are themselves interested in ideas, the students are likely to attend to them as well. If adult family members are bigots, cheat on their taxes, abuse one another, and waste their money, the kids get the message that this is the way to live. If teachers do not value learning, their students rarely do either. A careless community breeds careless people.

A wise school's goal is to get its students into good intellectual habits.[3] Just which habits can be grist for properly endless debate, but the extent of agreement among Americans on these is very high. For example:

The habit of perspective: Organizing an argument, read or heard or seen, into its various parts, and sorting out the major from the minor matters within it. Separating opinion from fact and appreciating the value of each.

The habit of analysis: Pondering each of these arguments in a reflective way, using such logical, mathematical, and artistic tools as may be required to render evidence. Knowing the limits as well as the importance of such analysis.

The habit of imagination: Being disposed to evolve one's own view of a matter, searching for both new and old patterns that serve well one's own and others' current and future purposes.

The habit of empathy: Sensing other reasonable views of a common predicament, respecting all, and honoring the most persuasive among them.

The habit of communication: Accepting the duty to explain the necessary in ways that are clear and respectful both to those hearing or seeing and to the ideas being communicated. Being a good listener.

The habit of commitment: Recognizing the need to act when action is called for; and stepping forward in response. Persisting, patiently, as the situation may require.

The habit of humility: Knowing one's rights, one's debts, and one's limitations, and those of others. Knowing what one knows and what one does not know. Being disposed and able to gain the needed knowledge, and having the confidence to do so.

The habit of joy: Sensing the wonder and proportion in worthy things and responding to these delights.

Most of these habits may be cast as skills. Ask the student: Can you analyze this matter for me and then tell me what you find? However, the purpose of education involves more than that. Education is so to convince an adolescent of the virtue of these skills and so to give opportunities to practice the skills that they become almost second nature, and graduates live with them fully after they leave school. *Of course* I listen. *Of course* I insist on knowing the facts. *Of course* I am not fully sure about this new matter, but I know what I know and what I do not yet know. *Of course* you may have a better idea than mine, and I'll listen to it carefully and with an open mind. *Of course* I'll do something about this if the situation warrants it. Having the skills today is but a small part of the whole. Being committed to using them consistently tomorrow is the crux of it.

Habit, obviously, relates to disposition: I have to want to apply these skills. Therefore I must be convinced of their utility and reasonableness. Good schools endlessly labor at this task of persuasion. Good schools self-consciously display these habits in their own functioning. Everything about these schools reinforces the argument that the habits are worthwhile.

These habits reflect value. They neither denote nor connote mere technical expertise, usable skills. They are loaded with judgments, for teachers and parents as well as for students. The lines between habits that are good and bad, slovenly and devoted, personal and collective are blurred. There is no escaping this. A school devoted to the inculcation of certain sorts of intellectual habits — the qualities of mind that engender respect — will tangle endlessly, and revealingly for their students, over matters of judgment. Good schools welcome this. In fact, only from such tangling can those habits we most respect emerge.

Good schools focus on habits, on what sorts of intellectual activities will and should inform their graduates' lives. Not being clear about these habits leads to mindlessness, to institutions that drift along doing what they do simply because they have always done it that way. Such places are full of silly compromises, of practices that boggle commonsense analysis. And they dispirit the Horace Smiths, who know that the purpose of education is not in keeping school but in pushing out into the world young citizens who are soaked in habits of thoughtfulness and reflectiveness, joy and commitment.

Further, mindless schools may show students a superficial picture of that which is to be most highly valued, what the school puts forward as its most respected students. Kids with high scores will always be ridiculed, human jealousy being what it is. But they will fare much better in a school which knows that the display of knowledge, however accurate or rich, is only a beginning, and that students who can use knowledge, who are seemingly in the instinctive habit of using it, are the ones deserving of highest honor.

"How do you teach habits?" the school board member wanted to know.

"Drill, drill, drill." The response from Coach drew laughter.

"How boring," said the second student.

"But that's what you do in my class." The young English teacher pointedly addressed his student. "You read closely, over and over. You write, over and over."

"Boring!" shouted Patches. Lots of laughter, with the young English teacher reddening with anger as well as embarrassment. He was saved by the mathematics teacher.

"Come on, come on . . . good habits take practice. You can't just be told something, practice it twice, and then move on. Nothing sticks . . . You have to stay with things."

"Boring?" Patches still was at it, but this time seriously. He would not tease the mathematics teacher. No one ever did.

"That's our task, to make sure that the practice is fresh, that it connects but still reinforces the serious work . . . ."

Horace: "But how can you do that, with all you're supposed to cover in the Math Department syllabus?"

"We can't, and I don't. Better to learn a few of the most

important things well than to have superficial acquaintance with lots of things . . . We've got to focus, to choose, to select, to emphasize what is the most important."

"But all those tests favor knowing lots of little things!"

Patches: "A plague on such tests."

A parent: "You mean to say that the students will do better if you cover fewer things?"

"Yes. Precisely," said the mathematics teacher. There was a silence. He went on: "We must give the basic tools, the basic ideas, and show how these ideas were derived and can be used. We must get the students into the habit of such use and into the habit of learning on their own-by means of this use . . . If we do this, we'll wean them from us, from their textbooks, from the lists of facts that we give them, from the little crutches for using their minds that we in schools construct for them. Going deeper, insisting that serious understanding is there, is at the center of our work." Silence followed this heavy speech from a man not well known for extended disquisitions.

"And that's not boring," the first student unexpectedly intruded on this very teacherly talk. "Finding things that one can do with math on our own is challenging. It's fun."

"That's fine for you, and I appreciate you very much." Margaret smiled at that student known for her academic prowess. "But is it boring for other students?"

"It can't be." A vocational teacher stepped in. "That's our job, making it so that kids will take it, will dig in."

Margaret: "So this kind of 'less is more' argument applies to all kids?"

"Absolutely," Horace replied. "All kids need these habits. We should no more ignore the need to put the right sorts of pressure on the kids who have never shown an inkling of interest in college as we should avoid the fact stuffing of the academic seniors preparing for the College Board Achievement tests."

A parent, laughing: "Pretty idealistic stuff!"

Horace flared. "Isn't it about time that the schools got a bit idealistic?"

"But we have to be realistic," the parent replied.

"Let's not let realism get in the way of the much higher standards we must have for all students." The two men stared at each other.

"Less is more," repeated the visitor. "Lots of decisions would flow from this." No one challenged her. The discussion appeared stalled; tension rippled the air.

Patches broke the silence. "How do you assess habits?"

"We can tell by how the boys play," answered Coach.

Green demurred. "But that's just their display of gridiron ability. It doesn't show that the kids have any sort of good habits."

Coach retorted, "They can't play well without good habits."

"But there are exceptions." The mathematics teacher mentioned the names of some students who got by on the football field largely on their raw physical talent and considerable size. Coach did not challenge his argument.

"We don't want *any* exceptions," stated Margaret. "Further, the analogy to sports is not at all perfect. We're talking about intellectual habits that are called on by every one of us every day of our lives."

"So," Patches repeated, "how do you assess habits? If we can't figure out how to assess them, we can hardly figure out how to teach them."

Observations tumbled in. The first student: "It isn't really a habit unless it's expressed unknowingly . . . that is, the test of the habit has to be hidden, secret . . ."

"Inconspicuous?" suggested Margaret. The student went on, "Yes, inconspicuous. You practice a habit without thinking, but it's an example of how you really think." She stumbled over this apparent paradox, but her point clearly struck a chord.

"Habits form and are expressed over time. We can always crank up our good habits when we need to, like when Grandma comes to call . . . or when Grandma is my math teacher." Laughter.

Horace summarized: "Over time . . . inobtrusive testing . . . a measure of how one does in the everyday situation?"

Margaret: "What's called for is a project, and a record of that project. We'd watch how that project develops, unobtrusively if you must."

"Habits cover all sorts of things. When is a habit math and when is it French?"

"Just the point," interrupted the visitor. "Are these habits which you've identified 'subject specific'?" The silence indicated a unanimous no. She continued, "Then a project or portfolio Exhibition could cover everything. It could be a kind of culminating test?" She twisted her assertion to sound like a question.

"It couldn't be only at the end," the second student complained. "To make our first try our only and final try wouldn't be fair."

Horace: "Are we agreed that we should try to find an Exhibition — or several Exhibitions as the students go along — that addresses the habits we've identified as important?"

"Why not?" said Patches.

An Exhibition: Two Projects

Please meet with your adviser and agree on two year-long projects. One should relate to some important matters arising from classes here at Franklin High School. The other may be broader, an enterprise that is extracurricular or even conducted well beyond school.

The purpose of these projects is to give you the opportunity to shape a subject of your own choosing, to develop it over time, and to demonstrate to yourself and to us that you can persist in an important effort, that you can be self-conscious about your own work, usefully and accurately critical of it, and that you can identify and learn from your own mistakes. We hope that you will gain pleasure as well as experience and self-confidence from this exercise.

Examples of the "in school" part of the project: carefully following and even raising an issue in City Council, for example an examination of "redlining" practices of local banks; working for a local or regional political action group, such as Right to Life, both to understand its arguments and to analyze its political practice; working with a seriously handicapped person not only to assist him or her but also to understand the nature, causes, and effects of that person's disability; breeding, raising, and studying several generations of mice, interbreeding them to

79

establish the dominance of a particular trait; creating a new arrangement of a major musical work (e.g., adapting the central themes of a Liszt concerto or a medley of soft rock tunes to solo piano), practicing for, and performing the work.

Examples of the "out of school" part: helping to launch a soccer program for elementary school youngsters in the area and coaching them; serving as a tutor and eventually as an assistant teacher in a Hebrew school; developing an independent carpentry business or helping a small contractor expand his or hers; organizing and running a community service program as part of a nearby hospice.

For both projects you must keep a journal, to be shared with your adviser on a schedule mutually agreed on. After the two projects are chosen, you must take the initiative to meet with your adviser once every two weeks for the first three months and no less than once a month thereafter. You are expected to keep a portfolio of materials about the progress and performance of your effort. Your adviser, and several other people whom you and the adviser will identify from within and without the school, will assist you. They will periodically "drop by" your activity to see how it is proceeding. Your success in meeting the terms of this project will hinge on your enthusiasm, dependability, willingness to work out problems that arise, and skill in keeping track of details.

In special circumstances, advisers may allow students to work in pairs.

This Exhibition allows a student to demonstrate not only qualities of mind but also of persistence, habits of organization, and the ability to apply "classroom knowledge" well beyond the confines of the school.

It differs from the usual project (the primary purpose of which is often a product like a science display) to the extent that the process — the display of habits — is put first and is attended to by both the student and his or her adviser. The products are important but secondary.

It gives scope to a student's particular interests.

Its duration is long enough to allow for the correction of false starts. There is sufficient time for a fair chance at success.

It runs through summer months, allowing for full-time activity when school may not be in session.

It can produce income, a necessity for some students. It can thus happily operate as a formal apprenticeship.

It permits activity not normally associated with public school regimens, such as participation in a business and teaching within a religious setting.

It is an expression of the school's concern for independent effort, for the ability to use that which has been learned in classes, and for a display of habits (as it must in an exercise of this duration).

It allows — indeed, expects — the student to act as a grown-up in a significant part of his or her schoolwork.

It allows teachers and others systematically to observe a student, obtrusively and unobtrusively, judging the formation of habits.

At the same time, these exercises are very time-consuming for faculty. The hours required must be budgeted if these Exhibitions are to be taken seriously.

7

Learning by Using

THE COMMITTEE had had a grueling session with the faculty the evening before. There had been small group discussions, this time without parents, students, or other community members. The resentment and suspicion among the faculty had been evident.

"Some of them just don't want to listen," Green complained.

"They put us off . . . They don't want to hear anything we say because they think it's criticism."

"The ones who annoyed me the most were the ones who said nothing. They just sat there."

Patches: "They're waiting us out. They think that all this is one more little fad and that nothing will happen." Horace was quietly delighted that his old friend referred to the committee as *we*. If this old historian can come aboard, others will too. They'll follow him. They'll fear his acid response if they demur.

Margaret added, "The burden will be on us. Everyone else can criticize and complain."

"Or just sit on their hands, denying what we're saying." Patches wore a smile, not conspiratorial, just smug, ornery.

The first student: "We've got to get them to react. They can't just ignore us!" Her anger had been growing since she learned how the faculty reacted: the backstabbing, the maneuvering, the refusal to doing anything, as a form of sabotage. Even after Margaret patiently explained to her that this kind of behavior could be found in any workplace, not just in schools, her anger did not subside. Actually, Margaret had confessed to Horace, her sustained fury was an asset: the teachers would feel the heat of the disappointment of a respected and influential student.

"How do we get them to join us?" The griping turned constructive. "Throw them questions, not just a report; it's nothing more than our answers to our own questions. How *boring* . . ." The young English teacher mocked the earlier discussions.

"Take them on trips. Have different groups go with you to other schools. Get everyone talking someplace away from school and its familiarity," suggested the visitor.

This was an option, Horace knew, because money had been made available. Local businesses had pledged for what they called the "R and D cost" of the committee's work if the school board would match it, which it did. This funding covered travel expenses and the associated needs for substitute teachers. Most important, it gave some relief from the classroom: the workload of every teacher on the committee was reduced by one course for the spring semester, and substitutes hired.

Horace and some of the others were sorry about this. He liked teaching, and he knew that there were some students who had "saved up" for his course and were now under the tutelage of a stranger. Yet he knew that this adjustment was necessary. The work of the committee was demanding and could not be piled on top of everything else.

The only people on the committee who did not get any relief were the students. It amused Horace that it seemed easy for them to take on this big extra load without any apparent cost to their studies. The kids, Horace knew, spent over ten hours a week on it, given all their chatting around school about the committee's ideas, the small meetings they called, the polling they did. Maybe "good" kids like these were in fact underworked. Or understimulated. The committee's deliberations were a new venture for the two juniors. But there was more: the committee members took them seriously. They were treated like everyone else. No hall passes were required. Horace knew what this meant and hoped that others had figured it out too.

Horace was not surprised when the school board member buttonholed him at a coffee break. "The kids aren't working hard enough," she said, and it was clear that she meant all the youngsters at Franklin High School, not just the two eleventh-graders.

She realized that such accusations publicly aired would damage the group. Its collective skin was thin at this point, she believed. She went on: "We aren't tough enough on them. We know what it takes to learn, and it's more than we insist on now."

Horace thought that she should add (but wouldn't): *Look at me! I learned. More kids should get what I got, and do what I did to learn. The schools are flabby places, and the kids run wild. Let's bring the kids and the teachers back to the standards and practices that I experienced.* That's implicit in her charge, Horace guessed. He knew that her view was widely held in some politically influential quarters. Indeed, he largely agreed with it.

"My students get into good colleges," Horace replied. He wanted to add that several just this year were Phi Beta Kappa. *They appreciated what I did for them. They come back and tell me about it. I'd like to do more of what I do for even more students. I know that I'm a good teacher. I know what works.*

The terse conversation broke off.

Most American students do not work very hard and in a sustained way in school. Most are as academically docile as they are genial. Some kids get into demanding colleges and some do very well there, using the skills they learned in school. A prized handful remember to thank their teachers.

But the school board member and Horace missed the mark. Apart from the reality that there were not any Good Old Days in American secondary education (rosy eyeglasses notwithstanding), the school board member should not have been saying how effective her education was; she should have asked why it had not been much better. After over fifteen thousand hours in school classrooms, why didn't she know more? Why couldn't she do more? And Horace should have asked in the public sessions of the committee why there were so few "good students." Why do so many adolescents not really care about much of importance? Sure, they're kids, but why are they seemingly so careless about their futures?

One of several likely answers is that we persist in viewing school learning in simplistic ways, with unhappy consequences for students. We accept the conventional modes of teaching and learning with more generosity than they deserve. We too rarely recognize that today we know far more about the stunningly complex processes of learning and teaching than we did ninety years ago, but the template of American secondary education that was struck then is very much in place. Indeed, we seem almost afraid to ask fresh questions about learning and teaching, perhaps because of what we might find.

Even a little shift in the way we characterize "school" can be upsetting. Take, for example, a variation of a school's stated purpose from readying the students to *display* knowledge to expecting them to *use* knowledge. The difference here is more than semantic. Using knowledge assumes a student to be markedly active, inventive. Displaying knowledge can be done with relative ease by a passive student. Use requires the student to be a fundamental part of the process. Further, if to that purpose we add the objective of expecting the student to *want* to use knowledge — to be in the *habit* of acting in a knowledgeable way — the distance beyond display is substantial.

It is a truism that we learn well only when we are engaged. That is, if we do not pay attention, we will not "get it." Our attention is caught by things that interest us, that so intrigue us that we are compelled to find out more about them, that we believe we had better attend to or we might miss something.

It is a further truism that sermons do not work well in engaging us (we are expected to listen passively) or in taking into account the particular spark that each of us might strike (there is one message, one text, responsive only to the minority of listeners who are ready for that particular message). Learning by listening is inefficient for much of serious education. The fact is, however, that the most used pedagogy in high schools is "telling," either by us teachers or by our equivalent in the form of films, videos, and textbooks.[1] While it has its uses some of the time — narrative when employed well is a powerful tool — as a central pedagogy it is demonstrably inefficient (though it may be practically necessary to control students whom we do not know well and who come at us for brief periods in large numbers). We bore young people. And they do not learn well.

All this is common sense and is widely accepted by thoughtful teachers. But remedying the faults implies once again ambitious change on a scale that many find threatening. So the teachers usually say, Let us not raise such issues about our work, least of all in a committee meeting. Let's just try to do more of what we now do. That doesn't threaten us as much.

However, we know that serious school reform absolutely requires that we raise such issues, formulate good responses to them, and carefully think again of the purpose and functioning of schools. Fussing with what we have is not working.

A good — a necessary — place to start is with how to attract and hold the students' attention, how to instill in them a commitment to think hard. Without this, there is nothing, just the shell of a school. Two steps are minimally necessary. Teachers must know each student well to capture that young person's mind and heart. And the "destination," the place we wish the student to reach, must be clear and compelling. The young person must know when she gets there that she has achieved something that her teachers and her community all value.

The school should so deploy its resources that each student can be known well by his teachers. Habits are unlikely to be mass-produced, and the kind of Exhibition that demands and fosters the student's habits of thoughtfulness requires a mentor who knows that child deeply. Just as no teacher should be responsible for more than eighty students, all teachers should be able regularly to consult with the adults who have taught each child. That is, every student would be the collective concern of the faculty who at that moment are working with her; and there would be both the expectation of, and time allotted for, discussions by those teachers and that student about how she is doing.

The "knowing well" is only the beginning. Teachers should have substantial control over class time, materials to be used, and the ways of teaching in order to shape these factors in the interests of each student. The school would be personalized, each child addressed in a respectful way and treated as an individual even within the class programming. The governing metaphor for the school would be student as worker. To learn means to work, sometimes drudgingly, sometimes joyfully.

Being busy is not the same as being involved, a point some teachers miss. They assign piles of worksheets, which the kids listlessly fill out. Or they plan colorful but directionless games that the students may join with the gusto appropriate to an elementary school recess period but that do little to stretch their minds.

No one learns well solely from exposure. To sell effectively a new insurance product, for example, we are briefed and then hold practice sessions where each of us makes a mock pitch to a colleague and is criticized on it. These sessions are most useful if they bring up new situations, unexpected but legitimate twists. We thereby get the hang of using resourcefully what we were briefed on. Later, we do best when our first calls on real clients are in the company of a colleague who knows the product well, because it allows for further debriefing — and a usable understanding of the product. Such a sequence makes as much sense for adolescents as it does for adults in the world of business. Put differently, apprenticeship — working alongside someone better qualified — is a productive learning mechanism. Students who are apprentices to respected teachers — Horace Smith's theater groupies — or even to older and more experienced students learn thoroughly and well.

"Working" means working the mind. No one works his mind unless he wants to. Faking is easy. Intellectual work is often fatiguing as well as exhilarating. One condition for getting a student to be a worker is catching her attention, enticing her to concentrate, to focus, to puzzle, to persist.[2]

Although no two people are similarly disposed, there are useful patterns to follow. Students respond when a matter at hand connects or seems likely to connect with something important, even if the importance is at the moment recognized only by a teacher whose word is valued. Students go along with adults they respect. But they especially go along when they can see that such a journey will affect their own lives in some purposeful or intriguing way.

The inherent interest of the matter is also influential. Is the puzzle it presents challenging? Is it interesting? Questions are usually more interesting than assertions or answers, and the most appealing questions are those which are genuine — dealing with matters of manifest importance in the world — and have no easy or total resolution. Is a progressive tax fair? What are, in fact, the fittest in a biological realm, and what may this mean? Why does *pi* work?

Further, the connection between what a student knows and what the new issue portends must be clear. He needs to know that he has the tools to start comprehending this new domain. While the totally new has its allure, its effect is blunted if it only confounds and confuses. For a student to work resourcefully he has to have confidence in himself. For adolescents, this confidence is often gossamer, changeable, troublesome for teachers to plumb. Without it, students find it difficult to learn, because learning involves contemplating the new and unfamiliar and, what is even more challenging, being open to change in the face of new evidence.

Students at work create various kinds of noise. They talk and measure and puzzle out and make the audible messes that an assistant principal is supposed to abhor. Their activity also exposes the inconvenient truth that some kids do the work faster than others. The neat march over the material that is possible when only the teacher sets the pace of the journey cannot be maintained. Some kids sprint; some kids crawl. Each has his own pace. The variation wreaks havoc with orderly syllabi and precise fifty-two-minute periods.

But students must do the work themselves if they are to learn. We can so arrange things that they will be disposed to do that work; we cannot force them to do it. They can be enticed, persuaded, provoked. Ironically, what we have long called homework — the assignments done alone by each student in study hall or out of school — become the heart of the matter rather than something that is added on and all too often ignored.

Inhabitants of the real world are doing homework, not listening to someone else tell them what they should know. Provoke a student into the habit of doing important homework, and his task of becoming a self-propelled learner will be easy.

Good schools are suffused with talk, with all sorts of constructive conversation. Most of high school should be about productive and resourceful thinking, what the research community has come to call "higher order thinking skills." To oversimplify somewhat, basic schoolwork involves the systematic learning of skills — writing, drawing, reading, for example — and of simple, easily believable content: if you have three apples and I have five apples, together we have eight apples; George Washington was the first president of the United States of America. Higher order thinking skills demand of the student's own analytic and imaginative powers; they involve understanding judgment, abstraction, temporary suspension of belief, sophisticated concepts of causality.[3]

The experience of veteran teachers and the evidence from recent research both argue that these intellectual activities are most effectively developed by a dialectical process, by testing and reacting, by *conversation*. What counts is the quality of that conversation, the standard set by the adults as well as by the students. The questions the teachers ask by themselves set a standard; the willingness of all in the conversation respectfully to challenge incomplete or shoddy thinking creates a culture that endorses constructive reflection.[4]

The real world demands collaboration, the collective solving of problems. The clichés are familiar: *Two minds are better than one. Many hands make light work.* Learning to get along, to function effectively in a group, is essential. Evidence and experience also strongly suggest that an individual's personal learning is enhanced by collaborative effort. The act of sharing ideas, of having to put one's own views clearly to others, of finding defensible compromises and conclusions, is in itself educative.[5]

Collaborative learning serves other, humbler functions. It is difficult to hide one's slothfulness if one is part of a group that is expected to produce collective work. The congeniality of a group sparks one's energy (and also can, of course, be a distraction).

One learns how other people, peers as well as teachers, see matters, a kind of perspective not easily achieved when the only authority is the teacher's voice and the textbook. And conversation requires sustained, challenging communication, possible only when there is the expectation of collective inquiry at a high standard.

Such a conversation requires a subject: there has to be something to talk about, a situation that gives meaning to the particular focus of study. It is not enough to ponder the intentions of Falstaff; the student should see the character in the context of the entire play and in light of her own sense of the human condition. If matters are placed in context, she will gain a quicker and richer grasp of their meaning than if they are presented as independent blocks in the construction of a building. Better to see the possibility of the whole, even darkly, before starting with the specifics. If a kid sees how the German language flows in an overall sense, he can understand better the placement of verbs in a sentence and readily appreciate their effect.

These threads of understanding about learning intertwine. Effective conversation demands rich situations and contexts. Conversation requires collaboration, and vice versa. Being known well and having respect paid to his particular interests and concerns is a considerable incentive to a student to make an effort. Having a clear academic destination — what he has to Exhibit in order to demonstrate success — also provides an incentive: he has an idea where he is going that makes the effort of getting there more comprehensible; and if reaching that destination requires the employment of useful habits, he will have the incentive to develop them.

These practices square with common sense. They are followed in other sorts of effective educational efforts, in business, the professions, the military. They arise from a fair body of research. The rub comes with their implications. For the student to have a destination and the means of knowing when she has reached it, the teacher must create a clear view of the nature of that destination and a system to judge whether the student has arrived. These are remarkably unfamiliar tasks. If "using history," for example, is a desired destination, what practically does this mean? What sort of exercise would serve to display a student's ability to make sense of the present and future through a knowl-edge of the past? How can the teacher ascertain that the student is in the habit of using the past? What sort of work is necessary to ready her for the Exhibitions? Few educational administrators or teachers are used to addressing their work this way — plan-ning backward, as it were.

More problems: as the youngsters become better known in those wise schools where teachers have no more than eighty students, their particularities become sharply evident. They do not learn at the same rates at the same time in the same ways. Further, they keep changing: securely packaging them as this or that sort does not work. Their chronological ages do not help administrators much. The tangle of kids makes an awful bureau-cratic mess. What to do? Simplify and loosen up the program; adapt to the students rather than making them adapt to the routines. Give substantial authority to the adults who know the particular students — that is, their teachers. Inevitably this will mean once again setting priorities, because most American high schools are a riot of programs that make schedules and routines so rigid as to preclude sensitive adaptation for particular students. Further, such adaptation takes the time of teachers, even in its planning. The time must be built into teachers' days, a further cost.

Collaboration, conversation: these activities are unsettling, noisy; they are invitations for kids to screw around. Girls, boys, the social game, hormones, the endless distractions of adoles-cence . . . Organizing activity for them that is rigorous and at the same time sufficiently engaging to draw them into significant work is difficult, certainly more so than merely positing that "today we'll cover the future tense of the verb *être.*" Further, the fifty-two-minute periods that circumscribe life at Franklin High do not often work for this kind of schooling. Making the kids' wandering talk and their start-and-stop collective efforts intellectually coherent is an endless, tortuous process, impossi-ble competely to plan for. How is one to prepare next week's lesson plans? How could a substitute teacher take over on a moment's notice?

It all seems daunting to Horace's committee: so much would have to change.

* * *

To break loose some fresh ideas, the visitor suggested a trip to another school, one that had grappled with many of the issues now freezing up the Franklin High group. The members focused on one unit in a high school that, while roughly the size of Franklin, had decentralized its work into small, semi-autonomous schools within the school:

Fifty-some students, representing half of this high school's A Unit, were spread across two large, adjacent classrooms, and the two teachers, one technically of mathematics and the other of science, moved quietly among them. These were new students, just up from middle school. Their task for these several days was to observe, describe, and identify any living organisms found in samples of water each had brought from a source near home.

Youngsters clustered around tables and took turns using the microscopes arranged on the benches along the walls. At first they were dumbfounded to find so much life in what they had previously thought was only "water" and so much variety among the organisms in the different samples. They worked quietly, talking with one another at the tables. It was soon clear that each table was a team, the members of which were to help each other. Some were drawing pictures of what they had observed. Others stood at a long spread of tackboard on which were pinned charts describing some of the forms of water life found in this region. They looked there to find their own animals. The room was full of quiet bustle at this midmorning moment.

One student stood apart both from his team and from the microscopes and the tackboard. No one bothered him; the class seemed to go around him. Another student muttered intensely to herself as she wrote up her notes, disturbing other team members but not too much. They ignored her, pulling away to their end of the table. A couple of others kept getting up and down, stretching, going first to the tackboard, then back to the table, then over to the books in a case. Restless types, clearly, but they seemed to be getting on with their work.

The teachers kept circling, commenting, criticizing, chiding. Periodically, one would say to the kids who bopped up and down, *Settle down, guys.* To which they replied, *We're working, Mr. Sanchez.* The loner was ignored by the adults at this moment; they knew that getting him to join in would be an extended and painstaking process, and doing so now would cheat the other kids. They would get to him, and he knew they would. He seemed morose as well as disengaged, but, as the teachers said later, he was there, in class. Previously, he had been often truant.

Some kids were completing their work, in the form of written reports including diagrams. They checked these with the teachers. Most were found wanting, to the students' obvious annoyance. The teachers pointed out inaccuracies, incompleteness, messiness, imprecision, clumsy sentences — *But this isn't English class, Mr. Sanchez* — and more. The final products would go into the students' portfolios, there to be seen by their parents as well as by other teachers. *You're making a record here,* the kids were told. *This is the beginning of your science portfolio . . . It's got to be something you'll be proud of.*

Downstairs, in the library, several of these A Unit students were sprawled around a table poring over biology books. The teachers had allowed them to come down — indeed, had sent them. The charts in the classroom apparently had not included some of the creatures the students had found in their water, and they came to dig in books here. It soon became apparent that the group was working on only one team member's sample, and that it had curious characteristics. The entire team had put aside their work to focus on this sample; again with the blessing and encouragement of the teachers. The kids were absorbed with it. They were periodically noisy and had to be shushed; their sprawl was ungainly and their papers and books littered the library. But the librarians quietly applauded their effort, encouraging them regularly and helping out with the catalogues and listings and computer searches required eventually to identify the mysterious organisms.

The rest of A Unit was also spread across two classrooms, each with about twenty-five students, one class split in groups and the other in "plenary session." The first, in clusters of four, was reading aloud from short stories, each student rendering in turn a paragraph to the other three. There was a hum in the room, but the students seemed to heed it not at all. Some of the students could, in fact, barely read. They strained, stumbled, froze, struggled. Their peers helped some of them; others were left to suffer. Boredom showed on some faces; fright on others. This exercise clearly could not be pursued for long. It was agony: the students displayed what they could and could not do, for themselves and all to hear. The teacher circling around concentrated on praise. *That's wonderful, Phyllis. Try again, you can do it, Rachel. That's nice help you all are giving, over there.* She seemed to have ears everywhere and eyes in the back of her head.

The plenary session was focused on voice: Who is speaking in this story? What is my personal voice? Each student had prepared a presentation on his or her personal voice. *When you listen to me, who do you hear?* An embarrassed boy, taller than most in this group and already with a mustache, gave his offering in halting phrases. *You must know that I come from the South . . . I didn't grow up here. I haven't gone to school with white folks until this year . . . They make me nervous.* (Laughter all around; he grins.) *I don't like English . . . I don't like to talk . . . No one listens to me much, and that's all right with me.* His peers listened intently, politely. This new classmate was creating a focus of himself for them, albeit painfully.

The four A Unit teachers of these one hundred students met later. They discussed the desperation of the unconnected youth in the biology lesson. They wondered whether some of the semi-literates could get ahead in a respectable way in science, given the standards of the expected reports. They talked of the painful process of "letting each kid know what he does or doesn't know." Could this be done in a less bloody way? Could the kids build a sense of collective responsibility for all their peers, not just those they liked?

The teachers knew that this was yet early in the year, that they were building not only skills (for example, careful observation, both of organisms in water and words read aloud) but also thoughtful conduct (staying with a problem until it has been solved; finding things on one's own; working constructively with other students without much adult monitoring; taking responsibility for oneself by going alone to the library). These A Unit teachers agonized over how long some kids were taking, how bad their habits were. Most of all, they swapped observations about the students. They planned how they would adapt what had and had not been accomplished that morning to the studies they had planned for this two-week period. They joked about how compulsive and angular most of the young kids were.

This sort of activity could be found in most schools, but Horace's committee knew that it was the exception rather than the rule. The endless talk, the anticipation of regular performance (Exhibition), the expectation of personal engagement on which the teachers would insist, the honesty about one's accomplishments and about a standard to be met, the availability of substantial blocks of time to push a project to its finish: these infused this school. There was noise and the appearance of disorder, but there was little listlessness, on the part of students or teachers. It was a place full of busy-ness.

These classrooms were not without pain and pathos and distraction and frustration. With all this, however, their world evinced striking respect for students, a high demand. The kids showed up. Most of them understood what their schooling was about — not just in the sense of getting a diploma, but substantively. They knew they had to do the work, and most of them saw it most of the time as worth doing.

These qualities did not just happen. The school had made fundamental changes in its organization, in how its staff was deployed, in the means of instruction, in the expectations for the students. Compared with its earlier self, it now was a simpler, more focused school. It had made possible a team of four adults for one hundred students. It put the students' performance first and let everything flow from that — rearranged student assignments into teams; gave each team's teachers collective responsibility for the success of their students and authority to carry out what they deemed best; scheduled a day broken into as many pieces of time — "periods" — a team wanted; provided a library that was a tightly coordinated partner with each team; and, above all, radiated an attitude that the central point for each student was to be able to use knowledge easily in a useful, purposeful manner.

Common sense, obvious stuff. But, as the Franklin committee members knew, rare.

If the habits of learning to use ideas are the end of schooling, then schools must give students practice in the craft. Serious use of the mind is difficult work, learned by doing, by sustained apprenticeship in the processes of the intellect. It is strange and demanding work for most adolescents. It does not come easily. It is not "given" to them. At best, it is provoked. The practice of schools is the practice of sensible provocation. To do it well requires many different routines, and different assumptions behind those routines, from what obtain in most high schools at present.

Paralyzed though he often feels, Horace understands that. Getting it right will erase the school board member's complaint of "softness." Horace chuckled to himself: the day should come when they chide us for being too hard!

"This sort of teaching is difficult." That Margaret admitted this meant much: she seemed such a natural when she ran her classrooms. "We have to ask more questions and give fewer answers. We must coach, must question all the time . . . we must keep the students at it . . ."

"As Mortimer Adler has preached . . ."[6]

"Yes," said Margaret, "Adler's *Paideia Proposal* ideas are sensible, but they push us to new kinds of teaching. Lots of us try to teach that way now, and we often do, but it's difficult to arrange and to sustain. The kids fight us sometimes. They'd prefer not to work . . ." The student members of the committee smiled at her. "Let's remember the watching and challenging and provoking that we saw in that water-samples biology class."

Green: "That just didn't happen. Getting that exercise set up right was a big job. Making sure that the research materials were available for any organism that might show up must have taken hours."

"A solid library is crucial," said the one of the parents.

"And tolerant librarians!" said another.

"Teaching this way will mean we can't cover as much." The principal shifted the topic. "All that time on a few academic questions : . . How will the kids do on the tests?"

"We keep coming back to that. It's simple. Get better tests," said Patches, predictably.

"While it appears paradoxical," the visitor reported, "many students taught this way — provoked to engage, given time to get on with their own learning, with high expectations for using what they've learned — do better on traditional tests of presumed coverage. They seem to be in the habit of figuring things out."[7]

"And most of the tests can be conned, drilled for, in effect subverted," interrupted the young English teacher. His colleagues knew that he moonlighted on the staff of the Princeton Review, a company that helped high school students prepare for the Scholastic Aptitude Tests and other offerings of the College Board.

"That doesn't address my objection," persisted the principal. "Do we cover less?"

Margaret: "You will and you won't. If you start early enough getting the students actually to learn on their own . . . and this means the slow work of getting them to apply knowledge and skills . . . lots of practice . . . you can expect more of them later. You won't have to cover everything from the front of the classroom. They'll get it on their own — if you demand it."

No one rebutted this argument. Coach added, "Get 'em out as Pop Warner players; that'll give them a big head start when they're older." He was referring to the football programs in many communities for middle school boys.

"We need the academic equivalent of Pop Warner."

"Without it, we won't be able to pull this off. Unless the kids are used to being expected to do the work, we'll spend all their high school years hassling them into new habits."

"We can't blame everything on what goes before!"

"It's all the *parents'* fault!" Laughter, particularly because the remark had been made by one of the parents.

Horace pressed: "So we're agreed, are we? We involve the middle school in this plan?" The committee seemed stunned. This hadn't been a new idea, but, put so directly, it was startling. Someone finally replied, "We have to." There was no dissent.

Patches returned to the tests. "If we want something different from our existing course tests, those tests of recall, the ones that show the kids can use the material, what could we use?" The committee turned to specific examples, ones less grand than the Exhibitions they now regularly talked of, the ones from their various disciplines.

Exhibitions: Knowledge in Use

A. FROM AMERICAN HISTORY

"In the eye of the Constitution, in the eye of the law, there is in this country no superior, dominant, ruling class of citizens. There is no caste here. Our Constitution is color-blind, and neither knows nor tolerates classes among citizens . . . If evils will result from the commingling of the two races upon public highways established for the benefit of all, they will be infinitely less than those that will surely come from state legislation regulating the enjoyment of civil rights upon the basis of race. We boast of the freedom enjoyed by our people above all other peoples. But it is difficult to reconcile that boast with a state of the law which, practically, puts the brand of servitude and degradation upon a large class of our fellow-citizens, our equals before the law. The thin disguise of 'equal' accommodations for passengers in railroad coaches will not mislead any one, nor atone for the wrong this day done."*

Please explain what this segment from a decision of the United States Supreme Court says.

Speculate on the subject of the case represented here and on

---

*From Justice John Marshall Harlan's dissent in *Plessy* v. *Ferguson*, 163 U.S. 537 (1896)

98

the period of American history during which it was rendered. Give reasons for your opinions.

Extract from this segment its enduring constitutional principle, cast it in the form of a hypothetical case that might reach the Supreme Court today — a case arising from today's particular social realities — and express how you personally would act on such a case if you were an associate justice of the Court.

B. FROM SCIENCE

Act as the school's nutritionist: the cafeteria has $2.56 to spend per full single serving for lunch. Design three menus, each of which is (1) within that budget allowance, (2) maximally nutritious, and (3) maximally attractive to students in your school. You will have to consult the various tables and data displayed in the current nutritionist's guide available in the library and the cafeteria office. Be prepared to defend your definitions of "nutritious" and "attractive" and your particular menus. You will submit your entries to an all-school poll, and the winning six menus will be served during the next term.

C. FROM MATHEMATICS

1. A recent study reported that of the two million cancer deaths in this country each year, three hundred are related directly to an improper diet. The study went on to state that the overall life expectancy of cancer victims would have increased by three months if all victims had followed a proper diet. Several of your classmates argue that three months isn't much to gain for sacrificing some favorite foods for the rest of one's life. Explain how the report has seriously misled your classmates. Provide mathematical evidence rather than philosophical reasoning as the basis for your explanation.

2. A. Describe how you would measure the distance between your ears without using calipers. B. When you are satisfied with the method you have devised, compare the result with that obtained by using calipers. Discuss what you would need to do to make your method almost as reliable as using calipers. C. Carry out your plan and describe the results. D. Critique your work, describing what, if anything, you might do differently in the first three parts of this task.

3. You have decided to buy a used car. You must choose between a 1988 Ford Tempo, priced at $5800, and a 1988 Toyota Corolla, priced at $6700. Both cars have had one owner and been driven about 36,000 miles; both have four doors and mediocre but working stereo systems. A mechanic friend of yours has verified that they are both in good condition.

You have saved $1100. Since you are too young to qualify for a bank loan, your parents will lend you the remaining purchase cost at the terms available from a bank. They will also add your car to their insurance policy, but you must pay the additional premium. You have a part-time job, at which you work eighteen hours a week and for which you are paid 15 cents per hour over the minimum wage. Your employer likes your work and has told you that you will get a raise of 12 cents an hour every six months, beginning three months from now. For ten weeks in the summer, you may work forty hours a week, less any vacation time you want to take.

Determine the cost of buying and operating each of the cars over four years. Indicate which car you will buy, describing your reasoning and showing your calculations. Assuming that you must spend money on entertainment as well as on your car, explain in detail the implications of purchasing whichever auto you decide on.

4. Estimate the number of rubber molecules peeled off a tire at each revolution on an asphalt surface. Be prepared to explain both the procedures you selected and the variables attendant on your solution.

The Exhibitions, of varied difficulty, draw on topics widely accepted in history, mathematics, civics, science, and home economics.

All ask for straightforward analyses, the first with close reading of a simple legal text, the second with the use of a detailed manual, and those in mathematics with observation and calculation of ascending difficulty, the last requiring a knowledge of chemistry and considerable ingenuity. All ask for analyses that go beyond the data presented; that is, they expect the student to do autonomous creative work. (Even if a student recognized the legal text, she would have the same next task as all the other students.)

All call for realistic decisions and defenses of those decisions. All involve topics that are of interest to most adolescents. All require judgments that most teenagers would expect of thoughtful citizens in real life.

All are in some respects easily graded (i.e., the menu costs no more than the dollar amount per serving allocated); some depend heavily on the judgments of adults monitoring the process (i.e., the definitions of "nutritious" or the shaping of a contemporary meaning of the identified constitutional principle).

All draw from academic scholarship — legal history, mathematics, chemistry, and physiology — and connect it to sensible decisions in a prudent world.

8

Substance and Standards

"WHAT'S THE CURRICULUM to be?" asked the young English teacher. Horace feared that his neophyte colleague was groping for the List of Things to Cover, that beginning teacher's salvation. Mercifully, Green rode in on her hobbyhorse: "We've agreed to plan backward. Tell me what the student should be able to Exhibit, and I'll give you your curriculum."

Others broke in: "How can there be only one curriculum? We've spent hours agreeing that kids differ. If they do, then what we give them should also differ."

Horace: "The point is not what we give. It's what the kids learn." He had made this point so often that his colleagues kidded him about it. No sermons from Horace.

"The Exhibitions will drive the curriculum. Kids will get to them in different ways. But what of those matters which can't readily be Exhibited?"

"How you teach is itself a form of curriculum. It's not just the stuff I put forward; it's how I put it forward . . . how the kids receive it." The remark was flipped mischievously in Horace's direction.

Patches: "There's too much in the curriculum now, too many courses, too many promises, too much stuff. We know that most of it is covered superficially, and we know how confused the kids are — those kids who bother to think about what we teach them." Patches was referring to what the committee members had learned from "shadowing" individual students over the course of a day, an experience that had radicalized more than a few of them. At the end of trekking behind a student for seven periods, their behinds were sore, they had been bored by being talked at so much, they had witnessed the cumulative intellectual chaos of a typical sequence of courses, French to physics to English to phys ed to mathematics, none planned with any reference to any of the others, and all before lunch. There was, most of them had agreed, no coherent sum to be totted up from these disparate parts.

"So what's the solution?" a parent member asked. "A core curriculum?"

"Back to basics?" The second student snorted at that. "Give us a break." This assertion was expressed not as a plea but as an attack.

Patches: "What's wrong with a core curriculum?"

The student: "We deserve some choice. We don't want to learn just what you want us to learn."

Patches, scornfully: "How do you know what you want to learn when you don't know anything to begin with?" The student flushed but held his tongue. The teachers stiffened.

The mathematics teacher: "Franklin is trying to do too much. We have no priorities. The curriculum is there because it's always been there. It's completely divided up by departments, and tested accordingly. Somehow we've got to break all that."

"You can talk that way because you know that math will always be there, and you'll have a job. Art is just as important as math, but when people get into core curriculum and the basics and all that stuff, art gets cut out. Goodbye to my job." Others nodded, all teachers of "elective" subjects — art, foreign language, the vocational courses.

The first student, quietly: "The curriculum that *we* have to take really reflects *your* jobs, and whether or not you'll keep them. Nobody asks what *we* like and need. That's not fair." Her remark slapped across faculty faces.

"What about the colleges?" The effort to shift the discussion from the faculty and onto a scapegoat was transparent. "All they want is the traditional subjects." Horace turned to the visitor for response.

"The colleges want apt students with good academic habits. Some college admissions offices are still mesmerized by the technicalities of transcripts and the rest, but most selective colleges are looking for resourceful kids, and if your school can prepare its students far better than it's doing now, the colleges will beat a path to your door. They, their faculties, would like the direction you're taking here."

"And the SATs, Advanced Placement, and the rest?"

"As you well know," the visitor answered, "most tests are limited and limiting, and their content lags behind changes in scholarship. Some, particularly some of the fact-stuffed Advanced Placement and Achievement tests, reward the mere display of knowledge, and thus distort teaching and learning. The worst ones are easily drilled for, and I know schools that do the drill, get their kids their high test scores as early as possible, and then get on with true education. They play the game. But keep in mind that there really are very few truly selective colleges. Behind all the talk about tough admissions standards is a college that wants your graduates on almost any terms. Don't let the colleges scare you. Figure out what's right and then sell it."

Easy for her to say, thought Horace. She doesn't have to answer to bitchy parents, the test-score/rank-in-class/my-son-the-president-of-the-student-council terrorists.

"Let's have some standards here . . ."

"Where are we going?" Frustration.

"It's a mess, I agree," Horace admitted. "Getting hold all at once of the various pieces — the courses and their syllabi, the Exhibitions and the ways we teach — is very tough. But let's not be too hard on ourselves: we've never really tried before. Planning backward is new and hard."

"What's to be Exhibited?" Horace asked the visitor, privately, after school, away from the committee, off the record. He wanted to know what she thought. Her formal role had been mostly that of clarifier, cheerleader, suggestor of places to visit and books to read. Horace knew that this was deliberate: the committee had to do its own thinking. He thought of his group as her class. She's the coach. Or Our Lady Socrates.

"So you want my opinion. What should be Exhibited? At a very general level, habits of perspective, analysis, imagination, empathy, communication, commitment, humility, joy — as I have previously argued."

"Fine." Horace Smith snorted. "*Such* a nice, long list. Lovely polysyllabic words. You must have it fully memorized." He smiled. "Typical Professor's Pedagogical Precepts. Mush. Motherhood."

"Come on, Horace," the visitor replied, laughing. "Note the word 'habit.' What it says represents a real shift from the traditional wisdom, and it ups the teachers' ante considerably."

"Come on, yourself," Horace persisted. "Be specific. And keep the list small, manageable. Less is more, you say. Practice it, please. And put it all in terms of the kids, what they'll get from whatever investment they make in school."

Horace's comments were justified. Serious learning — and habits of learning — are not quick studies. They demand persistence, engagement, repetition, patience. All that takes time. The typical American high school offers an abundance of opportunities and curricula, and most kids sample this and that, becoming informed about many things but unable to make much use of anything. The essential offerings are those which are most useful and most generative — that is, the most effective in leading to more knowledge. They must connect with one another and be as coherent as possible.

Horace and the visitor talked the matter through. They struggled, and often laughed, over what they frequently sensed was pretension and pomposity in their conclusions, what they sincerely believed was the heart of schooling. Perhaps schools *should* be pretentious, they concluded. Schools are to be places of hope, places that help young people not just to survive but so to live their lives that the world is better for their presence. Horace summarized later for the committee their meandering conversation:

Students must be able to tell us what they think, clearly and in a variety of ways, with written and spoken languages, visual and musical devices, gesture and stance. Their arguments must be informed, measured, sensitive to others, and, when appropriate, logically persuasive. The students must be aware of the tensions between appearance and reality and be able to sort out the relevant from the irrelevant. They must find the personal authority to stand up, respectfully, for what they think and to handle, gracefully, reasonable challenges to their views. They must be able to hear well what others tell them.

They must have some sense of how the world works — and be interested, ready — to discern an issue or puzzlement and know how to make some sense of it (say, the relationship between a chemical that is possibly toxic and ill infants who are exposed to it). They should be versed in the language of relationships — mathematics — which allows the shape of these relationships to be used.

The students must display some awareness of history — our communal memories — to figure out why we are where we are, how we represent ourselves, the meanings and value of those representations — written, designed, somehow shaped — which define us. The students must display awareness of some of the values that shape their culture and others and how these have played out in practical affairs in the past.

Horace and the visitor had gone further, designing Exhibitions that represented their general ideas. Again, Horace summarized these for the committee:

Explain to us some idea, using several means of communication. Root the argument in fact and present it appealingly. Handle well our commentary. Be able and willing to dig out more evidence to support your position or to serve as the basis for a new, better position. For example, convince us why we should support a proposition on the state ballot adding the death penalty to the penal code.

Figure out how to understand and perhaps use some important matter in the physical world, drawing on existing skills and developing new ones demanded by this new situation. For example, devise a way to remove a heavy, bulky object now lodged in a building's exposed cellar; defend your solution on the basis of specific physical laws.

Tell us how to know your sense of, your feeling for, your taste about an important matter. For example, make us realize the torment of a teenage soldier after his first firefight on the Kuwait-Saudi border in ways that go beyond straight exposition, that plumb feeling, that draw powerfully and richly on the perception of such torment felt by others.

Show us that you know your roots, and those of others. For example, prepare a brief for an American secretary of state about to negotiate a trade agreement with a Muslim country.

Horace and the visitor agreed that all these Exhibitions would require the student to work on new ground but with familiar tools, to bring "old" knowledge to bear on new situations analogous to the challenges presented by the real, and thus changeable, world. The student would have to display his existing knowledge and control of skills by applying them in an unfamiliar situation. Schooling is about equipping people to deal with the fresh, the new, the unknown. Youngsters learn how do deal with the unknown by practice with the known — which is, in many respects, yet unknown to them. Their task is not merely to know the known and to appreciate it; it is to develop habits of using it. This focus profoundly affects the way learning, and therefore teaching, proceeds.

Horace pondered all this and asked the visitor, "What familiar disciplines are represented in this list of Exhibitions?"

"There are four areas here. The first, in most respects generic, deals with manners of communication and with forms of inquiry, ways of seeing the world, ways of puzzling things out. The second draws on mathematics and science; the third, the arts, including literature; and the fourth, history and philosophy."

"That's all?"

"That's all. And all kids should work at all of these matters all the time."

"All kids? How will you keep the attention of all kids?"

"That's the pedagogical challenge. We'll have to tailor the material to our particular kids — without cheapening it. The skills and knowledge implicit in these Exhibitions and what lies behind them are fundamentals for *all* citizens. No one is exempt. The kind of 'dealing with the new' represented in this approach affects the future gas station owner as well as the brain surgeon. It's fundamental general education. It's also fundamental vocational education. And civic education."

"It's barebones."

"Actually it isn't. Practice for using knowledge takes time, energy. Casual acquaintance won't do. This will be a demanding regimen for everyone."

Questions about the substance of schooling and of standards or changes of any scale in the existing high school regimen inevitably provoke controversy — in a word, politics, most particularly the politics of subtraction. A high school that proposes to simplify its work sets itself up for violent criticism.

Americans seem to like their shopping-mall high schools, where there is something for everybody, different sorts of subjects at different standards. The subject is there if you want it, but you don't have to take it. That is the mythology of American comprehensive secondary education. The hard fact is that comprehensiveness is an illusion. Not everything is offered, and the culture of an individual school influences choices among those options which are available. The mall indeed has a limited number of stores, and the pressure to choose some over others is often very strong.[1]

Nonetheless, students like the choices: it puts them to some degree in charge of their own learning. And the choices allow adolescents to sort themselves out by their interests, by how hard they want to work and by the station in life to which they aspire (or to which others have quietly assigned them). Needless to say, the process is at best capricious and often appallingly wasteful.

The mall is the system's response to the truism that kids differ. The reality is, though, that most students remain names or numbers but not people; they select their courses pretty much on their own and attend classes where they are little understood. The mall gives the appearance of respecting differences, but in fact is set up in such a way that a majority of the kids remain essentially anonymous, and the teachers can never creatively and effectively address the promise of their particularity. There are too many of them facing each teacher for that instructor to know more than a handful well enough to teach them resource-fully — the condition that leads Horace to compromise.

Critics usually brand the narrowing of a school's program a step toward rigidity, one providing less well for student differences than does the mall's many courses. In fact, the opposite can be the case. Simplifying the program and expecting students to stay with a generally defined subject for a substantial time can, if combined with parallel and reinforcing rearrangements, create a program where teachers have few enough students to know them well and to know them for a reasonable length of time. Teachers can then "use" the interests of individual students, in effect giving them electives, albeit and properly within the selected areas. Ironically, then, the simpler the program, the richer it can become, more attentive to serious and deserved individual interests.

Further, the process of creating a simpler program — the politics of subtraction — can restore a necessary set of priorities for the resources of schools, focusing on that which is the most important function of schooling, the development of intellectual habits, even as legitimate student interests and diversity are respected.

A different sort of politics arises from the need for accountability, for authorities (political and parental) to know whether the resources they have put into schools have been well spent. In an earlier day, merely the provision of handsome schools was enough to re-elect political leaders, but since the 1960s expectations have become more demanding. How well are the students doing, the "products" of the schools? How do they stack up against one another and against their counterparts in foreign countries? What standards should we set for the graduates of American high schools?[2]

The answers to the first two questions are dismal. When compared with some rough abstract of how well adolescents should be doing and with high school graduates overseas, American students fall short. Such findings helped to swell the number of reports critical of American education during the 1980s and by the early 1990s created a climate tolerant of reform, at least to some degree. Lurking behind all of the rhetoric and effort remains, however, the third matter: *What are proper standards for Americans?*

Unfortunately, the answer has become entangled with the mechanics of assessment, with testing. Talk about standards seems always to jump almost immediately to the design of tests. We seem fixed on the notion that one cannot have quality without precise measurement.

Much contemporary discussion of standards follows a seductively simple argument. National and state policymakers must decide on the standards to be met. A syllabus will be issued to help schools aim at these standards. Tests that measure achievement of those standards will be administered to all kids. Those who pass will get diplomas. Schools will be compared, and those which have lots of failing students will be humiliated into reform or be taken over by higher authorities.

The argument sags badly when examined closely. Who in America has the hubris or the right to set specific measurable standards for all the people? Are the standards in things we value — taste, complex reasoning, historical meaning, economic fairness, imagination, the relative value, say, of life and property — widely agreed on? Or do reasonable people, including scholars in these areas, disagree? If there is sincere disagreement, how can there be common standards? And would the imposition of such standards be consonant with intellectual freedom? Would the selection of a common standard necessarily be the wisest choice, and if not, what would the costs be?

Some proponents of national testing say that tests should be voluntary, with states and districts developing their own versions. The national standards would be promulgated on the basis of expert "calibration" of those tests. That is, a group would rank the tests according to its definition of rigor and would publish the results. Control would then be with the calibrators. By whose standards would they play?[3]

Can formal tests discern and evaluate a student's intellectual habits? Tests may usefully tell us what a student can display at a given moment, but can they predict for us the promise of a student's disposition to use knowledge effectively when faced with important new situations? (That is, presumably, what most Americans believe students should learn at school.) Are precisely similar tests administered in precisely the same manner necessarily fair? How are the differences among students — not their position on a single scale of presumed ability, but their richly varied ways of addressing the world — to be gathered in, accommodated, honored?[4]

What of those curricular matters which are properly political — the texts selected for literature classes, the emphases in history classes, the choice of topics in biology lessons, and more? While we Americans might readily agree on the substance and standards for reading, expository writing, and computational mathematics, we would not necessarily agree on the substance of that which arises above those thresholds. The struggles during the early 1990s in several states over textbook selection and the nature of a "multicultural" social studies curriculum are evidence for that. Reasonable people disagreed — often hotly.

They should disagree. The curriculum will demand judgments, and these judgments will involve contested values. Given that unavoidable fact, who should make those decisions? A parent will argue: what is at stake here is the mind of *my* child; and while I cannot expect to make every such decision for my child's curriculum, I want to be able directly to confront and promptly to affect the educators who do make the decisions. If they are made by some remote committee, particularly one accessible neither to my direct vote nor to my protest, I am denied the right to affect political decisions about the ideas to which my child is exposed. The issue for me is not, thus, merely a scientific one about testing techniques. It is, rather, a matter of philosophy, of intellectual freedom. *How much control should the state have over my child's mind?* Is there a limit to state authority here?

Would the reform of schools and the improvement of standards be moved by an assessment system that failed to take account of important qualities that mass testing cannot distinguish, qualities expressed as habits of thoughtfulness? If the name of the educational game is getting high test scores, and the tests measure only what is technically testable, then the other goals will get short shrift — or so recent history suggests. Thus, is a system of standards based exclusively on what can be "scored" in the American interest?

The proponents reply that tests must be improved, must be more authentic — that is, closely connected to the activity being measured. (For example, to show their writing ability, students would be asked to give a sample of their own writing rather than to answer in machine-gradable form questions about someone else's writing printed in their examination book.) To measure what students should care about in high school — their ability to shape and maintain a position or proof or opinion — the tests would have to include dialogue. Some argue that this might be computerized and thus scored; but is the effort to build in this crucial capability far enough along to rest the standards of a national education system upon it? And what about dialogue that cannot be reduced to a keyboard?

The technology of "authentic assessment" is primitive, the scoring apparatus cumbersome, and the costs likely to be astronomical. America has never spent money for more than simple tests. Will they tax themselves five to ten times as much for a better kind of testing? Do Americans — in practice, not in the rhetoric of some of their leaders — exhibit confidence in the fairness and utility of existing mass testing programs?[5]

Ironically, recent political concern over educational excellence has created not only a promising climate for reform but also an impatience and intemperance that could take the schools from their existing inadequacy to one different only in character, little better or even worse. The myopic belief that mass testing is the only way to achieve accountability and thus higher standards is dangerous; it clouds our thinking about those high standards themselves. To assume that national examinations provide the only way to improve the system is both arrogantly to overrate our ability to create decent mass tests and — when we make international comparisons — to engage in a tricky non sequitur, to argue that because those nations we think produce better school graduates have national examinations, it is therefore the central presence of those examinations which primarily creates the quality we admire.

For some, taking a position against such national examinations does not, as some critics would have it, indicate an indifference to the low quality of American schools or inattention to the importance of clear academic goals. Exhibitions are, of course, themselves tests. Teaching to the test is eminently sensible if the test is worthy, and a travesty if the test is corrupt or mindless. The issue is how far the test can and should be from the student, from his or her family and community, from the professional teachers who know their students well.

Good Exhibitions can be effectively designed close to a particular group of students, even if they relate in a specified, if limited, way to a larger standard. They are public and thus a source of close and visible accountability. This closeness allows for the protection of the individual. Each student taking the test is known to her examiners; her dispositions and record over time are widely understood; and she and her advocates, such as her parents, are part of the process leading up to and including the Exhibition. Given the inescapable crudeness of assessment machinery, the need for such care and for advocates is simple justice. Further, as demanding tests of intellectual habits require the documentation of the student's performance in a variety of ways over a substantial period of time, local administration is a practical and financial necessity.

The question still persists: What should the standards be and who should set them? The existing system is a jumble, with states and localities often marching to different drummers, with a variety of texts and tests on the market, and with a fog of professional and special interest pressure groups — from the National Council of the Teachers of English to Phyllis Schlafly's Eagle Forum — swirling about.

We could discard this mix of influences as hopeless and replace it with a more unitary authority, with the state setting the examinations and laying out the curriculum, leaving the communities and the schools to worry about the means of education (as though one can neatly separate ends and means in the daily life of a classroom). Or we can accept this mix of influences as a necessary evil at worst and a fundament of democracy at best and figure out how to improve it. The latter approach is much to be preferred, especially for America, a nation blessed with sweeping diversity, enriched as well as tortured by cultural dissonance. We are not Japan or Germany. Our demographic variegation is essentially defining. And at this stage of world history, with its fresh outbreak of community and nationalistic jealousies, our ability to manage this diversity may provide direction for how an ever more populous world can live with itself.

We must learn to value variety and see it as the basis for a richer rather than a thinner standard. The setting and maintaining of standards must be *shared* in the deliberate creation of parallel and competing systems of standards. Let the state assess some things; the districts, others; the schools, more; and parents and students, exercising their choice among schools, even more. Let the states take educational audits — tests of samples of students from samples of schools — and not with a single instrument, but by means of a number of competing instruments, ones that can lessen the likelihood of a monopolistic assessment bureaucracy erecting an unstormable bastion for itself.

To argue for competing interests in the setting of educational standards is to argue for the same sort of messiness that has resulted from the balance of powers embedded in the United States Constitution. What our children think is too important to be left to any one group; and as long as we believe that schools profoundly affect — or should affect, if they were effective — how children think, these schools must be subject to the same sorts of pulling and hauling that characterize democratic government at its best. We are not dealing here with a commodity citizens can ignore. We are dealing with the habits and convictions and understandings of young citizens who are compelled by the state to attend school. No sector of American public life is more fragile, more at risk, and more important. No small group, however noble its intentions, should have disproportionate power over it.

What is needed is raised expectations within the various agencies that now affect standards rather than their demotion and replacement by a more centralized system — a sustained and deliberate effort to build strong and necessarily competing influences on standards for American schools. A loose system without rigor is unacceptable, and so is the oxymoronic unitary system of standards from the top. *The task is the creation of a loose system that has rigor.*

The search for such a system starts with two realities — the inattention of American culture to serious learning and the misdesign of the schools.

Most Americans do not care about rigorous high school education and thoughtlessly accept, for example, the convenience of the massive employment of teenagers on school days and the exquisite entertainment of Friday night football, however it may undermine the players' academic progress. Leaders lie, misuse facts, deliberately distort. The country happily tolerates mediocrity and the conviction that anything which sells must be good. It is difficult to insist on academic rigor in such a climate. High educational standards are impossible without high civic standards.

The misdesigned school — the one that forces Horace into his painful compromises — is more easily reckoned with than is American apathy about schooling. However, current policies that address this matter obliquely, by means of "choice" plans or external examinations to show up the laggard schools, have the unintended effect of misdirecting public attention and reinforcing incompetent practice. Public policy must, rather, address the issue of standards by attending directly to the two barriers to excellence — public attitudes and ineffective schools.

Horace Smith can do little about public attitudes. His committee, if it has the grit, can help to address the functioning of its own school.

"Cut out the Advanced Placement courses and you'll reap a parental whirlwind," the principal warned.

Green: "But that's just a small group of kids!"

"With a powerful parental lobby," Patches added. The school board member was nodding her head.

"AP means tracking, and tracking is unfair."

"Not all tracking is unfair. How do you teach a Shakespeare sonnet to a kid who can barely read? How can you teach functions to a kid who can't add? Is it fair to ask a student to do things that he can't handle or to repeat simple material that he's already mastered?"

"They can be put in the same classroom and taught together, the abler helping the slower . . . different work for different kids."

"That's not fair to the abler. They need to be pushed and helped too. The extras shouldn't always go to the slow kids."

"But they don't now! Look at the size of those AP classes. There are only eight kids in the advanced, BC, calculus section." Eyes turned to the mathematics teacher, who had that class made up of the swiftest mathematicians. "They deserve the challenge . . ." He trailed off.

"But if they do, some other class is overloaded. Someone wins, someone loses. It's usually the kids in the middle who lose. The AP kids get a break and the special needs kids do, and the noisy or troublesome ones do . . ." Laughter, but brief.

"What about vo tech?" Coach questioned. "The teachers there can't have more than fifty kids, by state regulation." He was immediately rebuffed by the shop teacher: "How many boys are there per coach on your football team?" There was strain in the air. The politics of jobs was ever present. The teachers could feel the students watching them.

"The part of tracking that bothers me the most is how it starts so early. The signal goes out that some kid is a loser when he's barely thirteen, so they send him to the shops." This remark caused most to glance at the shop teacher. He stared ahead.

"Kids change. We all know that. The later we make up our minds about them . . . or they make their minds up about themselves . . . their parents too . . . the better."

Patches: "All kids should meet common, fair, but demanding high school diploma standards. The differentiation — the *curricular* differentiation — should follow that."

"Do you mean like English O Levels and A Levels?" Margaret knew that Patches had been a Fulbright exchange teacher in Oxfordshire some years previously.

"Yes and no," he replied. "We want all our kids to get some sort of 'ordinary' diploma. No one should be left out, and that's our job. Lots of English kids never get that far. And our version of advanced work should be broader, richer, less encrusted with the pointless scholarly hazing you see in the British system."

The shop teacher: "That's where vo tech should be. Maybe in the community college. Let them come to us after an early high school diploma."

The committee pondered. The members had earlier drawn in the middle school, and now were talking about something additional at the end.

The visitor: "It's appealing because it's sensible. The ramifications are very interesting. There may be a better allocation of staff in such a system. There have been efforts at this in the past. Have you heard of Simon's Rock, the early college? What's happening in the community colleges here?"[6]

A flurry of talk followed. The crux seemed to be a definition of an ordinary Franklin High School diploma and what could be responsibly forwarded at public expense as appropriate advanced work. As always, Green brought them back to the Exhibitions. "Give me some examples of what kids who were 'advanced' would have to do to deserve the extra diploma?"

Exhibitions: Exercises for an Early College

A. THE ARTS AND SCIENCES
Assemble from metal pipes a wind instrument. Write a piece of music that uses it and perform this piece for us.

Present to us design drawings for the instrument and be prepared to explain precisely how and why it works.

B. ENGINEERING, SCIENCE, AND MECHANICS
The engine and drivetrain of the 1983 Chevette before you has been "sabotaged" by us in a number of ways. Please troubleshoot the problems and repair them in the shortest amount of time and with as few new parts as possible. Draw up a description both of the problems and of your specific remedies; include a bill for the owner. (You should assign your labor time at the rate of $28 per hour.) Be prepared to defend your troubleshooting strategy, to explain why the sabotage caused flaws in the engine's functioning; and to tell us whether there were remedies you considered and then discarded.

These exercises are both demanding and familiar. However, they usually appeal to the interests of students with very different career goals.

Each results in a completed entity — a musical instrument or a functioning engine and drivetrain — and each requires the student to go beyond that product, to explain it and his puzzlements about it. Each requires theoretical understanding as well as skills of application. They mix "fields" (including notation and performance, engineering, chemistry, and arithmetic) in realistic ways, and they call for an appreciation of the constraints that each field imposes on the others.

They require substantial equipment and materials — a limitation where budgets are very tight. But both can be jury-rigged, with scrounged materials and tools from local shops.

Either could be completed by an individual or by a team.

9

Thoughtful Places

"WHEN WE GET to recommendations, Horace, be sure to insist on a copier machine for every department . . . or least for our department." Laughter. "And a fax." More laughter. "What about a coathook?" Groans.

"Let's not get into details yet." Horace tried to brake the discussion.

"This isn't a detail," Green demurred. "It stands for something, a symbol of something bigger."

A chorus of complaint suddenly rose. No phones for private calls. No place to lock up one's materials. No offices. Inadequate washrooms. Glacially slow responses to book orders. No access to the building except when students are there.

Gripes continued. The kids get away with murder. The parents don't care . . . just how many came to the last Parents' Night? Parents treat the staff like servants. Parents always complain. They never say thank you. We're cursed with the students' goddam cars, and with easing up on the kids so that they can earn the money they need to pay for their hotrods. The school is amoral: What about the sheepish reactions to teenage unmarried parents? What about our own hypocrisies, pretending not to talk with the kids about pregnancy and abortion while in fact we're doing so? Why is there so much cheating at Franklin High? Why do we tolerate, glorify, violence in athletics . . .

The two parent members listened, aghast. The two students smirked. The face of the school board member was hard. She spoke: "This is remarkable talk from professionals . . ." the last word spat out almost as an insult. She herself was startled at her reaction. So were the teachers.

Horace turned again to Green. "What did you mean when you said that the copier problem was bigger?"

"They don't respect us."

"Who's 'they'?"

Patches, scoffing: "We shouldn't respect ourselves." The school board member thought she had an ally, but she was quickly disappointed. "The school board," Patches continued, "simply doesn't understand what it takes to teach well. They starve us, and we just accept it. Professionals, indeed."

The school board member flared. "Money doesn't grow on trees in this town, you know. We do our best, and you know it. And your union's demands need some looking after too . . ." She paused. The room was tense. "How much respect is there in all those union demands for rules about what teachers can and can't do? The union tells teachers precisely what to do. Is that respect? Doesn't the union believe its members have minds of their own?"

The two students were fascinated by the confrontation. Horace deflected the talk from the union issue and tried again: "We must suggest some changes, whether they're for additional copiers or something else, and we have to keep our plans within a reasonable budget." Patches snorted.

The second student: "Treating us better isn't a matter of money. We could rewrite the student handbook." More snorts, now from others as well.

The mathematics teacher: "Treating students better. Treating us better. It's all of a piece. It starts with how we get along, with how we feel about each other and our work."

"Feeling takes time." It popped out of a student. People stopped at this observation, silly on the surface but provocative below.

The mathematics teacher: "Sure it takes time. But if we had a sense of what we want here, a sense of community about that, a goal that spoke of this school as a decent place as well as a producer of high test scores . . ."

"Yes," Green agreed. "It's what sort of community we are." She eyed Patches, knowing that any kind of "community" talk riled him. He didn't react. She went on: "It's not that complicated . . . it's just what we believe. If we could settle on that, we'd be able to get some ideas, some priorities."

Inwardly, Horace sagged. He knew that Green had the essence here, if it could be strained out. The kind of place Franklin could become was crucial, far more so than copiers or a new syllabus.

So much about what makes up a good school is simple, obvious, supported by common sense and often by research. The pity is that many schools, and the system as a whole, often seem to operate with different rules.

People tend to copy those whom they respect. People of all ages are likely to work harder when they feel they are valued and respected. The essence of respect is being known. Those who are mere numbers or whose identity is characterized solely on the basis of paper credentials or scores or race or gender or age are demeaned, their personhood belittled and their ambition denied.

People with the power to adapt their work to its immediate demands act on that opportunity and take responsibility for the result. People who are not trusted act as though they cannot be trusted.

If people have the right tools and the appropriate amount of time to use them, they do their jobs better. People who are denied the tools and time they need quickly become discouraged; they believe that those responsible for their work do not respect it. Neglect breeds cynicism.

In jobs that require judgment and that by their nature cannot be subject to routine, time must be available both to arrive at judgments and to consult with informative colleagues. In jobs where the knowledge or technology required is in constant evolution, time must be available for workers to keep up with it.

Friends make better teammates than do strangers. Teams that share values are successful. Values for sharing cannot be summarily imposed from the outside.

People who are distracted work poorly. People who feel that their workplace is hostile or unsafe cannot be effective. People who are asked to do too much either cut corners, depreciating their own efforts, or give in, collapse.

People like to know why they are asked to do things. They value an enterprise whose purposes are clear. Most people like to care about the communities in which they work. Most appreciate symbolic rituals that affirm the collective enterprise.

The joys and pressures of each part of one's life affect the other parts. The worker frightened by a situation at home works poorly. The employee with two jobs attends scantily to the one that seems less interesting or important. A hungry person engages sparingly. A community that cares little about a person's efforts saps that person's resolve.

Respecting people means attending to their special needs. Schools that welcome new students all during the year, for example, cannot merely assign them to existing classes, there to sink or swim. Respectful schools have "reception" units to smooth the way for often disoriented and frightened newcomers. This usually calls for new or reallocated resources.

Respect means assuming that the file of a student — test scores, personal data — is a bare beginning in an understanding of that student, and that time has to be allocated regularly for his teachers to consult on how best to serve him. Respecting students means asking much of them and giving them the time to meet that standard. In most schools this means narrowing the tasks the student is asked to take on and raising the standard that the student is expected to meet.

Respect is modeled. Students who eat meals at school should help to prepare them. Students who make messes should clean them up. Respectful communities do not signal that the Good Life is a right to a free lunch, and they do not farm out their own scutwork to be done by others. No one is wholly another's servant.

There is nothing radical about such propositions, but they

represent values rarely accommodated in typical high school programs. They are indeed *values*; they reflect fundamental moral — democratic — convictions, ones long embraced by Americans. Individuality means something, we believe. If so, then it must be addressed. If, on the other hand, we believe that students are the school's products-in-the-making, then we can treat them as if they were fenders awaiting installation on an automobile assembly line. Adolescents who sense this drop out of school, usually psychologically, sometimes physically.

Adults who themselves are accorded respect are likely to respect students. Put alternatively, teachers who are shabbily treated are likely to treat their students the same way. If your judgment is not respected — for example, if the performance and potential of a student are judged largely on the basis of brief examinations, with no heed paid to the considered opinions of teachers — it stings, and you readily begin not to care. *Why should I worry about this kid? Even if I did, I couldn't do anything about it. No one wants my opinion.*

It is hard to stay at the enervating business of helping a hostile kid learn to read when the system does not give you appropriate books to do the job.

It takes stubbornness to persist in making copies of recent and relevant articles for your students if the system denies you ready use of a copier machine.

It takes special loyalty to a student when you make the telephone call to her home on your quarter at an overused public telephone in the hallway. It requires doggedness to insist that your students come by for one-on-one chats when you have neither private place nor dependable hours.

It tests your sense of community when there are few faculty meetings, and those which are held deal only with administrative trivialities. It is impossible to build a team of teachers for any purpose when staff assignments to the school are made by administrators in a distant central office solely on the basis of technical certificates and seniority.

It requires the tolerance of a saint quietly to accept an overstuffed curriculum designed by strangers for students who are not like yours, and which is to be covered in too few days and by all students equally. It is difficult to retain a sense of your own scholarly and professional growth if the time formally allotted for that purpose is pre-empted by programs devised by strangers in a central office. It is insulting to be "in-serviced," particularly when nothing follows from it.

Respect for students starts with respect for teachers, for them as individuals, for their work, and for their workplace. Who could disagree? Yet the conditions that reflect disrespect, however unintended, persist. The rhetoric of a different school world is widely heard, but meaningful substance is rarely achieved. The practical implications of taking these commonsense matters seriously are daunting.

Behind this matter of respect lies the issue of purpose, of a common resolve around which the teachers and, all hope, the students can rally. The kind of school — its character — gives all a focus, a basis on which to make decisions of priority. This character arises less from a particular orientation, such as that commonly associated with magnet schools ("This is the High School of the Performing Arts"), than from its nature as a functioning community, a school infused with the practice of thoughtfulness. As is so often the case, the character is difficult to describe accurately; one has to sense it.

The school with more than a superficial mission has an air of collective assurance, an ease, pride. One sees it in the ability of many of its students to describe substantively what they are working on and why. One feels it in the interaction of adults; they are colleagues, not free-lance professionals sharing a building and students and functioning by the rules of an administrative hierarchy. A school's assurance arises from its knowledge about what its core values are — and from having the authority to act upon them. Given traditions of top-down bureaucracy, such schools are rare.

People of all ages learn best when they are not distracted, when they can engage with ideas long enough to grasp them, when the culture of their school reinforces careful, thorough work, when they are not physically and acoustically crowded together. This takes time, an intellectually coherent program, and widely understood standards. Such a culture requires agreements on what is more or less important. It is, in sum, the antithesis of the shopping mall high school, full of every sort of curricular, extracurricular, and social activity. The very richness of offerings confuses; the frenetic choosing sets bad habits. Distraction abounds, whether from the student's perspective ("This morning I still have French, then math, a study hall to do my English, a meeting on the newspaper, time to catch up with Janice, then chemistry, lunch somehow along the way in D period with lacrosse after that, an away game, and I'm baby-sitting tonight . . .") or from the school's perspective ("Welcome to our high school. Let me show you our many programs . . . the Course of Study Guides are here and the student handbooks there . . . The marching band just won State . . . We offer Japanese here . . . We just got these new computers from IBM"). This kind of school is wonderful, colorful, well intentioned, almost breathless in its wealth of possibilities. Yet it lacks a center. It all too often devastatingly distracts, and, being much of many things, is little of any one thing.

High school, of course, absorbs but a fraction of an adolescent's time. Even for dutiful students, high school casts a shadow over but eight months of the year and attracts attention for about six hours a day for five days of the week. Few students do much more than an hour's worth of serious homework each night, if that; a student not physically at school is usually not engaging with the school's agenda. Further, the flat and lifeless nature of much of traditional school work makes distractions all the more potent. Lectures in chemistry have to compete with the soaps on TV and the cute girl across the classroom's laboratory table, mathematics problem sets vie with football games, the reading from a text about early Mesopotamia with a job. School's residual attraction for many kids is simple: it is where their friends are.[1]

And so teachers have to struggle for their students' attention. The effort is made all the more difficult when the student's world beyond the school is not only unmindful of what a good education implies but, intentionally or unintentionally, is hostile to it.

Media that mock schools and teachers, political leaders who blatantly lie ("I misspoke . . .") and engage in grotesque hypocrisy, employers who press kids to be on duty long hours, businesses that hawk anything that will sell, however tawdry or corrupt, parents who show no interest in their children's school work or who belittle it, communities that abuse and frighten children: the list is stunning and well documented.

Further, some Americans do not see the schools as engines both of information and of intellectual liberation. Indeed, they find the latter — especially when so described — to be intolerable. The schools, they insist, are to teach young people what is true, what is right, and what is wrong. Anything beyond that is anathema. Their argument is seductive but flawed, especially when one gets to schooling beyond the rudiments. There is too much information to purvey, and choices have to be made. And what is right and what is wrong are, however much we may regret it, uncertain in most important matters. Should schools teach a particular kind of certainty? Or should they attempt to teach the craft and habit of deciding for oneself, on the merits? The only "good" that they would teach (perhaps) is a respectful commitment to the facts, to the logic of an argument, and to an awareness of when one is working at a level of principle or opinion rather than of provable fact. They would encourage opinions to be freely expressed, particularly to those who want deeply to conform.

Some find this approach both wishy-washy and dangerous. They prefer that the schools teach *their* definition of truth, at the expense of that of (presumably misguided) others. They fear that teachers will use their authority to force students to adopt other opinions, or at the least to keep open the possibility of other ideas winning out. The bigger fear for all of us, though, is that students may have no opinion at all.

However, most communities rarely even debate these matters. Parents and teachers are all very busy. School is school. The kids should be there, "preparing for life," having enough of a good time to stay with it, and not rocking many boats. Indifference is school's major enemy.

A veteran high school principal once promised an audience,

"Let me control one thing and I'll run you a perfect school." What was that "thing"? "Let me choose the parents." School reform does not start with schools. It starts with families, with their communities, with the culture. At the least we should start laughing at the ironies. Only a forlorn society could believe that it is helping education by running state lotteries ostensibly for the schools' benefit: lotteries absolutely depend either on a citizenry ignorant of simple mathematics and the laws of probability, or on desperate individuals addicted to gambling.

Good schools are thoughtful places. The people in them are known. The units are small enough to be coherent communities of friends. Amenities are observed. There are quiet places available as well as places for socializing. No one is ridiculed. No one is the servant of another. The work is shared. The entire place is thoughtful: everything in its routines meets a standard of common sense and civility. At such places do adolescents learn about the thoughtful life.

"All this is so idealistic. It asks too much. We can't do this."

This came from a middle school teacher, one of the three who had joined the committee when it decided to start its plan earlier, with younger children. She was a practical sort, a highly skilled teacher of both mathematics and science. She had won the state's Teacher of the Year award. She had been touted as a "local heroine" in the city's newspaper. She let these accolades slide over her: her realism dominated. She was the veteran's veteran, an old pro.

"What can't we do?" Horace asked.

The veteran explained: "There's so much here, so much expected of so many people. We're asking for a change in the community's attitudes right down to how the budget is spent."

"That's right. Can we do otherwise?" Horace pushed back.

The veteran paused, eyeing Horace. Then: "I suppose we do have to be idealistic. But how can we expect so much of others if we can't get our own act together?"

"Who are 'we'?"

"Us. We teachers. Us people."

"What do you mean, 'us people'? What's wrong with us?" Some of the high school faculty were getting defensive.

The veteran paused again, looking steadily around at the others. They waited her out, and she knew they would. "Let's take the — your — English Department, for example." Horace tensed. "You can't get much done as a group. You are not a group, a thoughtful community. You get from day to day by avoiding one another. You don't meet much because you'd fight like cats and dogs. Each of you goes his own way. Everyone knows that. The students know that. And now we want to build some sort of collective commitment, a 'thoughtful community'?" She let that sink in. "Let's get some thoughtful communities within the departments for starters."

The committee seemed frozen. The two students, now joined by a terrified eighth-grader from the middle school, were rapt. No one argued with the veteran or asserted that she was wrong.

Horace finally broke the silence. "Our department doesn't get along not because we disagree about educational matters. It's about personalities." His language was unusually clumsy because of his emotion.

The veteran kept the pressure on. "If it's not educational matters, then what is it? You're all friends in that department."

Indeed they were. Most had joined the faculty together, several years after Horace had come. They were mostly now in their mid-forties, colleagues who had been in collective harness for almost twenty years.

Horace explained: "We know each other too well. I suppose that we compete, though I doubt whether any of us really wants to. I guess it's that we're bored with each other, bored with the kids and the routine. We love it, but we don't love it. Its familiarity is a joy and a pain. The only new thing we seem able to do is chafe each other. It's not happy."

The veteran continued to press. "So, what do you do about that? Your own lives are getting in the way of school."

"No, they're not," Horace flared, but he knew that they were, and he knew that every other teacher there sensed that the chippiness in the high school's English Department arose not from disagreements over the program but from abrasion among its members. He knew he was floundering. "What do we do with this?"

The veteran, now that her point was made, pushed further, constructively. "We've got to shake things up, get some newer, better things on people's agenda, something more important to worry about than the staleness of being forty-five years old at Franklin High School . . . Change for change's sake, almost. A new mountain to climb." The clichés multiplied but were apt.

"Something worthy of abrasion," said Green. "Getting on with the idealistic. We should go for it. The school needs something bold, for its own morale, its own soul even."

The veteran swung toward Horace. "Sorry for picking on the English Department. There's much that can be said about all of us, at both schools."

"We deserve it," said Horace, relieved.

"How are we going to get people off the dime, away from their old squabbles?" asked the visitor. She admired the veteran; the committee had moved abruptly forward since the middle school teachers had joined in. Curiously, the tension the newly arrived teachers brought seemed to accelerate good thinking. The members surely knew that they were at points of importance because these were often points that hurt. The little wars within the departments, for example, had finally surfaced, to be recognized and addressed.

"The school itself can be a part of the curriculum." The principal spoke. Some thought she was trying to turn the discussion from the high school's faculty squabbles.

The principal pushed ahead. "That sounds mushy, but it doesn't have to be. What could be done to create a better environment here that also advances the academic goals we've agreed on?"

"You mean," said Patches, "what's curricular and what's extracurricular?"

"We don't have time for the truly extracurricular," said Green. "If it isn't important for the overall goals of the school, it shouldn't be here at all. Everything is curricular."

The gasps were audible. The second student: "What happens to Student Council? The yearbook? The band? Sports? Come on . . ."

"You misunderstand me," argued Green. "Everything we do, and that can include sports and the school newspaper, must tie in to the goal of making this a thoughtful school."

"Just my point," said the principal. The fact that she was arguing this way encouraged Horace. He had been skeptical of her since she joined the school the previous year. At first she seemed weak, but what she had been doing, wisely, was lying low, figuring out the place — or so many of the older teachers now believed. She had a pleasant but reserved style. She didn't feel that she had to be a Leader — Franklin's Joan of Arc. She led now; that much was sure. The kids knew who their principal was. But with the teachers, she played a more collegial game. When she suggested things, they came across as though they were from a colleague rather than from a superior. She seemed to trust the faculty, more so since she had served on this committee. She clearly was a "teacher"; she thought and reacted like one. She knew kids, and they liked her. Horace felt that this boded well for the group's work.

The school board member: "If it's important for the school's central program, you'll have to be able to see it when it happens. Are there Exhibitions here?" The suggestion jolted some: Exhibitions for matters not tied directly to courses?

This question appeared especially to galvanize Green. "That's just right . . . We always try to make important extracurricular things into courses, the newspaper into a journalism class as though it were like Biology One . . . It doesn't work . . . What we need are activities, not ones that meet as though they were formal courses, activities that help kids prepare for Exhibitions . . . general sorts of Exhibitions. This will give those activities importance, make them a real incentive for the kids." She paused. "So many of these extracurricular-curricular things that are just classes are taken by kids who want an easy time and credit for their college applications."

"It's not that way in sports," said Coach.

The school board member pressed her question again. "How

can there be some Exhibitions that give the students a rigorous, serious, and academically useful target and at the same time strengthen this school in its effort to be a thoughtful place, a school that models what it hopes for the students?"

To which Horace added, "And give some new life to a school engrossed in its old little personal battles."

Exhibitions: Learning Thoughtfulness
by Thoughtful Practice

A. A newspaper will be published each week during the school year covering events of the previous week, announcing immediate events, and commenting on the school scene. Each of the school's five Houses (or some other categories depending on the school) will have a full newspaper staff; these staffs will produce the paper in rotation. The costs of the paper will be covered by advertisements from local merchants that have been solicited by a single business staff. To the greatest possible practical extent, production will be at the school, superintended by the students. An outside committee of local journalists and others with related interests will provide regular and public criticism of the publication.

B. Recycling of all sorts of waste will be organized and supervised by a schoolwide committee, reports on its effectiveness regularly issued, and analyses of and comparisons with similar efforts elsewhere published.

C. When communicable diseases appear among the school community (strep throat, measles, viral conjunctivitis), surveys will be promptly made by interested students, the patterns of the diseases' spread described, and information about them and their treatment quickly published.

Such activities characterize healthy, thoughtful communities.

Some can be used as Exhibitions for some students. To that degree, they are part of those students' academic programs. Others can be justified not as Exhibitions per se but as activities necessary for the conduct of a community that lives in a thoughtful way.

Some activities, such as the frequent publication of a timely newspaper, require the use of academic knowledge in very practical ways.

The line between adult and adolescent responsibilities blurs, a desirable occurrence in any thoughtful high school community.

Such activities must be allotted time to be successful. Their educational value — for example, the "science" involved in studies of recycling or the "civic learning" expressed by fair and accurate newspaper reporting — must be understood and accepted by the faculty and the community.

10

The Committee's Report

IT WAS JULY. The round of community meetings was over, having followed a three-day workshop of the faculties of both the Franklin High and Middle Schools. All had been thoroughly covered in the local newspaper. Horace got a bit of joshing for the string of articles, which had been written by a former theater groupie of his. He liked to think, however, that the columns were even-handed. Indeed, he was proud of their content as well as of his former pupil's style. Unquestionably, they had been supportive.

The polls and surveys of various special groups — parents, elementary school faculty, local business leaders, and some college admissions deans — had been summarized and analyzed. District and state authorities had been briefed and queried. The committee felt sodden with feedback, tired, bewildered, and curiously depressed. People seemed unwilling to accept the complex problems facing the schools — much less the overarching problems, distractions, and temptations facing adolescents these days. It was as if every person had his or her little focused agenda. What the committee got from all this consultation was chaos, or at best a laundry list of desires lacking any sort of realism or cohesion.

And yet there *was* feedback; the community clearly cared. One of Horace's friends from his liquor business told him more, that the interest was not there until the committee had struck the spark. "No one ever asks us," the friend had said. "We like to be asked. Of course we responded."

"What if we don't give you what you want?" asked Horace.

"We don't really know what we want. Not specifically. But we like to be listened to, to be a part of all this. And we want to know that people like you are leading the effort."

"Then it doesn't matter what we recommend?"

"Not as much as the fact that you're recommending it." That support braced Horace, and he passed the message along to the committee members. They did not believe it. Only Patches rose to it. "They think that we really are professionals and know what we're doing. What an absolutely stunning thought," he remarked. But there was little sarcasm in his voice. He knew well that the committee, by its very openness and candor, had built substantial credibility.

The committee by now fully appreciated how vital the superintendent and principal had been. The superintendent, having launched the effort, had kept apart, in touch primarily through the principal and the school board member who was on the committee. He publicly and repeatedly backed the process he had started. How he would come down on the details would be known only after the report's issuance. The principal had told the committee, however, that she would let it know whether the superintendent at any point was concerned or upset about any major issue. And everyone knew that the school board member would do likewise.

The committee started its detailed walk through the final recommendations. A big question was the length of the school year. More time was what seemed necessary to many of the committee members. If they were to expect more of the students, they would have to give them the days and weeks required to meet that expectation.

"The community will never buy it. It'll wreck vacations."

"Who'll be the lifeguards?"

"What'll it cost?" The arguments against more time in school seemed endless.

Coach pushed back. "If we want the kids to be well trained, we have to give them practice time . . . time to get into those habits we admire."

"And that the community will admire," added the school board member. She went on: "The public usually wants the schools to change without any inconvenience — no new taxes, no changes in the school bus schedules . . ."

"Just give 'em another test!" Patches sneered. The committee had been dismayed by state and federal leaders' reactions to what they themselves labeled a national crisis: they called for more tests.

Horace: "If we recommend a longer school year, will that arouse so much hostility that no one will notice anything else?"

Margaret: "Let's not be too political. Let's tell the community what we believe. Let's take up the political issues as they arise." The visitor nodded. So did the superintendent, who was sitting in during this hour of discussion.

"This isn't the only red flag," Green said. "How are people going to like seeing their programs cut?"

"They won't, obviously."

"They'll accept it if they see that *everyone* has to change and that *everyone* still has a job, a new job."

"We've been over that. Is it realistic?"

"Only if people have the courage to try the new things that are needed, and we are able to get beyond personal agendas."

"They won't."

"Some won't. They will leave . . . have to leave . . . will want to leave." Margaret said it slowly. Everyone was quiet. They knew that she had put it fairly.

"We can't dodge this reality," said the young English teacher.

"People have to be helped with the changes," said the mathematics teacher. Coach nodded. The shop teacher watched, almost expressionless. He was as crucial to the credibility of the committee's work as he was reticent in its meetings.

"Will you accept us?" the shop teacher asked. The question

stung. The teachers in the academic departments knew what he meant but cared not to address it.

The mathematics teacher: "You'll have to knock some of the rust off your math. But you can teach us a lot about how to teach. We talk too much. You give the kids the tasks . . . You know about Exhibitions. We have much to learn from each other . . . We have some rust to knock off too, and learn some new ways of teaching . . . from you." No one followed; the subject was painful. The committee's drift toward a program focusing on the traditional intellectual areas of the curriculum — for all students — obviously threatened some of the teachers of vocational courses.

"Will parents like some of us teaching 'out of field'?"

"No," Horace said. The visitor added: "They'll accept it when they see the tradeoff. Their kids will be 'known,' and the strength of the teams will guarantee better quality than what we have now."

Everyone knew what she meant: more than a few Franklin teachers, whether certified in their fields or not, were weak scholars and did not have a thorough grasp of their subjects. They lay low, each one autonomous behind the shut door of his own classroom. Another of Franklin's dirty little secrets, Patches had frequently reminded the committee. "Don't hide behind those silly certification requirements or all those education degrees," he had repeatedly said. "Ask them if they read anything important, if they stay up with their fields, if they get a serious daily newspaper, if they do some work on their own." The school board member had added, "Teachers at private schools are good," referring surely to the competition Franklin felt from a local Jesuit high school. The issue of teacher standards was as much one of appearances as of substance. It also was one of power. Which pressure group could keep its programs unscathed?

This would be a touchy issue. One even larger finally surfaced. Unlike many others, it had remained largely implicit, pushed aside by discussions of particulars. Some of the changes the committee ardently desired had profound effects on all areas of the school. One could not put these new practices into place without changing almost everything else. Would the community support such a sweeping overhaul?

"They won't stand for it. They believe that these are good schools, that only some fine tuning is necessary, nothing more."

"They're wrong and you know it."

Horace pressed. "*We* know it. We know that we can do much better . . . much, much better. The question is: Can we sell our conclusion and the changes it implies? Who will support a longer school year? Who will understand our two diplomas and Early College?"

The veteran: "We can count on the support of the governor." Some committee members did not understand. She explained: "The state wants us to take some good risks. Heavens, they gave us this money to plan. Do you think that they want just more of the same from us? If we make our arguments well, and don't expect to start the changes too quickly, we'll get support. We'll have to build it." She paused. "We'll have to get ourselves a lobby."

"Let's get the governor to convene it!" The suggestion was greeted with laughs. Theirs was a big state.

The committee pondered. No one, clearly, could yet answer the question of how much support they could count on in the faculty and within the community.

"How do we know until we complete our report?"

"How can we write the report without keeping our constituencies in mind?"

"How can we present a coherent plan if it's compromised at every turn by some special interest group?"

"Pressure groups like us!" Green erupted, lancing the tension.

"Let's push a plan forward, one that satisfies us," the principal said. "Let's not be too wary of the critics, not at this stage."

The visitor agreed. "You've got to say what you believe. Don't play complicated politics at this point, especially politics that you don't fully understand. You don't really know who is for or against what. The quality and force of your report will shape the politics. You've got to show the community what you believe, as boldly as possible, with practical considerations taken into account, but the politicals at this point kept in check."

She went on: "Make sure that the report is practical, that its program is roughly within the existing budget. Show in enough detail what can be done so that people won't knock you down over some extraneous matter to protect their special interests. Show how you deal, for example, with state regulations and tests. But don't get very far into the nitty-gritty or you'll lose everyone in the detail."

Horace: "We've got to show them what they could have, but we can't be rigid. We want to point a way . . ."

"Aha," said Green, ever on to her Exhibitions. "If you know where you're going, it's easier to get there!"

"Exactly," said Horace, amidst groans.

"But shoot high," counseled the visitor. "And you'll be happy with what you finally get."

"Yes," said the principal. "We must design a Cadillac even though we might end up with just a serviceable Ford."

The Report of the Committee on Redesign of the Franklin High and Middle Schools

September 15

To: Board of Education
FROM: The Committee on Redesign of the Franklin High and Middle Schools

Our committee herewith presents the recommendations for the redesign of this city's high school that you requested eighteen months ago.

We were charged to present a plan for the improvement of our school, drawing both from our experience at Franklin and from evidence in recent general studies of American secondary education.

We have read widely, observed other schools, and talked endlessly. We have tried to "visit" our own school in new ways, becoming "students" and trying to sense the worlds that are Franklin from a variety of perspectives. We have forced ourselves to ask all the essential questions about schooling in fresh ways, this to protect ourselves from unintentionally and unwisely accepting habitual but inappropriate ways of perceiving learning and schooling simply because we have long relied on them. We have endeavored to be honest with ourselves and with our schools, recognizing the good and the bad, both the generosity of this community and some significant unfulfilled promises to our adolescent citizens.

It is no attack on this community's energy and good intentions to assert that Franklin High School deserves fundamental redesign. Indeed, only a very strong and proud school is capable of handling the changes we will recommend. The boldness of our report is an expression of special confidence in the strength of this school.

As you will discover, our deliberations included Franklin Middle School: our plan encompasses the program for students from about age eleven up to and beyond high school graduation. When we hereafter refer to "the school," we mean both the middle school and high school.

We are intensely aware of the importance of the work of our elementary school colleagues, which undergirds all we do. We acknowledge it gratefully; and we further acknowledge that many of the convictions long played out in practice in primary school classrooms here in the city are ones we wish now to borrow for the secondary level. The redrawing of the Franklin Middle and High Schools will be readily consistent with much of existing elementary school philosophy.

We present to you the framework for a new secondary education for this city. The details to fill out this framework will follow and must be shaped by the particular people at an immediate time charged with carrying out pieces of this plan, because the details will necessarily change — as the students and teachers and community values change — from term to term, year to year. Good schools are organic places, always in constructive and sensitive motion. The function of an effective school structure is to provide a sensible and expansive context — most usefully in the form of a cluster of essential informing ideas — within which the best school possible at a given moment may be shaped.

Our recommendations are inevitably compromises, the adjustment of several central ideas so that they mesh effectively. The committee members got a bit here and gave a bit there to shape a common vision. The result is a unanimous report.

A. Beliefs. We introduce our report with statements of the several beliefs that inform our recommendations.

We believe that the school's central focus must be on the intellect, on helping each young citizen learn to use his or her mind resourcefully and well. Other enterprises, however worthy, that conflict with this goal must yield.

We believe that this goal applies without exception to all students and that those who seem weakly disposed or who take to serious intellectual effort with difficulty need more of it rather than being switched to something less demanding or pressing. The twenty-first century will require thoughtful citizens and workers; to deny any person a serious education is to assign him or her to a second-class existence and to put the rest of the community at risk. Further, high school is not primarily about sorting people out, the presumed abler from the less able; it is about educating *all* children, generously and without qualification.

We believe that our school must model the thoughtful life that should infuse a civil and rich democracy, that it must be a safe, engaging, inviting, and joyful place for students and for adults. Learning is risky business; it requires one to absorb unfamiliar and often challenging ideas, and it frequently requires one to change one's mind. For learning to proceed, schools must be trusting places, where confusion and error can be acknowledged and thus remedied.

We believe that everyone at the school should be accorded the respect of being known well, that the particular strengths and weaknesses, worries and hopes of each young person should be understood and accommodated. Personalization is not just courtesy; it is the necessary condition for efficient and effective teaching of each student. Every teacher should know his or her students well and should have the authority to act flexibly to capitalize on the special qualities of each. No teacher should be assigned more students than he or she can teach effectively.

We believe that our school should be driven by specific goals in the form of Exhibitions through which the students can display their grasp and use of important ideas and skills. The school's program would be to the largest practical extent the preparation for these Exhibitions. We are aware of the danger of this approach — for example, the trivializing of schooling and its reduction to that which can be inexpensively tested — but we believe that today's well-intentioned but largely directionless program harbors greater risks.

We believe that incentives are the heart of serious learning. Adolescents as well as adults learn only what they want to learn, what they are convinced is important, what inspires them. Exhibitions that are appealing as well as rigorous provide one sort of incentive. There must be others as well. Further, we know that coercion and humiliation are poor incentives to serious learning.

An affirmed student learns; a hectored student resists. Such is not only warm sentimentality; it is cool efficiency.

We believe that effective education must be coherent in at least two senses: there should be a sensible sequence of activity for each student over a number of years, and the academic demands for this young person should be clear and connected. We are aware that we all aspire to such ends. However, as much as we wish it were otherwise, in reality middle and high school are for most students a daily procession through unconnected subjects, and each year is a wrenching new experience, with little cumulative knowledge gained from earlier study.

We believe that if schooling were more efficient — more coherent, more engaging, more demanding — it would be notably more productive. We believe that the typical Franklin student would be able roughly by the age of sixteen to work at a standard now widely accepted for admission to strong colleges and that many of our students could continue for a second, or honors, diploma at our school in what we have termed the Early College.

We believe that serious learning in school is hard work, requiring involvement, intensity, and loyalty to the task. Such hard work cannot be done by anyone but the learner; school must be a place where students seriously engage. We care about students knowing things — being able to recall what the teachers or texts "told" them — but we care even more for the ability of the students to use that knowledge, to employ it in a new setting. We care about the student's habits of the use of knowledge: Do they "instinctively" act in thoughtful and effective ways?

We believe that adults today underestimate the ability and trustworthiness of most adolescents and that much more responsibility and accountability can and should be given to students at high school.

We believe that the community must understand and support this school and the others in the system. We further believe that such fresh support depends on the school's demonstrating a more effective approach to education than that which is now practiced, and with roughly the same resources. We therefore propose (with several special exceptions) to pursue a new design that requires adding no professional staff. We have, rather, redefined the roles of existing staff and of the students themselves. Reform by addition is easier, obviously, but such a luxury is neither available to us nor do most of us believe that it is necessary.

B. The Basic Design. We present eight specific proposals based on the foregoing beliefs.

1. That Franklin High School's requirements for a diploma culminate with success at Exhibitions to be offered both in each of the school's three central academic areas — Mathematics/ Science, the Arts, and History/Philosophy — and in some "cross area" exercises. The Exhibitions will call for the resourceful use of knowledge more than only its display. Franklin should also require a student to be "in good standing" — to have been a good citizen — in order to receive a diploma.

2. That Franklin High School offer two diplomas — a Diploma of Secondary Education (DSE) and an Advanced Secondary Diploma (ASD). The first would reward successful work in all three of the school's central academic areas and would represent solid accomplishment worthy of college admission. Determined efforts should be made to have the majority of Franklin's students achieve this level before their seventeenth birthday. The second would recognize the completion of advanced academic work at Franklin's Early College program, such as Advanced Placement courses or their equivalent taken at nearby colleges, structured apprenticeships, and substantial independent study. The ASD would be awarded on the basis of a contract struck by the student and the school following that student's receipt of the DSE. No student beyond the age of legally mandated school attendance would be required to proceed immediately to work toward the ASD.

3. That a common program be created across both the existing Franklin Middle School and Franklin High School with the academic offerings in both organized into three curricular units — Mathematics/Science, the Arts, and History/Philosophy. The faculty in each of the units would share responsibility for basic

work in language and the skills of expression, for techniques of inquiry, and for study habits.

4. That for students preparing for the DSE, the middle school and the high school should be organized into units of 200 to 215 students, each served by twelve to sixteen faculty. These units, to be called Houses, would be largely self-contained academic and administrative entities — in effect, small schools. Entering at about age eleven, a typical student would progress through some three years in a first-level unit, some three years in a second-level unit, and, if the student wishes, one to three years in the Early College. Movement from one level to the next would be on the basis of successful Exhibition, and the high school diploma (DSE) would be awarded on success at the second level. Obviously, some students will take longer or shorter periods to meet the standards; these variations in rate should be expected, readily accommodated, and honored. Students continuing in the Early College would be grouped in a single unit.

5. That deliberate and concerted effort be made to affect the attitudes and raise the expectations for schooling by students, teachers, parents, educational administrators, and the community at large. Students will have to engage effectively to meet the Exhibitions' standards; they must accept responsibility for their own education to a degree today all too rarely seen. Teachers will serve less as deliverers of information and more as coaches to students developing the habit of learning on their own. All in the school will have to understand and to value the shape and demands of their institution — their particular unit and the entire school — as it is deliberately devoted to modeling and thus bearing witness to the value of thoughtful learning.

6. That the school calendar be lengthened from thirty-six to forty-two weeks a year with a school day running from 8 A.M. to 4 P.M. We further propose that the schedule of these weeks be shaped to allow for four terms, each preceded by a week for special or introductory activities that cut across the several units. Finally, we propose that the daily schedules in each House be wholly controlled by the faculty in that unit.

7. That Franklin launch this "new school" with two pilot units, one at the middle school and one at the high school, staffed by

volunteer faculty and interested students, with the clear expectation that more units will be added as experience grows about their detailed operation. We wish to stress that our recommendations are not addressed to the creation of an interesting "alternative" school; our concern is to affect directly the core school, because it is there that flaws must be rectified.

8. That plans be so designed that their cost is no more than at present and that state and private funds be gathered to underwrite the required planning, training, and development costs.

C. The Curriculum: In describing our recommended academic program, we wish to stress two points we considered in addressing the matter of the substance of the course of study.

First, we find that the current program is superficial — there is too much offered in too little time — and fragmented — courses on this and courses on that — each undoubtedly with its own internal logic but as a whole fostering confusion rather than learning. We must make choices about what is essential and encourage all students' appropriate and sustained involvement with this most important material. We should insist that they "make sense" of the cumulative knowledge.

Second, we believe that the curriculum can no longer be viewed as "what is to be covered" and "what the students should show us that they know" by simple recall. Asking students to display what we have previously told them to memorize, to look up in the dictionary, or to read is limited in purpose. We must expect more: the students must be able to use this knowledge, to acquire the habit of its thoughtful use. We do not sneer at the "well informed." However, we emphasize that our culture and our times demand more of students than that they be well informed, and expect school in all its aspects — its teaching, its texts, and its tests — to define and set such a standard.

Acquiring the habit of use takes time, which is another powerful reason for us to sharpen and focus the academic program. The teachers can cover material only as fast as each student learns to use it resourcefully. The more that the material makes sense in the world of the student, the stronger and deeper will be his grasp of knowing. Clustering subjects in ways that respect disciplinary lines and are persuasive as reflections of the real world is necessary. We recommend three such clusters, these to engage all of the students all of the time, until each student Exhibits successfully for the first-level diploma.

Over the last decade there has appeared a series of important reports on teaching the various academic areas, and we have depended on them extensively. Although these documents were issued by different groups about different academic areas, they have in common some significant themes, and these are reflected in our recommendations.

For example, accomplishment by all students (rather than, say, only by a percentage of them who are assessed as gifted) is expected. The 1989 report of Project 2061 of the American Association for the Advancement of Science puts the matter right in its title: "Science for All Americans." Its language is unequivocal: the AAAS

> set of recommendations constitutes a common core of learning in science, mathematics, and technology for all young people, regardless of their social circumstances and career aspirations . . . The national council is convinced that — given clear goals, the right resources, and good teaching throughout the thirteen years of school — essentially all students (operationally meaning 90 percent or more) will be able to reach all of the recommended learning goals (meaning at least 90 percent) by the time they graduate from high school.[1]

"Everybody Counts," the 1989 report of the National Research Council on the future of mathematics education, asserts that "secondary school mathematics should provide for all students a core of mainstream mathematics in which different student groups are distinguished not by curricular goals, but only by speed, depth, and approach."[2] This assumption is itself crucial: not all students are alike, think alike, or learn alike. None of the reports recommends a monolithic curriculum; all counsel attentiveness to the rich differences among students. The attention, however, must be directed toward a common general standard of achievement.

All recommend the goal of a student's being able to use knowledge rather than merely displaying it. Teachers of the arts, of physical education, and of writing, for example, have long assumed such a goal, but it now is explicitly expressed elsewhere. In writing of the social studies performance of American students over the last decade, a panel of the U.S. Government's National Assessment of Education Progress argues that "to foster the types of learning desired, teachers will need to act more as facilitators of learning and students will need to become active doers and thinkers in the classroom rather than simply passive recipients of information."[3] Most Americans would not challenge this goal, but the fact is, NAEP found, "fewer than 17 percent of the students [in their national sample] reported that . . . instructional approaches" indicative of this objective were used weekly in their classes.[4] Universally, the reports urge engagement. "In science, profound understanding comes from having concrete experiences with a phenomenon before it is given a name or a symbol," the National Science Teachers Association asserted in 1990.[5]

This NSTA committee in its program on "the scope, sequence, and coordination of secondary science," argues for "less" coverage to ensure more thorough knowledge.[6] So do several of the other groups, explicitly. The AAAS "Science for All Americans" document is very blunt: "A fundamental premise of Project 2061 is that the schools do not need to be asked to teach more and more content, but rather to focus on what is essential to scientific literacy and to teach it more effectively . . . To ensure the scientific literacy of all students, curricula must be changed to reduce the sheer amount of material covered."[7] The National Research Council's Committee on High-School Biology Education clearly asserts a less-is-more philosophy: "The central concepts and principles that every high-school student should know must be identified, and the curriculum pared of everything that does not explicate and illuminate the relatively few concepts." The committee goes on, arguing much as we here argue:

Those concepts must be presented in such a manner that they are related to the world that students understand in language that is familiar, and they must be taught by a process that engages all the students in examining why they believe what they believe. This requires building slowly, with ample time for discussion with peers and with the teacher. Particularly in science it also requires observation and experimentation, not as an exercise in following recipes, but to confront the essence of the material.[8]

Many of the committees, even when charged with reporting on a particular academic discipline without regard to other subjects, argue as we do for greater coherence in the overall curriculum, for interrelationships and connections. The biology panel, for example, recommends, "We should begin now to plan and support models for integrated or parallel programs in biology, chemistry, physics, and mathematics." The AAAS group from the start addressed mathematics, science, and technology, including engineering, as a single, coherent unit. The Bradley Commission on the teaching of history and the social studies recommended a curriculum whose core was history, with the other social sciences related to it. The joint project of the American Historical Association, the Carnegie Foundation for the Advancement of Teaching, the National Council for the Social Studies, and the Organization of American Historians reports on the need for coherence, for "the *systematic* and *interrelated* study of people in societies, past and present."[9] The call from many quarters for "writing across the curriculum" is now commonplace, as are skill and understanding in computer science. Our appeal, then, for a newly focused and systematically integrated curriculum is a voice in a national chorus.

We are intensely aware that such appeals for "coherence" and "interrelationships" and "engaged students" and the display of cumulative knowledge are easy to make and that to respond practically to them is difficult. We know, too, that the existing, familiar routines of schedules, courses, and teaching styles do not serve to reach the ends on which we all now largely agree. Our recommendations for changes in these routines are no bolder than are the recommendations for curricular reform by the scholarly and professional groups. However, they may appear more so because we have calculated carefully what it would take in the actual conduct of the Franklin Middle and High Schools to achieve what is widely accepted as desirable. We have tried honestly to bring the cosmic to the level of the nitty-gritty of schoolkeeping. Realistic means must be gathered to reach agreed-on ends, and as the ends we seek are ambitious, so too will be the means.

To repeat: we recommend two stages — conventionally described as grades six through eight and nine through eleven — where a unified curriculum, organized into the three areas of Math/Science, the Arts, and History/Philosophy, is pursued each year by each student. Across these three areas the entire faculty would carry a collective responsibility for what we call the tools of inquiry and expression. Movement from Stage 1 to Stage 2 and out of Stage 2 to a high school diploma (DSE) would be accomplished by Exhibition. Stage 3 — Early College — of advanced opportunities would be voluntary for those students beyond the age of compulsory education who have received a DSE.

Let us turn first to each of the three areas, recognizing the necessity to be succinct at this stage, only generally descriptive. We present here not a curriculum but, rather, the concept for a course of study. We focus primarily on the activity preliminary to the receipt of the regular high school diploma, the DSE. The necessary detailing of any curriculum must be done by those who will teach it, and must reflect the characteristics of each group of students. Further, we want to sketch simply a forest; too much detail will lose us among the trees.

For our area of Mathematics/Science, we strongly endorse the line of reasoning and the recommendations of the Project 2061 report of the American Association for the Advancement of Science. We hope that the AAAS leaders will maintain their focus, resisting the temptations to pile too many topics into their new course of study. Happily, the thrust of that project's work distinctly parallels that of the National Science Teachers Association "Scope and Sequence" effort and in many respects the "Everybody Counts" report on mathematics by the National

Research Council: arithmetic, algebra, geometry, statistics, functions, taught in a context of constant use. Common themes in science, mathematics, and technology: systems, models, constancy, patterns of change, scale. The physical setting, the living environment, the human organism, human society, the designed world, the mathematical world, the language of science. The relationship of science with history, and the interactions of cultural movements and events and scientific discovery. Scientific habits of mind, matters of value, and skills in computation, manipulation, and observation. All this is a sensible list, demanding but attainable.[10] Recent work on standards in mathematics forwarded by the National Council of Teachers of Mathematics is also helpful and constructive.

Beyond this, responsibility for the best of the traditional concerns and activities of health education and physical education (excluding competitive athletics) would be lodged within the Mathematics/Science area.

Regrettably, the Arts are blessed with no studies of the quality and reach provided for the sciences and mathematics by the 2061 report. The area is so fragmented that many barely see it as an area at all. Only as we look at the matter from the angle of aesthetics, as did Philip Phenix thirty years ago in his provocative study *Realms of Meaning,* or from the perspective of the varieties of human learning, as has Howard Gardner in his *Frames of Mind,* do we see something different from the conventional arrangement with literature as part of English, art (meaning the visual arts), music, and more or less in most schools, theater and sometimes dance, with all of these operating largely in isolation from one another.[11] While together they are part of the aesthetic domain, few high school students will ever realize that. Painting studios are miles from English classrooms or music halls.

The College Board in 1985 published a report, "Academic Preparation in the Arts: Teaching for Transition from High School to College," which suggests useful connections but strongly implies that the traditional distinctions among the arts are clearly fixed. Each — visual arts, theater, music, and dance, is a discrete subject.[12] Much more helpful is the work of Elliot Eisner of Stanford University, who, though his focus is primarily on the visual arts, paints a broader, more inclusive picture. In a report for the Getty Center for Education in the Arts entitled "Beyond Creating: the Place for Art in America's Schools," he writes:

> Why arts in the school? The answers for me are clear and straightforward. As content, the arts represent man's best work. Our children ought to have access to the intellectual and artistic capital of our culture. We also tell the young what we value for them. Surely then arts are among the things we ought to care about . . . But the arts are not only important because of what they represent, they are important because of the ways in which they engage and develop human intellectual ability. To learn to see and to make visual form is a complex and subtle task. The child needs to learn how to look, not simply to assign a label to what is seen, but to experience the qualities to which he attends. Artistic tasks, unlike so much of what is now taught in schools, develop the ability to judge, to assess, to experience a range of meanings that exceed what we are able to say in words.[13]

Our committee accepts this view, but by incorporating literature, in both English and a foreign language, as one of the arts, we go measurably farther. We want students to learn to understand in words *and* in other forms, separately and in combination, and to appreciate the ways in which varying forms of human expression, separately and in combination, have rendered rich meaning in the past. As Eisner says, "There is no verbal equivalent of Bach's Mass in B Minor. Words cannot convey what the music has to say."[14] Some might say, albeit from a different viewpoint, the same of MTV. Obviously, too, there are domains where words transmit richer meaning than does music, and so forth. A particular idea or feeling draws on some of the arts more effectively than on others. A student should understand this, have a clear sense of the repertoire of the arts, and be able to use it. It will introduce him or her to traditional high culture, and also open up the contemporary public arts and the ways of most deliberate modern communication, such as advertising, that displays in multiple forms.

We are well aware of the challenge in asking our faculty in English, the foreign languages, art, music, and physical education to start anew in thinking about Art and its indivisibility, then about the Art*s,* and only finally about each teacher's personal artistic discipline. Yet we believe the task also to be liberating, and we know that addressing the Arts in this way will properly serve the students. The world of adolescents is not divided into the neat subject distinctions that give us comfort, and it is their world — in fact, our real world too — that should direct our effort. The current formalism and myopia in Arts education is very costly.

The Arts faculty should take special responsibility for superintending the schoolwide obligation in "expression," in writing and reading in English and a foreign language, in drawing, in making music. That faculty would also have responsibility for sponsoring musical, theatrical, and related enterprises in the school, including a student-produced weekly newspaper. These activities, generally now treated as extracurricular, will more often than not serve as Exhibitions. They come into the middle of the curriculum, then, claiming their fair share of time, faculty attention, and high standards.

There is much argument as to whether social studies is a discipline or, rather, a gawky agglomeration of social science subjects more or less attached to the disciplines of history and political science. The Bradley Commission argued in 1989 that the schools would be well served if they assumed the central role of history, but the National Commission on Social Studies in the Schools — not surprisingly, given its title — argued for the retention of the traditional area.[15] To us this argument is largely semantic and not helpful, but we tend more to favor the practical Bradley solution. We are intensely aware of the sweep of this subject or subjects, of the political pressures for all kinds of substantive inclusion or exclusion, of questions of moral and doctrinal position that inevitably and properly infect classes. We recommend calling Franklin High School's area History/Philosophy, by which we expect the narrative history of America to serve older students as the central thread of the story, with major and deliberate thoughtful digressions both to society beyond these borders — the relationship of particular British and African interests to the slave trade, for example — and to allied social science disciplines — for example, the economics of worldwide depression in the 1920s and 1930s. The narrative of life in this place, America — selected because it is where we are, not because it somehow is more important than any other place — provides the coherence that the subject, as now taught, seriously lacks. We accept the trade-off of sweeping breadth for focus and depth.

We recommend a framework similar in some respects to that suggested by the National Commission on the Social Studies. Stage 1 — conventionally described as grades six through eight — would concentrate on people in time and place through a sequence of topics drawn from pre–1750 communities such as Athens and Sparta, Confucian China, the Incas and Mayans. The focus would be on understanding the relationship of individuals to their immediate groups and to larger groups. Stage 2 would not precisely center on what the National Commission calls "World and American History and Geography" but, more narrowly, on the American experience in the world. Our recommendation allows some three years for this material, in contrast to the fewer than two suggested by the National Commission.[16]

We expect to be criticized for this seemingly narrow and chauvinist view, but we persist in believing that some such center of interest is necessary if we are to get beyond the superficial encounters with the sophisticated assumptions and materials of understanding time past, different cultures, and people who are driven by unfamiliar ideas that now characterize the social studies. An "American Experience in the World" — an America in geographic, political, cultural, and economic context — is the most workable fulcrum that we can devise. Study of matters far from our shores will proceed, but in the context of their relation to the American experience — our "multiculturalism" against a global framework.

We recommend philosophy, the rational investigation of principles, for two reasons. First, such careful study is necessary to understand the central essence of constitutional democracy as well as other systems. For example, it is not enough to "know about" the Constitution; the arguments in the Federalist Papers and their successors must be grasped if a student is to be able to "use" history. Philosophy, then, is an enabling subject.

Second, no members of an age group — except perhaps the

aged — face as many critical life decisions in such a short span of years as do adolescents. Self-expectations, careers, friendships, spouses, parenthood, even personality (What kind of person do I want to be? How do I want other people to perceive me?) all crowd in on young people in what often is but two score months. Most adolescents want to address these matters (even as they mask their interest, out of bravado or embarrassment or because they think that no adult would be interested). Although the schools have no business in offering therapy or anything of that sort, systematic *intellectual* efforts powerfully attract students and serve them well.

Properly, faculty in this area would take the lead for matters of House and school governance and in appropriate personal and career guidance. A student's "good standing" will be their special concern, as will thoughtful and fair discipline.

Visualize our curriculum as a pie, sliced into three pieces, each representing one of the areas outlined above. The space in the center where all three join is in effect a fourth area, what we call Inquiry and Expression. All faculty, by Houses, must take responsibility for its objectives. The central position in the pie is symbolic: proper ways of thinking and learning and communicating and conducting oneself are critical for any kind of serious thoughtful activity.

The areas of concern are familiar: the ability to read efficiently and accurately. The art of writing and speaking clearly, economically, and even with grace, in one's own language and in a foreign language. The methods of nonverbal communication, received accurately and delivered with sensitivity and color. The technique of organizing ideas and data, of sifting through them, of arranging them wisely, of making sense of them. The skills of memorization and study, even (if one can choke back one's hypocrisy) of the tricks of test taking. Habits of reflection. The practice of thoughtfulness.

None of these skills can be taught well in a vacuum. They are most efficiently embedded in areas of study already chosen for their substantive importance. The problem usually is that the skills get short shrift from teachers who believe that the sub-

stance is the only matter for which they have clear responsibility.
Who tests the writing ability of students on a biology test? And
who takes the time to teach all students the tricks of memorization or the operation of a word processor?

We recommend that there be schoolwide standards and expectations for skill in writing and reading in English and, ordinarily,
in at least one foreign language; in speaking and listening and in
communication using nonverbal means (visual art, music, theater); in the use of computers (including word processing, with
an emphasis on computers' capabilities for communicating and
expressing in multiple media); in study and memorization skills;
and in civic behavior (the ways and means of getting along in a
community, this one in particular). Some activity of this sort is
now attempted, such as with writing-across-the-curriculum efforts, but the attempts are sporadic and are usually starved for
time. Most important, usually no one is accountable: these are
rarely unequivocal facultywide responsibilities.

Even worse, some of these areas, like those symbolized by
custodial and food service activities, are now operated in a coun-
terproductive (or countereducational) manner. If we ask little of
the students — even politeness and respect in the cafeteria —
we are implying that it is all right for those healthy adolescent
students to expect someone to look after their creature needs
and to clean up after them.

We recommend that the culminating Exhibitions include exercises that call for command of the matters of this Inquiry and
Expression domain. The entire faculty in each House will be
held responsible for the work of its students.

We recommend that the first few days of each quarter be
exclusively focused on these "common" matters, thus giving a
regular and intensive attention to these skills.

Further and explicitly, we wish to stress several points that
will be new to many at Franklin High:

Within each House, each student will have a faculty adviser
and be part of that teacher's Advisory Group. Coordination of a
student's academic program will be the responsibility of the student himself or herself and that adviser.

At the earliest possible date, all students will be proficient in the use of computers for basic research, computation, and communicating purposes. (Needless to say, this will involve special initial and sustained funding by the district.)

There will be Housewide policies on homework: the work load on students is a collective responsibility.

To the greatest possible extent, each House will offer a single foreign language, and the entire House will shift into that language on regular occasions. (This implies, of course, that those faculty who do not know the language will make an effort as good-humored as it is serious to start to learn it on those occasions.)

The House, and the school as a whole, will take the time self-consciously to conduct community affairs in a thoughtful manner. To the greatest possible legal extent students will maintain the building and operate the food service facility. (Custodians and food service workers, in time as retirements occur, will be fewer in number and will serve as teachers and supervisors of students rather than only as workers in their areas of responsibility.)

Finally, the Early College. The Early College serves students who have acquired their DSE and wish to continue or must continue under the state's compulsory education law. Franklin High School should encourage all to continue, at least through their eighteenth year. The program would be individually tailored — a contract between the faculty and each student — and would consist of a variety of opportunities, in their specifics changing as the needs of students change.

First, there would be advanced academic courses of a traditional kind, those part of the Advanced Placement program or its equivalent. Some of these may be "basic" courses but in a wholly new area, such as Japanese language. Others may focus on a particular occupational field, such as data processing or accountancy. Some of these opportunities would be available at Franklin High and some, by arrangement, at nearby four-year colleges, community colleges, and technical institutes.

Second, there would be structured apprenticeships on the pattern of currently effective work-study arrangements. These apprenticeships may be in traditional occupational education fields, such as business office practice and auto mechanics, or in newly opened ones, such as apprentice reporter for a local newspaper, assistant teacher in a primary school, and foreign language mentor in the school system. As students will already have their DSE, their choices of courses relating to their apprenticeship could span a considerable range, again drawn from those offered at Franklin or at other institutions in the area.[17]

Finally, as resources are available, there would be independent study opportunities for a student to work closely as an apprentice with a faculty member on, say, a research project on a local endangered species or on the mounting of an art show at a local gallery.

The Early College serves as a bridge between school and college or work. Despite its title, it is not elitist: there is something of consequence for every adolescent here, whatever his or her academic interest or serious career goal may be. It demands a substantial level of independent responsibility on the student's part. It allows for rigorous advanced work for the chronologically or socially "younger" student who got his or her DSE "early." It provides a sensible transition into a variety of trades and fields for those who elect this career route. With its freedom, it serves as an attractive incentive for young people to buckle down to the preparation for the DSE.

D. Exhibitions. We recommend a focus on Exhibitions for three reasons. First, by making clear what the students should be able to do in order to earn the diploma, we point to the ultimate destination of their journey and provide an incentive for getting there. The prospect of mastering an Exhibition of recognizably high standard and unquestionable value can usefully spur a student as well as focus his or her effort.

Second, Exhibitions present the faculty with a basis for deciding how to design and apportion the resources of the school. By casting a shadow backward, they show how we can best use our time and effort in order to prepare students to meet the standard of these Exhibitions.

Finally, Exhibitions provide a basis for accountability, especially to the student (How am I doing?) but also to the teachers

(How are my pupils doing?), to parents, and to the public. While effective Exhibitions rarely are amenable to precise quantified grading, their matter is not imprecise. At their best they provide — even in and especially due to their complex richness and attention to student diversity — a fair picture of how the student and the school are performing.

The curriculum, even as we have described its framework above, should be shaped by a particular House faculty's choices of Exhibitions. We have stressed the culminating nature of these exercises, as they are used within each of the three curricular areas and also across them, within the area of inquiry and expression, and we have several examples of the latter to give you. However, Exhibiting should be a routine part of school; there should be repeated opportunities and expectations for students publicly to deal with serious material. That is how they practice the art of using their minds well.

We wish to stress the need for common general standards and varied means to express those standards. Students differ. A single sort of test addresses the skills of a single sector of the students. The world is not made up of such singular tests (nor, indeed, does it much use or value the stuff and procedures of most conventional standardized tests); it rewards all sorts of people who can accomplish important things in a variety of ways. School should be like the sensible real world.

Some will say that there can be only one standard — for example, there is only one truth in the expression $(2 \times 3) = 6$ — and that our recommendation for flexibility in reaching judgments is weaseling, a rationalization for low standards. However, serious work appropriate to a high school is not only about unequivocal expressions such as $(2 \times 3) = 6$; its matters require no less precision, but the final judgments about them are necessarily and thoughtfully lenient. Why did President Truman evoke the Truman Doctrine in 1947 and not earlier? Why is the character of Willy Loman in *Death of a Salesman* appealing and pathetic at the same time? How can one defend the use or the banning of powerful sprays to be used against a massive infestation of gypsy moths? The quality of the argument in support of a judgment is what is at stake here: its "grade" cannot be measured with uncontrovertible precision. And the way the student presents his or her argument, the manner and grace of its spelling out, itself must be accommodated. Grading must be rigorous, certainly; but it also must be respectful of the conditions of the exercise. We seek wise graduates, and wisdom rarely can be reduced to statistical scores.

We wish also to stress that Exhibitions are primarily educational tools rather than assessment tools. They are designed to help students rather than to help those who would sort out those students. They can surely assist those who must do such legitimate sorting; they are, at their best, good tools for "diagnosis." However, their function is not to measure as much as to guide, and that bias may make measurement more complicated than it would otherwise be.

We know that the district and the state — and parents — need some system of accountability for their schools, one that allows the institutions to be fairly judged by a reasonable regional and national standard. We recommend a four-part system.

First, Franklin students should be regularly subjected to a limited number of the best of standardized "mass" tests in (and only in) what may be called the critical enabling areas: reading, writing, and basic mathematics. Existing tests in these subjects are not completely satisfactory, but the substance they cover is relatively free of disagreement and politicization. There is much experience nationally in their assessment, the quality of the tests is being improved, and the danger of distortion of a sound curriculum in the schools and of unfairness to individuals is, if not limited, at least manageable. The annual record of all or, better, a fair sample of Franklin's students could be a benchmark of the school's effectiveness in these areas of obvious importance.

Second, each student should keep a portfolio of his or her work, a collection displaying evidence of progress and of performance over time on Exhibitions. This portfolio should be maintained with the help of the student's adviser and should be open to inspection by the student's parents, faculty members, and authorized representatives of the district and the state department of education. Analysis of the portfolios — in effect, an "educational audit" — by these outsiders would be a check on the standardized test scores and would give some indication of the development of students' habits.

Third, Franklin would welcome on a regular basis specifically assigned district and state officers, these to be advisers, "auditors," and friendly critics of the school and also individuals who, because they know the school well, can share an informed view of the school with those in authority, such as members of the local and state boards of education.

Fourth, Franklin would annually present to its constituencies a full report and hold a public meeting to discuss and answer questions about it. Further, Franklin would tie these reports into the regular accreditation apparatus of its regional accrediting organization, with the school's reports to that outside group being fully summarized and distributed locally for the public record.

Thus, Franklin should have a variety of accountability measures that together would yield a rich, fair, and thorough assessment of the school's worth. It also would give parents access to the work of their children. This system would correct the flaws of two current practices: excessively limited reporting to the local community on one hand and, on the other, a distorted and misleading accounting of the school on so-called wall charts, which summarize only the selected aspects of the school that can be reduced to statistics.

We believe that this four-part system will supply full and balanced information about the school to its constituencies. We also believe that such a thorough, fair accounting will attract support for the school from those same constituencies. Thoughtful and effective schools have no fear of worthy inspection.

E. Structure. Our intent is to create units that are large enough to encompass richness but small enough to allow every student to be well known. These will enable the faculty, grouped within the academically self-contained Houses, to work efficiently across traditional subject lines.

We recommend that students in the high school who are working toward the DSE be divided into five Houses, each unit serving 200 to 220 students and led by twelve to sixteen faculty members. A comparable organization would be established at the middle school. The Early College will be based at the high school and would likely enroll, full or part time, some 250 to 300 students. Faculty for the Early College courses offered at Franklin would be drawn from the Houses as necessary.

We believe that when many of the administrative and guidance functions are decentralized to Houses, a high school central administration of six people could meet the "larger" school's demands: for example, principal, assistant principal for program, assistant principal for administration, librarian, director of guidance, and coordinator of the Early College. Several of these positions could shared by teachers or held in rotation among the faculty. A similar complement could administer the middle school, but if the two were merged, new economies might accrue.

To the maximum feasible extent, each House would occupy coherent and convenient space in its building. Specialized laboratories and studios would have to be shared, especially with the Early College.

Each House inevitably would evolve its own character and style. These differences should be encouraged, and students asked to choose among the Houses.

Given the emphasis on work developed and Exhibited by the students, the load on the library will be much increased over present levels of activity. Faculty and students will have to assist in the operation of that facility, including its technology. Ideally, the Franklin High and Middle School libraries should be merged into the city library system, concentrating resources — and, too, signaling the seriousness of a library for adolescents. An easy and purposeful mixing of younger and older readers and researchers can benefit all.

We recommend that the allocation of academic time be controlled by each House faculty: they will know best what is needed during a particular period. Some hours each week should be reserved for the total school, for combined House meetings, and for activities where a large scale is desirable — interscholastic athletics, the orchestra, and similar organized enterprises.

F. Some Practicalities. This sketch of a redesigned Franklin High School and Franklin Middle School raises many legitimate concerns. The committee has identified some that deserve recognition even at this early stage of planning. They are most clearly expressed as questions:

What will a day in one of the Houses look like? We visualize breaking the hours down into a few major blocks of time, on a given day for one group of students, perhaps, involving Mathematics/Science and the Arts. Other days will be structured differently. The point is, however, that form follows function, that the schedule follows what a particular group of students needs during a particular day and week. The professionals who know these students best — their teachers — would make the decisions about the schedule.[18]

Will colleges and employers like what we are suggesting? They certainly will approve of an Exhibition-driven program, because the people they will be getting as freshmen or employees will have had to meet a public standard of some consequence. Graduates will not be able to hide behind "credits" they might have accrued long ago, as tenth-graders. Of course, the colleges will have to understand why and what we are doing.

How can the existing subjects, and their teachers, fit into the new, simplified curriculum? The Mathematics/Science area would house teachers in those traditional disciplines as well as some in physical education, home economics, health education, computer science, and several of the vocational/technical areas. The Arts would include topics and teachers in English, the foreign languages, visual art, music, theater, and some of physical education and vocational/technical areas. History and Philosophy would include social studies disciplines — history, political science, geography, sociology, economics — as well as areas of literary and art history and culture, and to some degree, guidance. Combining these fields must be more than merely adding up the old disciplines; a demanding scholarly exercise awaits us here.

Are teachers prepared for this new kind of work? No. We — and we teachers on this committee wish to put this personally here — will have to study again, and to evolve fresh teaching strategies. This will be new for most of us, but we welcome the change. All of us know that the current routines do not work well, that we are forced to make compromises in our work that we know do not serve our students. Further, we find patronizing the argument that we can properly teach only material for which we were certified many years ago on the basis of a list of courses taken in college. We wish to keep learning; we want that to be an expected part of our professional lives; we want to be respected for our scholarship, resourcefulness, and imagination.

But what about standards while we are "learning"? Well led, the teams protect standards — though this will require vigilance and the willingness to accept outside inspection. Each team will include experienced people in each of the key subjects, and all of us will have to meet the standards in each area maintained by its "expert." The team will operate as teams do often in other professions. The teaching profession is rare in that it operates as though each instructor were an independent entrepreneur, king or queen in his or her classroom. We need teams as a way to help us meet standards across the curriculum and bring the best advice about students as well as scholarship into our work. The Houses are the organizational vehicle for these teams.

Will the state approve? Most states support well-thought-out efforts at reform and provide waivers from constricting regulations. Most troublesome will be teacher and administrator certification laws, which currently rest largely on the assumptions that each professional is a totally autonomous operator and that "qualification" follows from the mere completion of courses, including what is usually an unsupervised and limited apprenticeship. The system is, obviously, profoundly flawed and must be changed. Committee members and our friends in the district office, most particularly the superintendent, have discussed our plans with state education department officials and found not only approval but active encouragement for our effort.

What about the unions? They are likely to be cautious and skeptical. Nonetheless, much of what we are suggesting squares with what leaders of both the American Federation of Teachers and the National Education Association have been saying for a decade. We believe that contracts can be amended and in time renegotiated or even fundamentally recast to accommodate what we recommend. Union officers are members of this committee and support our collective recommendations.

But, given the new roles for teachers we suggest, won't many people have to be replaced? Not if we can help it. Our view is that much has to change, that we all will be on relatively new ground, that there are no better prepared people out there to replace us in our jobs. Our motto is "Nobody will go, and everybody will change." Of course, some may not find our plan congenial and will leave of their own accord.

Won't this plan require a major change for administrators? Yes. The decentralization of authority to the Houses for many major functions alters the role of the central office to a considerable degree, from direction to support, coordination, and oversight. This spreading of accountability has to be recognized and appreciated by the district and the school board: Franklin's faculty will adopt a more collective responsibilty than one focused on a particular individual, the principal. This makes her job in some ways harder; but she believes, as do all of us, that the students are likely to be served far better than heretofore. Our high school principal has been an ex officio member of this committee from the start, and her counterpart at the middle school joined during our deliberations. Both endorse the committee's report.

What about traditional extracurricular activities, such as varsity sports? They should richly continue — after school.

What will all this cost? We have designed a new secondary education for Franklin using the same number of professional staff as currently serve. In effect, our plan will work at the same per day costs as those which now obtain.[19]

However, there are three exceptions to this condition. First, we recommend a longer school day (which is likely to cost only marginally more than the present arrangement) and, what is of more consequence, a longer school year. Our plan can fit into our current 180-day calendar as well as the 240-day year we recommend, though the latter is much preferred. We hope that the board will decide to extend the current school year; if it does, this will add only the appropriate additional per day costs, which we have roughly established.[20]

A second exception relates to capital costs. We foresee the need for considerable new investment in technology, with the service contracts and other expenses entailed. We also foresee additions to be made to our libraries. We know that accommodating the new House structure will require some renovation of the buildings. All these costs can be readily computed; they are not small, but are unlikely to require a bond issue or anything of that magnitude.

Third will be the costs of planning and development, the costs associated with making the shift from current practice to the new school. These could run some $150,000 to $250,000 a year for five years. Essentially, they buy staff time for planning and retraining. Without this kind of investment — as progressive American businesses have long demonstrated — significant change is unlikely to happen. However, funds of this magnitude will soon be available from the state. Further, our school system's business partnership members may be helpful in this regard; similar partnerships in other communities have been critical in helping schools move ahead. We are aware that there is a strong argument — again, from the example of effective private businesses — that such R and D costs should be permanently budgeted as a regular line item. The need for thoughtful reform will always be with us. This committee, however, is not making such a recommendation at the moment. We at Franklin need experience with major internally driven reform before suggesting mechanisms for managing wise change.

To recapitulate, the heart of the plan we recommend depends primarily not on budgets or restructuring or practicalities such as adapting the schedule and calendar but, rather, on a new way of viewing adolescents, how they learn, and how adults can help them learn deeply. Franklin's education will improve only to the extent that Franklin's students, teachers, parents, and the community are dedicated to thoughtful, patient, and yet demanding ways to achieve a better kind of schooling.

Today, this committee believes, we underestimate the potential, reach, and maturity of adolescents. We underestimate the complexity of learning and of growing up itself, and often trivialize and unnecessarily bureaucratize what is a humane process.

We in this community underestimate the threat to our children if they are not well educated. Soft and mindless schools will not prepare our young citizens for the harsh and intellectually demanding world that confronts them.

Finally, we underestimate our ability to break free from well-worn, respected, but outdated ideas about learning and teaching. We *can* make the leap from these, if we are honest about them and ourselves, if we are undefensive and resist any search for scapegoats, if we are patient.

Above all, we must remember that we are dealing with the most precious treasures that humans have, the hearts and minds of their children. We do well by Franklin's students now, but we must have the courage and confidence to do far better.

11
Policy and Power

THE REPORT had been issued to the faculty, the board of education, and the local newspapers. There was intense buzzing at the
school, particularly among the students. Given the extent of the
committee's consultation with various constituencies, many of
its members expected that no one would be surprised by their
ideas for Franklin. Yet many at the school reacted as though the
recommendations were new and radical.

"We're sunk," said Green.

"Everyone has something to niggle over," said the veteran.

Margaret: "No one challenges our criticism of the status quo."
She was upbeat.

The veteran: "They'll come around."

"There's so much new here that even those with whom you
talked a lot won't know yet what to think," said the visitor.
"Give them time."

The superintendent and the chair of the school board met with
them. How next to proceed was the matter at hand, and the plans
for these steps seemed as complex as the design for the new
school itself. Carefully designed and attractively printed bro-
chures were to be prepared and widely distributed: the community was going to know about this venture in great detail. Committees were formed. Contacts with local colleges and institutes

were initiated. A sequence of public hearings was scheduled. Local and state leaders were briefed, and those who thought well of the plan were to be recruited into special committees to explain the ideas to others — and to advocate them. Funding for the R and D was being solicited from local businesses: having this promptly in hand would be a spur to the process. A timetable was drawn up, with decision points clearly identified. Some community leaders were afraid of moving too fast, others too slowly: the superintendent looked for middle ground.

"We must be clear, we must be clear . . ." he repeated. "No appearance of backroom deals. But we must act, in due course but decisively."

Horace's committee was, in fact, encouraged by all the activity. The members had been asked to stay on, a steering committee for the discussion inside the schools. They knew that they had to listen, take all reactions, and adapt the best of them into the plan. "Their" plan, they now knew, was but a beginning point. Whatever design ultimately evolved would have to be that of a much larger group, certainly a significant piece of the faculty. The committee members would fight for their recommendations; they hoped that most would survive; but they were becoming realistic. What they were not prepared easily to accept was serious challenge to the *ideas* that formed the armature of the plan. Alter the tactics of responding to these, yes; but alter the basic frame? Only under powerful suasion.

The talk among the members wandered, reminiscent of the earliest days of their deliberations. There was a sense, curious to some of them, of sadness. With all their disagreements, and maybe because of them, the group had come together. Coach whimsically said that they should all quit Franklin and go off and start a new school to their precise specifications.

"What's going to happen now?" asked the second student, not fully appreciating that organizing talk was really action.

The superintendent replied, "We have to explain the ideas to the people. If they agree, policies will be changed. This takes time, persuasion, patience . . ."

"And pressure," added Horace.

"Power." Margaret finished it off, smiling. Patches nodded, smiling too.

Franklin High School does not operate in a vacuum. It is subject to all sorts of informal pressures within its own community — individual parents, booster clubs, the managers of shopping malls where kids congregate, probation officers of the juvenile court, vendors with products to sell to the school — and it is, obviously, an institutional creature of the district and the state. At some limited points, it even is the agent of the federal government.

These political entities have expectations and requirements. How they wrap around Franklin High School will affect whether that school, with its bold plans for the future, is warmed or smothered.

The instruments of the higher authorities — district, state, federal government — come at Franklin in the form of suggestions (for example, a teachers' guide for the teaching of writing), specific mandates (school will be open for instruction at least 180 full days), requirements (teachers at Franklin must have state certification for the subjects they teach or be equipped with appropriate waivers), and attitude (the way in which these authorities address those who work in the school, with courtesy or condescension). The instruments can be a clutch of directives collected over time, uninformed by any overarching set of ideas, even contradictory, canceling each other out. Or they can spring from policy, a set of coherent ideas that give direction and meaning to the sheaf of suggestions and orders that flow into the high school.[1]

The implications of the plan for Franklin High School and, more important, the commitments and assumptions behind it, affect district and state policy, and the shape of union-management collective-bargaining instruments, in areas best characterized by function. The term "state" will here serve to represent each of the several jurisdictions involved — state government, city, town or county government encompassing the school districts, and the labor agreements established by organized teachers and educational administrators with these governments. Indeed, one must lump these together, because they are fully interconnected.

There is the familiar and largely uncontroversial function of the state *to ensure fair and equal student access to and sufficient financial support for a "thorough and efficient education"* (to quote language found in many state constitutions). Franklin's plan little affects much of this familiar policy. The state provides sufficient resources to every school to allow it to function effectively. Funds are spread across and among districts in such a way as to ensure equity; no child in the region would be supported with fewer resources than are available to any other child by virtue of the place in the state where that child happens to live.[2] Special funding for the special student — the handicapped or severely disadvantaged or otherwise atypical youngster — are made available. To the fullest possible extent, given residential patterns, the schools integrate children from different racial, ethnic, and economic groups and work affirmatively to prevent the development of prejudice among them and discrimination affecting them.

Today these matters alone dominate much of the state's concern, and properly so. Within this familar agenda, however, the Franklin High School plan implies significant changes of practice. The state would be obliged to give wide discretion to each school to spend its money as the school decides is best for its students. This means, for example, that no two school budgets would be quite alike, that no two faculties would necessarily observe the same work rules, that the mix of faculty and staff would differ by school, that no formula would be applied to all school operations save those, say, of uncontroversial management matters such as energy consumption. This policy of unqualified delegated authority is the logical extension of the belief that places differ and schools differ. Expecting them to be the same denies reality, and insisting that they be the same guarantees mediocrity. Each school, obviously, needs to be accountable for its budget priorities; but a wise state and wise unions would give substantial latitude to each one.

Building and maintaining a school culture requires stability, including budget stability. Schools should be forward-funded, with "next year's" budget guaranteed to allow for planning during the entirety of "this year," thus permitting new appointments to be made in an orderly and careful fashion. Forward-funding is virtually unknown in American public education, but it is customary in some other governmental operations. The current waste and erosion of a cooperative school culture resulting from frequent last-minute major budget decisions is stunning.

Giving sweeping authority to the individual school shifts the role of the state from director to counselor, from boss to friend, from a giver of orders to the assessor of each school's work, from judge to advocate. It assumes that the state trusts schools. It assumes that teachers and principals will work together, creating a professional culture for their schools that ensures informed and thoughtful consideration of policy and practice. It assumes that schools are places where the adults — as well as the students — use their minds well.

Changes of this sort demand a profound shift in attitude for many educators who work both within and outside schools. As one policy analyst neatly put it, "We must debureaucratize the hierarchical bureaucracy."[3] Further, if the schools themselves take direct charge of their activities, far fewer central office people probably will be needed. A lean and supportive state department of education can replace the hierarchical bureaucracy. A tightly organized district office can function effectively. What is needed are state and district organizations that provide the critic-friends called for in Horace's committee's report rather than people whose job it is to check up in detail on whether schools follow the rules. Supervision of schools that must be "directed" is far more costly than support of schools whose integrity is from the start assumed — unless clearly proven otherwise.

A somewhat less familiar obligation of the state is *to solicit, assert, and assess the standards for students and for schools.* This obligation arises at the simplest level from state constitutions — the requirement for "thorough and efficient" schools —

but more is required, especially in a world far more complex than it was when the "thorough and efficient" doctrine was first expressed. In the last decade, most states governments have greatly expanded their testing programs — the preferred method of "setting standards" — because they are relatively inexpensive and can be kept neatly away from the hurly-burly of actual school operation. Most of these examination programs swirl in politics. Few are properly funded, and they garner paltry academic results and rouse profound disrespect from the individuals involved, of all ages.

Not surprisingly, many political leaders are looking for some means other than standardized testing as a qualitative yardstick and as an instrument to encourage students and schools to meet that standard. They seek tests that are valid in the sense that they "measure" qualities we desire rather than items that are but tokens of those qualities. These leaders are also concerned that what is measured should be the real power of a child, that child's enduring habits, not just what he has prepped for passing a test. These leaders are arriving at conclusions similar to those reached in its own way by Horace's committee.

Questions abound. How can Franklin High School simplify and deepen its curriculum if the tests continue to reflect the repeatedly discredited maxim that more is better and the 1893 description of the course of study as English–mathematics–science–social studies–language–physical education, each presented in isolation from every other? How is Franklin High to press students to show us that they can resourcefully use knowledge, and to display the habit of that use, if there are on the horizon few tests of habits and, in many quarters, even now still little interest in pursuing them?

Most important, who is the state to tell families the substance and standard of everything provided by a school? When so many thoughtful people disagree about the shape and substance of key ideas in several of the areas of the high school curriculum, what group can properly claim that it speaks for us all, setting a national standard, when the best minds and hearts in the country honestly and creatively disagree over such a standard? If schools are to be measured by that national standard, what does this say about the state's respect for community standards? Do not families have some rights of control of a public service? To put it most bluntly, are there not proper limits to state power over the minds of adolescents?

Franklin High School's plan suggests a wise division of labor and a separation of spheres of influence. The four-part system of accountability safeguards the proper interests of the larger community — the state — and those of the parent and student. There will be some limited standardized testing in certain areas. Portfolios maintained by and for each student will be accessible to teachers, the student's parents, and representatives of the state, who will conduct "audits" of the students' progress and, thus, of the school's effectiveness. Horace's committee desires assistance from the state's staff — friends who know the school well enough to describe, criticize, and defend it on its own merits. In this respect, the committee's report implicitly suggests an American version of Her Majesty's Inspectors of Schools in the United Kingdom, at least in their role as outsiders supportive, critical, and above all informed about a particular school. Franklin will make substantial annual reports to the community and will discuss them in public session. Added to this local accounting is the influence of accreditation by regional authorities, such as the North Central Association; their decennial reviews, if thoughtfully conducted, inform a community about its school's merit and challenge individual high schools to sharpen and defend what they believe and how they act upon those beliefs.

Also implicit in the committee's report, however, is the conviction that matters such as the literature assignments, the shape of history and science curricula, and the very culture of the school are all of such importance, delicacy, and sensitivity to reasonable debate that they must be left to local discretion. Families must feel welcome to address their concerns *directly* to the people who have the power to make or change decisions affecting their children.

Of course, local discretion will always be and always has been affected, however obliquely, by a host of influences pressing toward "national standards" — by regional accrediting associations, by competitive scholarship programs, by specific requirements for admission to individual colleges, by employers who insist on evidence of serious preparation, by the ebb and flow of scholarship, by choices made in the textbook-publishing industry, by prevalent notions, whether sensible or nonsensical. Serious people at the local level are no more or less smart about these matters than people at the state or national level; they are influenced by no fewer or greater political pressures than found at higher levels of government. Differences across schools may be not only the price of freedom but an excellent vehicle to maintain openness within American education.

The changes will be messy. Democracy is messy. Those who want an orderly solution toy with democracy, that form of government beset with flaws but better than any of the alternatives. Those who assert that "the people" can never be trusted with setting standards sing an arrogant, dangerous tune.

A third duty of the state is to *attract, train, and accredit professionals* to work in the schools. The attitude of the state is crucial here. If it sees its primary role as keeping out the incompetent, it follows one path; if, on the other hand, it sees its job as attracting and supporting the very best people possible for the schools, it takes different routes.

The present system rests on a set of shaky, indeed often false, premises. An individual receives a teaching license from most states after the satisfactory completion of a set of college courses that carry particular titles — for example, the Teaching of Mathematics, Foundations of American Education, Practice Teaching, the History of Texas — and sometimes a satisfactory score on the National Teachers Examination (currently a multiple-choice test on professional and basic academic subjects). A candidate presents a specialty — senior high social studies teacher, school counselor — and some of the courses required within that specialty. Having displayed a transcript, or having graduated from a university program that has had its list of courses approved by the state or its agents, the individual can teach, counsel, coach, or administer in the public schools. Some states require more "credit hours" to be "passed" every period of years; the system continues to be propelled by "courses taken."

However, there is little correlation at all between "courses taken" and success at teaching except, presumably, at the margins. (For example, the utterly uneducated candidate will flunk the National Teachers Examination, or the outstanding candidate will present a clutch of A grades, including one for practice teaching, from a demanding university.) At few points in the process is actual and sustained work with children seriously reviewed. Indeed, the record of supervision even of the initial and usually concentrated practice teaching is, by many reports, mixed at best.

Learning to teach is much like learning to write: one does it and, if lucky, is assisted by a perceptive editor. As with writing, the first efforts never see type, naturally; only when there is some mastery and enough lively stuff to write about is publication contemplated. And so it must be for teaching: assuming a rich background in the area to be taught, there then must be early immersion among kids, well before many courses in theory are taken. These theoretical courses make as little sense apart from practice as does grammar taught as a separate introductory subject; they make vital sense thereafter. A neophyte teacher should join a team at Franklin High School, teaching first under heavy supervision and surrounding himself with talk about the craft of teaching and the nature of kids and learning. It is here that Horace's school provides a special benefit; it is a place where novices can get a start in the craft by joining the work and the conversation of a group of committed and allied veterans, "editors of teaching," as it were.

The existing system depends on exposure to pertinent topics and the expenditure of time ("credit hours") rather than on performance. It most often puts practice at the end rather than throughout the course of preparation. It is a system as intellectually bankrupt as its equivalent in the high schools — credit counting, a discredited building-block theory of course sequencing and the reward of promotion based largely on accrued credits. There is rarely a substantial final Exhibition legitimated by agreement among an education school faculty as to what satisfactory teaching in fact may be. Indeed, a definition of "good teaching" is rarely a collective understanding, and the differences of opinion among college faculty are swept under the rug.

The roots of the existing teacher education system are very deep, their protectors also well entrenched, and the connections between certification authorities and the universities that provide the mandated courses uncomfortably close. Ridicule of this system by able candidates for teaching has been heard for over a half century, yet the old routines persist. The kinds of teachers needed for the new Franklin High must experience training that can stand up to commonsense scrutiny. The present regimen cannot, and state authorities who are serious about standards — and determined to attract the ablest, most humane, and conscientious recruits — have to evolve programs of intellectual merit and authenticity, programs that inspire rather than insult those wishing to enter the profession.

Horace's school carries three especially important implications for teacher practice and the policies that shape it. The first arises from the committee's call for a coherent and stable school culture, a place where the adults share many objectives and commitments. For the creation and nurture of such a place, the existing faculty must be in control of assigning new teachers. Assignment policies that shuffle people around a district on the basis of their credentials and their seniority absolutely deny this. Teachers' personalities — in a deep, not a petty sense — and their professional commitments are critical to the health of a school's culture. Further, a teacher who picks her school and is picked by it arrives there with a commitment that no contract can dream of matching. Franklin needs to select and evaluate its own staff, governed only by reasonable mandates relating to affirmative action, visible and reputable standards of performance, and the desirability of regular infusions of fresh commitment, energy, and wisdom.

Franklin's new curriculum is simple and its three scholarly areas deliberately broad. Each teacher must be sensitive to the imperatives of an entire area such as the Arts; he must be a vigorous student of that field, and, in part, a specialist in some aspect of it. The coherence of the program presented for the students, however, is the sum of the team's areas of expertise — the musician, the writer, the literary critic, the painter, and the actor *collectively* addressing the Arts, not one by one but each supporting the team's mastery of the entire field and each in her own specialty holding the team to a demanding standard.

There are happy side effects of teaming. Weak or uncertain teachers are put into a setting where more experienced colleagues have an incentive to help them, or even to counsel them to leave teaching. And absenteeism among teachers, an epidemic in many communities today, is far less likely when an absence will seriously hurt the very people with whom one must continue immediately to work. These side effects are not slight and should serve as further spurs to collective responsibility for teaching.

The necessary changes in teacher training and certification are obvious: the general education of teachers must be strengthened and their specialized educations treated not as separate entities but as part of a larger and more important whole. Teaming can be prepared for. Certification regulations must accommodate and support the realities of cross-field teaching by well-supervised teams.

As always, the doubters will be heard. This is impossible. Seniority must stand; teaching is so hard and so badly paid that we deserve protection. We tried team teaching in the sixties, and it didn't work. I don't want to be my neighbor teacher's keeper. I want no part of worrying about the quality of other teachers' work, much less their attendance. The mechanics of teacher certification across this very large state make attention to a particular school's teams impractical.

The fact remains, however, that common sense is on the side of Horace's committee. Sustained commitment to the needed policies is required even if it demands an agonizing rethinking of the very principles on which the current system operates.

The line between administrators and teachers has largely to disappear, except at the obvious extremes. The Franklin High that the committee envisions is not a place of managers and workers; its direction is in the hands of a "flat" hierarchy. People will have different sorts of responsibilities, but the overlapping among them will be more important than their specialities. The principal will be (once again, as was the case in an earlier day) the principal teacher. And teachers will take substantial responsibility for the institution as a whole. Many pivotal decisions — if they are to be properly informed decisions — must be made by those who know the individual students; the Houses and teaching teams are in effect consequential administrative units. The administrator-teacher distinction that arose from the early twentieth-century factory floor must give way, as it already has done in most progressive American enterprises.

Again, there will be objections. A principal may say, I am an administrator because I was tired of being a teacher. Or an instructor may say, I want to teach; I don't want responsibility for anything beyond my classes. My professional association expects me to meet the standards of my specialty; I have no interest other than being such a professional. These old assertions will die hard. Franklin's plan assumes that they must. Sensitive state policy can ease the process.

The state must *keep the record*; in effect, it must be the educational demographer. The task sounds easy but is in fact as difficult as taking any census. Where are the students? Who are they? From where are they coming? How many teachers will retire this year? What is the trend of tax collections, by community? While Franklin will have its own world, the movements of families and professionals and dollars across its region will inevitably affect the school's plan. The state must give warning of change.

Further, there is *research* and what it may mean for practice. What do we know about learning? What do we know about our schools and about schools like them? What seems to work where? How can the subject matters be freshly construed? What are the implications of recent Court decisions? And more. These are matters that require sustained study, an investment of time that the Franklin faculty, however able, cannot properly pursue on top of their school responsibilities. State and district authorities can, and they should make available, widely and usefully, what is needed.

The heart of the research is communication, getting the word out in a timely and stimulating form. Much of it also now plays out as highly organized activity labeled "staff development." Well intentioned though it may be, the term — and the programs gathered under its banner — is patronizing to many professionals who are not happy about someone else determining how they are to be "developed."

However, central office colleagues can be a powerful influence for good when they respond to the school's own priorities. No one likes an agenda rammed down his throat, and a district that consults only with some teachers and puts a few on a planning committee is not being respectful of the particular direction that a school's faculty has identified. Just as young people work harder at those matters which seem genuinely useful, so too teachers and principals. If the questions to be addressed are their questions, they will more readily seek and accept the help they almost always need.

Of course, some schools will sleep, ask for nothing, wish to be left undisturbed. The role of outsiders from the central office in these situations must be subtle. The activity of the best of Britain's Inspectors in the past gives a clue here; such a "critical friend" can shake a school out of its smugness or torpor with an unsubtle barrage of apt questions.

Finally, the state has *to coordinate related services for adolescents,* connecting them sensitively with the high school. Most of these are familiar: health clinics, special psychological or psychiatric services, employment agencies, college admissions offices, religious centers, community programs, police and court authorities, private schools, and private afterschool programs. Franklin's plan puts special pressure on libraries, and the state would be wise to review ways to concentrate its library resources, eliminating the distinctions between "school" and "public" libraries. Students and individual adults do have modestly different uses for information services, but the similarities among them are far more important. Getting adolescents into the habit of using general-audience libraries and expecting a mix of older and younger folk to work constructively there together are important ends in themselves.

Horace's committee's plan assumes, then, substantial changes in the system that towers over the school, changes for which there have been, to date, weak incentives. Few of the governors have directly attacked their own bureaucracies, much less the habits within them. Even since the torrid rhetoric of the 1983 "A Nation at Risk" report and the stir of activity that flowed from it, there has been remarkably little change in the habits of the hierarchical bureaucracy. Since the mid-1980s, it has handed down more directives and mandated more tests. It absorbs a great deal of money. Implicitly, it still assumes it knows better than the schools. It believes that only it can be trusted with standards.

Such impervious imperiousness has provoked radical reaction, usually presented under the banner of "choice." Let the standards be laid down, this argument flows, by the parents. Let their selection of their children's schools from among a set of competing schools create a market. The public's tax monies would flow to the schools chosen, just as federal dollars have long flowed to the college a military veteran chooses under the GI Bill of Rights. Good schools would flourish in this market. Poor schools would die. There would be little need for an attendant bureaucracy, for the state's inspectors, maybe even for superintendents and school boards. They would thus cease to smother venturesome schools, hassle parents, or soak up so much money — or so the case is frequently made.[4]

There are dozens of versions of this idea. Curiously, the idea of choice has attracted support across a wide political spectrum, albeit for often wildly different reasons. Underneath every version of it, however, is impatience and little respect for the existing hierarchical bureaucracy and the assumptions that govern its functioning.

There has always been choice for the affluent, who can either pay for private education or, far more frequently, move to a community that has schools they prefer. The federal government in effect subsidizes this choice through tax deductions of interest costs on mortgage payments. The family that does not have the financial ability to gain a mortgage in the first place cannot move, and certainly misses the tax subsidy its wealthier counterpart collects.

There is choice within many larger school systems, usually represented by "magnet" schools (the word itself is instructive). And there is choice within most larger high schools, among various programs or "tracks" (honors, general, vocational technical and so forth). The adolescent must go to school, but once he is there, he can choose from a variety of things. The fact is that once again the more affluent appear to work the choices to their children's special benefit. The various "shops" in the shopping mall high school are very often defined by social class.[5]

Horace's committee supports choice and rejects it. Franklin High is to have Houses, and they will inevitably compete. An unpopular House will provoke parental resentment, and changes would have to be made. The decisions about the Houses' nature rest within the school. No one has to go to higher authority to gain relief. At the same time, all students before getting to the DSE are enrolled in the same three areas: there are no specialty shops at Franklin. Here there is to be a common education. Individual interests are accommodated but are limited to the three academic areas.

The choice idea has much merit, as long as four conditions are met. Schools must be open to all. Franklin High is open to all, and such major curricular choices as are available — largely within the Early College — are accessible to all. Students who carry special burdens — physical or emotional handicaps or the stringencies, both material and emotional, of poverty — must not only be guaranteed acceptance but also carry a financial incentive for their school to serve them appropriately. That is, the monies following them into the school should compensate that school for the extra services they may need. Third, information about the schools — or the Houses or other programs within them — should be provided by a disinterested third party and be available to parents at the time they make a decision.

Finally, the schools must be given room to create their own cultures. The heavy hand of standardization, either directly through reams of specific mandates or indirectly through detailed examinations, must be absent. Serious choice requires serious options.

There will be choice among American schools in the future as there has been in the past. If there are innovations, some will focus on giving poor families the same options as wealthier families and incentives to schools to enroll the children of poverty. Others will lead to the creation of far more varied schools than we now have, ones that can compete as truly "different." Some will address the continuing problem of racial and class segregation in the public and private schools.

Lurking behind the choice issue is the matter of family — accurately, private — rights. The children are ours; we parents lend our children to the state for the community's benefit and we accept the need for compulsory education; but we resent the notion that what happens in school is to be decided solely by the state. It is this issue that particularly offends many who object to a national examination or any remote assessment device that determines which schools are to be considered meritorious, and thus are to receive bonuses, and which are not. Proponents of state power assert that the schools may have great latitude on selecting local means to the state's end or even to the locality's independent end. Yet the rating of that school is to be based on the scores of the state's choice of tests alone, and prestige and resources follow from this judgment. The arrogance of the examination enthusiasts' argument chafes, especially in the light of the well-known inadequacies of mass testing procedures and the unwillingness of most political jurisdictions ever to finance assessment sufficiently to provide a fair result. The fact that some strong advocates of choice are also strong advocates of a national examination is also peculiar. Yes, they say, you should have your own schools; but *we* will decide what the shape and standard of the product of those schools will be. The top of the hierarchy cannot seem to let go. They know best, in their view.

An accommodation is required, as Horace's committee outlined, with some central control of standards along with that arising from each school and community. However, the rights of parents for the public schools to address *their* aims — the private purposes of public schools — as well as those aims of the state must be strongly asserted. The school is one of the few settings left in this society that can mediate between the individual and the large institutions of our culture. The school can help a child protect her autonomy, learn how to cope with the state, with large business organizations, the mass media, even impersonal universities, in addition to becoming a responsible citizen. This private purpose of public schooling is profoundly in the public interest.[6]

Beneath the choice debate and concern for the issues of the private purposes for public schooling lies, of course, impatience with the status quo. Adjustments of existing policies and practices, the tactic of the moment, will not suffice. The hierarchy needs to reform itself, thoroughly and soon.

Policy without the promise of power is but a gust of wind, just as power without the compass of policy threatens disarray. And the existing power that affects a school like Franklin High comes in many forms. Some are explicit: the mandates of the state, the regulations of the school board, and the leverage of politically astute parents, for example. Some are indirectly applied: the political currents of a movement toward choice among schools, or professional currents such as those calling for more "collaborative education."

The explicit power descends from the governing bodies, themselves usually in competition. At the state level, there is the state board of education, the governor's office and staff, the education committees of the legislature, the legislature itself, the state department of education, the state teachers' and administrators' unions and associations, organized pressure groups such as those representing the interests of special needs children or vocational education or the business leadership and a variety of usually short-lived lobbying groups assembled around particular issues. All these have to find a way to work together, one that reflects the pressures of personalities and politics at the state capital.

In large states some powers are decentralized to regional offices. "Below" these are the districts, each itself a mélange of power groups: school board, superintendent, associate superintendents and their offices, semi-autonomous "special" units that answer to regulations set outside the district, regional superintendents (in some large districts), unions and other professional associations, organized special interest groups, such as parent-teacher organizations and sports "booster clubs." Again, these "estates" must find a satisfactory manner of working together. Each has its functions, authority, and dignity. The hierarchy does not behave like a stereotypical military organization, each leader saluting the leaders with higher rank. Rather, they often fiercely compete, even from adjacent offices.

All this necessary accommodation among the power groups has little if any relation to the particular needs of Franklin High School or the untangling of Horace's compromise. Much of their energy is focused on the politics of money and jobs — which is no surprise, since education is necessarily a labor-intensive enterprise. As the power groups involved are numerous and the stakes high, most of their agreements must be carefully balanced and intricate. The result often is precisely mandated and standardized requirements for the schools at the base of the hierarchy, practices that do not serve Franklin's students and teachers and cripple the kind of reform that Horace's committee recommends.

None of this centralized activity is surprising. No part of the hierarchical bureaucracy we have inherited happened because any one group expicitly rigged it that way. There is, alas, no scapegoat here to ridicule and humiliate for the satisfaction of the rest of us. The system's power is deployed in the way it is because we wanted it that way. We trusted hierarchies and "systems" more than we trusted teachers' judgments. We believed that wisdom was more likely to be found at higher rather than lower levels of government.

If policies implied by the reforms recommended by Horace's committee are to lead to practice, what changes must be made in the sources of power, the agents of control of money and regulation? There are obvious examples:

If more authority is to be given to the schools to chart their own courses, those agencies previously assigned to direct these schools must be eliminated. Keeping them around — "revising their mission" — is an evasion. If new missions derive from new powers, let them do so *de novo*. But asking previous "power centers" to give up power, and the habits that accrue with it, and to figure out something else to do is futile. They will not give up power.

If more authority is to reside at the school level, the union contracts have fully to reflect this. Authority can no longer be husbanded in the union's center or the district personnel office.

If accountability and assessment are to be deliberately shared at the various levels of government, the authority of each level has to be precisely assigned and the resources made available for each to meet its responsibilities and nothing more.

If authority is to devolve to the schools, the schools must have the resources to exercise it. Authority without money to buy the time and services of people at the school level is a cruel joke: it sets up the likelihood of the failure, which many of the existing power groups ardently desire.

If each child and her family is to be genuinely respected, those in authority must ensure that all voices are heard and must beware of the disproportionate power of those who merely happen to be organized, whatever the worth of their cause. A family must have direct access to an authority with the unqualified power to make needed changes.

Clearly, Horace's committee's recommendations suggest policies that require shifts of power, usually downward. A reform strategy toward this end at the state level, most logically initiated by the governor, that calls for the existing agents of authority to rearrange their power is unlikely to get very far. At the same time, an effort to circumvent the hierarchy entirely, for instance by "privatizing" the system by means of state tuition vouchers, is equally ineffectual; it sets against the reform all the sources of power, including those needed to win the necessary legislation.

We must seek the middle ground. Policy and power need to be seen as handmaidens, separate but interdependent. Choices among power groups have to be deliberately made: some are likely to forward new policies — such as those required by Horace's plan — and others are not. Where power should be sited but is not yet focused — for example, among various groups of the poor — it must be fostered. Alliances must be forged, and the indirect, but consequential pressures of a "reform movement" organized.

The intelligent exercise of leadership is essential. Ideas, well articulated, give power. The "insider" who galvanizes the commitments of the outside community to abet those best commitments inside the school, who accurately senses its concerns and articulates them, has power. The "outsider" — like the committee's visitor — who senses the climate within a school and can vivify and support it with fresh views from the general culture has power. Education is about persuasion: we must persuade our kids to learn, to get into the habit of learning, to value that habit. The way that power is properly deployed within education is again by persuasion: kids will not learn well from educators not themselves in the habit of expressing and using logical ideas.

The allocation of power has costs. There will be winners and there will be losers. Otherwise, there will be no new policy, no better ideas to steer the power the state enjoys on behalf of its citizens. Those in the traditional educational hierarchy need to recognize that they will have to change every bit as much as will the teachers, administrators, and students at Franklin High School.

If there is one quality that best characterizes the American school system, it is mistrust. The assumption is that no one can depend on anyone else. There must be "independent accountability systems" at every turn. The teacher contracts often nail things down to minutes per week. There are time clocks. The tests must be secret, often administered by strangers reading from texts the precisely worded instructions for the test takers. Paranoia is a professional epidemic.

No one has ever thought about assessing the quality of American schools by asking the teachers, or at least by asking them with something more respectful than a poll. The very thought would be considered quaint, charming — even though these people know their students better than any outsider does. Scores on thirty-minute tests are usually considered more reliable gauges of a child's merits than the opinions of his teachers. That is as sad as it is ludicrous.

The mistrust is so pervasive that we barely notice it. It is staggeringly costly. Checking up on everybody at every turn — or trying to, usually unsuccessfully — soaks up endless hours and saps morale. If the teacher concludes that *they* neither trust him nor see that conditions allow him to do his job well, why should he play the game? They don't care about his opinion; why should he try to have one?

Trust cannot be mandated. Yet it is the cheapest, most sensible, and, for us, most radical means for reform of the system that can be recommended. It is found in some prestigious public and private schools. The teachers there are respected, trusted — and they struggle to deserve that trust. The morale of such schools is high. And the performance of the students shows it.

Could there be an American education policy founded on the idea that everyone meant well and could be counted upon? Continuing to assume the opposite will surely be costly. Everyone will be testing everyone else. The prospect is ugly. Schools filled with such distrust — such disrespect — are hardly places in which to educate decent, thoughtful adolescents.

12

Will Horace Get His School?

THE PRINCIPAL of this middle-sized public high school, one with which I had had periodic contact over the past several years, had invited me to speak at the faculty's monthly meeting. I knew some of the people there, mostly the old-timers, and I liked them. The school served a middle-class and affluent community, disproportionately white. I was expected on this occasion to talk about recent research on American secondary schools in the hope (of the principal at least) that creative and useful discussion would ensue.

The teachers' contract called for such a meeting every month, from 2:35 to 4:00 P.M. The library was set up to accommodate it, with rows of folding metal chairs facing a podium. Clearly, and sadly, the expectation was for me to give a Lecture, perhaps even a Sermon. To my further chagrin, I saw no coffee or cold soda available. What all this appeared to promise was more of a Calvinist Sunday meeting than a gathering of professionals.

Teachers entered in clutches, most after 2:25. Once they were in the library, there was little talk among them or recognition of the superintendent, principal, or me standing off to the side. One old-timer came up with greetings. Teachers took seats, some pulling chairs out of the neat rows, others gathering at small tables that had been put off to the side. On these they placed piles of papers and books. These people, largely younger teachers, sat down, pulled out pens, and started, it appeared, to correct students' papers, oblivious of the meeting commencing around them. The black teachers clustered off to one side. Most of the white men and women divided, the former on our right, the latter to our left; it was an apparently comfortable segregation. There was little chatter, only some low talk, almost whispering.

At 2:45 the meeting opened. The principal spun out a string of announcements. Introductions were made. The teachers with their active red pens continued correcting, baldly in full view. Some others more furtively read books. One veteran teacher off to the side opened a newspaper. Most of the rest, the majority, simply watched.

I described work under way. There were no questions. I switched to stories about schools similar to theirs, stories I hoped would elicit some comment. No response. I asked questions directly, the "tell me about your school" kind and related matters, such as the student load on individual teachers. Most of the audience had a brief laugh about the heavy loads of the guidance staff and the physical education teachers, but nothing followed this brief engagement. I felt once again like the student teacher whose lesson plan had run out, whose students were in conspiratorial revolt. My "class" was not out of control, however; it just was not there at all, save physically. Nothing worked.

At 3:40 I simply said, "Well, that's it." Five seconds of ritual clapping preceded a rush to the doors. By 3:45 the room was empty. I felt ineffectual, humiliated, useless in this situation, intensely embarrassed that I had struck not a single spark. The principal abruptly left, saying that she had an appointment. The superintendent walked me to the front door. Neither of us mentioned the meeting. He seemed unconcerned, genial, but ready for me to go away. Apparently the session was just what he had expected, or had come to expect. I fled gratefully.

I visited another school, this one in a neighborhood that was home to many low-income and working-class families, not to Lecture but to watch and to join in as might be constructive. I spent an hour with a team of humanities teachers — at their formally scheduled, weekly (and not "afterschool") joint planning hour — as they argued about how to proceed with their unit on the American Civil War. There were six of them. Three student teachers were also at the tables; one looked to be in her forties, older than some of her mentors. Two others were there, professional visitors like myself, I assumed. I later learned that they were parents of students.

The give-and-take was open, sometimes raucous, often funny. The tensions among the black, white, and Hispanic teachers were patent, but there was a softness in their display: race and ethnicity were OK topics for these colleagues, evincing more respect and friendship among them than suspicion. The conversation swirled, more or less superintended by a staff member near a blackboard. I learned later that she was chairing the meeting simply because it was probably her turn and she had happened to sit by the blackboard.

It was impossible to join in, as I had been urged to do, because the talk revolved around prior meetings and a series of unit plans that had evolved over the past weeks. Further, the conversation frequently swung back to the students, to individuals. The two parents and I had little way of gauging what had gone before. The few points I raised, almost because I felt that I was expected to, were respectfully heard out and then quickly explained away. I was told, We considered and discarded that. Yes, we're using the PBS Civil War tapes. No, we're not making much of the movie *Glory,* because few kids will have seen the film. They don't go to theaters; it costs too much. I quickly understood that this was not a conversation that could be readily joined, and the fact that it had to produce something to be turned into classes within a fortnight added to its urgency. This wasn't a nice academic chat: this was serious planning.

The contrast between the two schools was dramatic. While my experience proved once again the limited value (to put it charitably) of one-shot professional visitors, it reminds me of the importance of the intangibles in healthy schools. Both of these places had structured staff-planning time, but there the similarity left. The first maintained the ritual. The promise of irrelevance had preceded my presentation; the inhospitable setting and careless attitude of the staff as its members arrived signaled the likelihood of an empty hour, something that had been woodenly planned for the teachers and perceived by them in advance to be useless.

The second school also had its structured faculty time, but it was built on what was of immediate relevance to the work of a group of the teachers with their particular students. This was not "in service," this was "service." Most important was the feel of the second school's work, the open association among the teachers, the candor, the commitment to shaping what was best for the students, the ease with which students' parents were included. The first school had long struck me as a place where autonomous entrepreneurs — each teacher with her or his own subject and classroom — plied their trades with as much independence from their colleagues and the community as possible. Their rudeness to one another (not to speak of their inhospitality to visitors) was in sharp contrast with the constructive raucousness and bluntness of the second school's humanities team. There the abrasions were smoothed by respect and commitment. These teachers believed that they had to join in order to teach well. In the first school the disrespect, however unwitting, was itself a ritual, an expected part of carrying out the contract. It's 2:30 to 4:00, and I may as well get some correcting done.

Analogous rituals abound in the system at large. Recently a large city school district decided that it needed to create "school site managment," the deliberate delegation of administrative power to individual schools. Wisely, it sought to give greater authority and flexibility to those professionals who knew their students better than did anyone else. However, the device by which this devolution was effected was deliciously, if sadly ironic. It was promulgated by the superintendent after virtually no prior consultation with any of the schools' principals. Schools wanting to be "autonomous" would have to apply for the privilege, following detailed guidelines of who in their school community had to be involved and precisely how. Central staff would decide which schools "won" the right to "manage" their own sites, and would monitor their progress thereafter.

Simply, authority was to be delegated only in the precise manner which the central authorities defined that it might be delegated. When I queried friends in the superintendent's office about this seeming contradiction, I was told that "principals do not know how to do this . . . They will not want it . . . They'll botch it . . . We must take leadership in training them." The assumption — the ritual — was that the central office knew better about how to run a school than its principal did. So does the hierarchy traditionally speak: whoever works below you is not to be trusted. That is why they are below you. Your job is to direct, to train, to supervise, and to assess. Inevitably, the effect on the school-level folk in this instance was ugly cynicism and reinforcement of their belief that central office leaders were hypocrites.

A governor long a leader in post–1983 school reform wished to advance the virtues of school and system restructuring. He wisely believed that authority had to be close to the children, that what worked well in a city might not work well in a rural area, that incentives had to be created to attract able educators to work in the schools and to lead them. Meetings were held all across the state, and a diverse group of progressive people — teachers, administrators, legislators, business and other civic leaders — began to coalesce as a force to produce and maintain this process. Most of these people had never been together before, and their conversations were meandering, sometimes stressful, and at first productive of little more than talk about goals for the state and the need for "change." Progress was not at all apparent. The frustration of the governor's staff finally peaked and a few friends in the state capital, joined by a couple of out-of-state consultants, quietly drafted legislation to cut through the talk. None of the drafts were shared with the people who had been earlier gathered to explore the ways to improve the educational system. In due course, the small group gathered the larger together and told them, You will restructure. We will tell you how to do it. We cannot wait. The president's and the governors' goals for the year 2000 must be addressed now. This is what we — you — will do. If you want, get behind it.

Not surprisingly, those who had given hours of time to considering the best approach to reform felt betrayed. They kept it to themselves, though. Publicly, they went along. The governor governs, doesn't he? Bold strokes are the essence of leadership. And isn't all the talk we've had with all those strangers — we've held three meetings over the last four months — leading us nowhere? No more meetings, please. Somebody up there knows best. That's the way things always have been done. And we'll go home and let somebody else worry about those adolescents, about the nature of the community in which we want them to grow up, about the values that should surround a school. That's all somebody else's business. It can't be ours: the governor himself tells us that by his actions. We're here to support his moves, not to counsel him on what these moves should be.

The gain for the governor? The appearance of action. The costs to the governor? Losing the political base for a broad-based, and thus powerful, movement for serious school reform — and having now to live with an ill-directed plan, superficial and unresponsive to the needs and hopes of the people.

Exceptions to this traditional ritual can be found, but the rule remains: those at the top of the hierarchy know best.

From such forays into schools and communities, one inevitably draws impressions about the prospect for significant change in American education — even about the likelihood of Franklin High School being modestly reformed along the lines suggested by Horace Smith's committee.

Since schooling is so dependent on the human condition — the personalities and dispositions and energies of thousands of people — one has to search for a constructive mood among teachers and others who are or should be involved with children. One looks for people willing to think anew about the routines and rituals of their professional and political lives. One strains to hear voices filled with both optimism and realism, with the sort of hope that has to pervade a school or a community if its adolescents are to believe in themselves enough to push themselves. One listens for folk who are patient, who understand the complexity of learning and growing up.

The search to date has often been discouraging. So many people appear distracted, impatient, stuck in their ways, the traditions of their contracts, their politics. If they are for change, it must be simple, abrupt — and be undertaken by somebody else. Few feel enough incentive to do differently much of what they do now.

While there are several reasons for this gloomy assessment, central among them is that serious school reform depends on our ability to change the way we think about learning and growing up and schooling. That is, reform is not a matter of reorganizing the resources now available in schools and school districts and states. Rather, we must look deeper, challenging some of the central ideas that originally shaped our schools. Much of the challenge is implicit in Horace's new school. The trick is how to create a climate for serious and undefensive reassessment of our enterprise, how to help children learn.

Horace's committee benefited from working with the support of its peers. It was not simply set afloat. It came about through initiatives of the school board, the superintendent, Franklin's principal, and Horace himself. The administrators were wise to give the committee's lead to a respected teacher, because only such a person could convince the several constituencies, especially the veteran faculty members, of the value of any sort of change. The committee went to great pains to report back to its constituencies at every turn. It sampled opinion during the entire period of its deliberations. It listened. It was honest with itself. It took the time necessary to do its work.

What lies ahead for Horace and his colleagues now is a selling job. The committee's recommendations will affect virtually everyone in Franklin High School — from the newest student to the principal herself. Because the design comprises necessarily interlocking parts, a piecemeal reform strategy will not work. As a result, to some considerable degree the community will have to buy at once much of what is recommended. Gradualism is possible only in instituting the Houses, which will be erected in phases.

The district and state will have to support the changes, from endorsing a diploma awarded on the basis of Exhibitions to giving authority and autonomy to teachers to assisting the evolution of a simpler yet more demanding common curriculum. The system will have to support, not direct; it will have to listen and watch. It must counsel as well as monitor, and intervene only if the school's work is demonstrably ineffective.

The design Horace's committee offers is fundamental because it rests on fresher ideas about schooling than those which currently inform Franklin High School. Still, it is realistic. It is full of compromises, but they take into account imperatives different from earlier ones. A fair example is the need to recognize that, because students differ, no teacher can serve more than eighty if he is to teach them effectively. If met, this imperative alone will profoundly change every school like Franklin. Better ideas spawn new habits, new expectations, new rituals.

It is on such new ideas that the burden of school reform rests.

Will American political and educational leaders seriously rethink what their schools are and what they do? I remember that they have not, for a long time, and I worry that they will not, this being a day dominated by the politics of slogan and sound bite, of short-range gain, where the higher levels of government are searching to take ever greater control of the schools. I fear that the preferred alternative to careful rethinking will be continued pushing, prodding, testing, and protesting our largely mindless, egregiously expensive, and notably unproductive current system. It is not a pretty prospect.

And yet there are glimmers of hope. The public criticism of the schools has been sustained now for over a decade. A generation of governors has staked their electability on platforms of school reform, and the White House and the Congress show signs of following some of their lead. President Bush and Secretary Lamar Alexander have called for a new generation of schools, ones that "break the mold." Criticism of conventional top-down methods of school reform, such as centrally imposed examinations unaccompanied by any other expected changes, are under fire: more people are paying attention.

Most important is a growing army of Horace Smiths, educators in the schools who are fed up with being relentlessly criticized and patronized, and at the same time ready to re-examine their own practices, their own ideas about learning, their own compromises. They get little leadership from their professional organizations, higher education, or the education industry; these monoliths are too inflexible to serve them well. The growth of the legion of Horace Smiths is as yet localized, inchoate, often barely known by the public; yet it is promising. If we gain new schools, it will be because these individuals have found among themselves a fresh source of authority and have asserted in community after community a new order.

Even if fully launched, Horace's new school is itself likely to be a temporary, transitional institution. Franklin High School is primarily a *place,* a site where the resources to help young people use their minds well are deliberately and generously concentrated. However, a place of this sort may perhaps become less important as American culture evolves. Getting educated and going to school are not the same, obviously. When the vehicles of communication were sparse and the population thinly spread, school as a place made sense. However, with a much larger and more concentrated population, with communication technologies of great power and low cost more readily available to the mass of the population, and with growing understanding of cultural diversity in this country, new ways of "getting educated" are likely to be formulated and accepted.

One key here is the Exhibition. If a student can convince himself, his community, and those whose approbation he needs (college admissions officers and employers) of his intellectual merit, who cares whether he has attended school for 180 days for each of thirteen years? No one — assuming the authenticity of the Exhibition. While ways of assessing the student's intellectual habits over time would be required, serious Exhibitions, ones with integrity, would make more sense as a qualification for a valid diploma than mere school attendance. Further, the specificity of these Exhibitions would provide an incentive for the students: they would know what and why they should study. They would know the standards and substance of the game finally to be played. Practice then makes sense to and for them.[1]

There will be the drifters, the youngsters who are distracted and careless, the kids for whom any sort of investment toward a thoughtful future seems worthless. Without question, their needs must be sensitively addressed. Yet their condition should not deflect us from pursuing the goal of a more open, more individualized secondary education, one that will serve the majority better than the current high school routines. Most American adolescents want to learn, and they appreciate sensible standards. They are eminently teachable as long as they are respected. It is this majority to whom a more demanding and Exhibition-based schooling can be directed.

Another key is technology. To date, most audiovisual, calculating, and computer technology has been deliberately harnessed to the traditional school cart: it is designed to assist the effectiveness of the existing system. In the past and present, it has usually been an add-on, a way to do the out-of-class exercises, the homework, some outside projects. However, if the destination is made clear — by means of the Exhibition — one is invited to construct the most effective means to reach it, and that may not be the familiar march through the familiar curriculum.

Technology can be a central part of an individual's new means to the end of a consequential education. Obviously, one need not attend school to have access to technology; it can be based in one's home, as are today most communication technologies, such as calculators, televisions, VCRs, stereo systems, and personal computers. If significant interactive technologies designed for educational purposes were soon to be cheaply available — accessible as a public right to the poor as well as to the affluent — "homework" could for many students become far more important than it is now, and "attendance" at school a more limited and very focused activity. The differences among children could be far more readily addressed, and the school site could become a place more of tutoring, seminars, and laboratory work than a place in which to pass on information. While a school building could serve as a sanctuary for children denied a safe or supportive home, the shape of most school sites would radically change, probably at great financial savings.

A final key is political, in particular the stresses arising from the fragmented character of American society. The consensus that brought us the apparent stability of the 1950s, for example, depended on the disproportionate leverage on the culture of an upper-middle-class white leadership, largely male. This group dominated the school boards and top positions in education's administrative hierarchy, such rituals as the White House Conferences on Education, the unions, and the universities; and the spectrum of its internal disagreements was narrow.

For good or ill, the spectrum of politics and of disagreement is wider now. As our power structure has become more democratic, our politics have become more confrontational and divisive. Efforts to paper this over, to fix it either by ignoring or denying it or by trying to impose cultural uniformity ("standards," as though they were above group conflict) by some sort of high-level governmental mandate will stir up fierce storms and will not work.

One way to accommodate the new stress is to provide for more choice in all sectors of life, usually through the deregulation or privatization of the public mechanisms of the society. Schools, however, may be the last to succumb to this movement. The fact that they serve (or, if effectively directed, could serve) the shaping of citizens' minds and values makes them especially important for the defenders of a self-consciously American (and thus unitary) system; and their recent political use in the attempts at the racial and economic desegregation of society makes breakup less palatable.

However, the pressures for an educational coat of many colors — rather than a coat of one blended color — increase. Some are ugly, all poignant. These pressures — especially when added to the refusal of the existing system so far to contemplate, much less get on with, its own reform — will favor new forms of schooling, new sorts of compromises within the American system. An obvious one is the practice that lessens the importance of school as a place and allows varied routes to agreed-upon credentials.

Fanciful! critics will say. Chaos! It lacks the order of the existing system. It threatens standards! It puts kids on their own. It mixes them in with adults. They will run loose on the streets. It means that some will graduate before others. Most of all, it trusts them. It will never happen.

It will, slowly. The existing system — even at the standard that the best within it (such as Horace Smith) strive toward — is too cumbersome, too expensive, too bureaucratized, and too inefficient to survive. Further, the political strains of running a unitary school radiating a unitary culture in a country now richly diverse will become too painful to tolerate, and the fact that the informal systems of education — the media and mass merchandizing — are purveying (again, for good or ill) a national culture inevitably weakens the argument for the school as the glue for the national culture. The new system will start haltingly, but it will start.

Entrepreneurs in the private sector may well first push this alternative.[2] There is a market out there among the forty-five million American schoolchildren, one beckoning for a system of "schools," each itself a congeries of opportunities that can be assembled to serve each student. The economically and pedagogically practical key for the mastery of this market is cheap, powerful interactive communication. The prospect is demonstrably there, if a decade or two off in its seizing.

Like any new venture, all this is alarming. We worry about what we will give up. We long for cultural stability, even if not one crafted, as in the 1950s, on the basis of one group's hegemony. The alternatives from which we can choose are not clear, and we are thus fearful.

Schools are important as children's minds are important. As the architects of the new system start their work, one prays that they will pay special heed to the heavy cultural responsibility they carry.

Horace lives in the immediate world. He needs to get his school right within the confines of present expectations. To take even the limited steps his committee recommends will require pushing the existing system hard.

Franklin's standards must reflect the best of its immediate community and that of the nation. Franklin and the system within which Franklin exists must accept the likelihood — indeed, the desirability within a democracy — of frequent tension between the local and the larger world, between local standards and expectations and those of the nation. Just as students must learn to make decisions and compromises, so too must the schools and the school system. Just as a wise culture values the constructive differences among its citizens, so too should it honor the wise differences among its schools.

Those who direct and care for Franklin must recognize that those who educate children have several masters, that an educated child is one who is in the habit of thinking for herself, that this is a proper and respectful private worth just as the ability of that youngster to become a ready worker and a sensitive citizen are respected public worths.

It is on this final truism that the success of the current school reform effort turns. The hopes for the nation, for the parent, and for the adolescent — the public hopes and the private hopes — are all legitimate. Rhetorically, and often substantively, these hopes are sometimes in conflict.

Unfortunately, the voice of the adolescent calling out to be Somebody and the voice of the parent asking that the personhood of his child be respected are not much heard in the current political debate. We hear often of our need as a nation to be economically competitive and little about an individual child's hopes and fears and need for a personal and decent identity. The absence of these latter ends, and the perception that America's political and business leadership has little concern for this absence, dulls widespread interest in school reform.

Only a generously broad and sensitive movement, as close to the grassroots as to the board rooms of big business and big government, will allow even the modest work of Horace Smith and his colleagues to proceed. Of course, grassroots politics are often contentious and fraught with frustration. However, trust in them, with all their messiness, is the price for wise educational reform. Rejection of them — worse, contempt for them — will lead to a reform of a different sort, hardly the sort visualized by Horace's committee, a reform that stiffens the ribs of an already rigid and dangerously standardized system.

Leaders must listen to the many voices of a people who stubbornly believe in schooling and who want the best not only for their children but for all children. Those who say such voices are mute have no ears, or plug them up with self-serving arguments. Leaders who press sensible policies to respond to all the legitimate voices calling for improving the schooling of children will begin to move the effort forward.

They will, of course, like Horace, have to compromise. Such is the way in sound politics, just as it is in sound schools. The trick is in the finding of the best compromises.

Appendix A

The Coalition of Essential Schools and the Re:Learning Initiative

If Horace's school were real, it would be a member of the Coalition of Essential Schools.

Formed in 1984 and building on five years of research arising from A Study of High Schools, the coalition is an association of school people and their colleagues at Brown University who agree on a set of ideas that they believe should inform all good schools. They also agree on the proposition that each school must craft these ideas into practices that are respectful of its community and that draw on the strengths of its particular faculty. That is, they agree that no two good schools are quite alike but all share principles that give shape to their effort. Horace's "new" Franklin High School is not a model of an Essential School. It is, rather, an example, one school's adaptation of Essential School ideas in ways that best serve its own time and place.

The coalition expresses nine common principles:

1. The school should focus on helping adolescents learn to use their minds well. Schools should not attempt to be "comprehensive" if such a claim is made at the expense of the school's central intellectual purpose.

2. The school's goals should be simple: each student should master a number of essential skills and be competent in certain areas of knowledge. Although these skills and areas will, to varying degrees, reflect the traditional academic disciplines, the program's design should be shaped by the intellectual and imaginative powers and competencies that students need, rather than by conventional "subjects." The aphorism "less is more" should dominate: curricular decisions are to be directed toward the students' attempt to gain mastery rather than by the teachers' effort to cover content.

3. The school's goals should apply to all students, but the means to these goals will vary as these students themselves vary. School practice should be tailor-made to meet the needs of every group of adolescents.

4. Teaching and learning should be personalized to the maximum feasible extent. No teacher should have direct responsibility for more than eighty students; decisions about the course of study, the use of students' and teachers' time, and the choice of teaching materials and specific pedagogies must be placed in the hands of the principal and staff.

5. The governing metaphor of the school should be student as worker, rather than the more familiar metaphor of teacher as deliverer of instructional services. Accordingly, a prominent pedagogy will be coaching, to provoke students to learn how to learn and thus to teach themselves.

6. Students embarking on secondary school studies are those who show competence in language and elementary mathematics. Students of traditional high school age who do not yet have appropriate levels of competence to start secondary school studies will be provided with intensive remedial work so that they can quickly meet those standards. The diploma should be awarded on a successful final demonstration of mastery for graduation — an Exhibition. This Exhibition by the student of his or her grasp of the central skills and knowledge of the school's program may be jointly administered by the faculty and higher authorities. Because the diploma is awarded when earned, the school's program proceeds with no strict age grading and with no system of credits earned by time spent in class. The emphasis is on the students' demonstration that they can do important things.

7. The tone of the school should explicitly and self-consciously stress the values of unanxious expectation ("I won't threaten you, but I expect much of you"), of trust (unless it is abused), and of decency (the values of fairness, generosity, and tolerance). Incentives appropriate to the school's students and teachers should be emphasized, and parents should be treated as essential collaborators.

8. The principal and teachers should perceive of themselves first as generalists (teachers and scholars in general education) and next as specialists (experts in a particular discipline). Staff should expect multiple obligations (teacher-counselor-manager) and a sense of commitment to the entire school.

9. Administrative and budget targets should include substantial time for collective planning by teachers, competitive salaries for staff, and an ultimate per-pupil cost not more than 10 percent higher than that at traditional schools. Administrative plans may have to show the phased reduction or elimination of some services now provided for students in many traditional comprehensive secondary schools.

These principles are directed inward, at the keeping of school. Public schools exist, of course, in a context of district and state policy and administration. The changes that several Essential Schools wished to make clashed early with regulations and expectations of the school systems of which they were a part. By 1988, it was clear that ambitious school reform of the sort which the principals and teachers at Essential Schools envisioned had to be achieved together with reform of the system that encompasses those schools. Fortunately, key political leaders in several states were coming to the same conclusion — that school reform and system reform had to proceed concurrently — and an alliance was struck by the Coalition of Essential Schools and the Education Commission of the States, a policy research center created and supported by the states since 1965, to encourage the reform effort "from the schoolhouse to statehouse." The initiative is called Re:Learning, and it is driven by the assumption that school practices which serve all children well should shape the system's policy and management.

By mid-1991, some two hundred schools in twenty-three states were involved, with seven states — Illinois, Delaware, Rhode Island, New Mexico, Arkansas, Pennsylvania, and Colorado — formally in the Re:Learning effort. Most of the schools were public; eighteen were private. Nine additional states were considering involvement in Re:Learning. Under informal auspices but with the close support of state departments of education, regional arrangements have been made in New York, California, Texas, and in New England. Several districts, notably Jefferson County, Kentucky, and Broward County, Florida, have also focused resources and policy to take account of the work of their Essential Schools.

What has been learned over the last seven years? Have adolescents benefited? How have the schools chosen to redesign themselves, and what can be learned from their processes of change? Frustratingly little can be said with assurance yet. Most Essential Schools are in the early stages of their redesign: Thayer High School in Winchester, New Hampshire; Walbrook High School in Baltimore, Maryland; R. L. Paschal Senior High School in Fort Worth, Texas; Hope High School in Providence, Rhode Island; Westbury High School in Houston, Texas; Central Park East Secondary School in New York City; and Brimmer and May School in Chestnut Hill, Massachusetts, among others. Each of these schools reports improved student academic performance, attendance, morale, and admission to college. All admit that the changes they envisioned have been difficult to achieve. Each school's plan is unique, sharing the nine principles but actualizing them in ways suited to each. As a result, comparative assessment of success or failure remains conjectural, but judgments from close observation are encouraging.

With the exception of a few wholly new high schools, such as Central Park East Secondary School and University Heights High School in New York City, most Essential Schools have followed a process not dissimilar to the one of Franklin High. A faculty steering committee, sometimes including parents, students, and others, has produced a plan and a timetable for the recommended changes to be instituted. Most often this committee work was done on top of other obligations; the luxury enjoyed at Franklin of released time for the teachers and moneys for travel and the visitor was, sadly, rare. The coalition staff has learned that plans evolved quickly and by tired people are at best incomplete and at worst trivial. The problem is not just insufficient time for the committee to work; the lack of financial support from school authorities signals to the committee members that their venture has been given a low priority.

Many schools have started by focusing on a few of the most promising and apparently least threatening of the nine common principles, usually those of student as worker, personalization, and Exhibitions. Many have adopted a school within the school — an experimental unit staffed by volunteer teachers instructing volunteer students. Such a small-unit plan — like that espoused by Horace's committee — is often the only practical way in which change can be attempted. In many situations it is difficult, both practically and politically, to reshape an entire school all at once (although some smaller Essential Schools — such as New Hampshire's Thayer High School and Massachusetts's Brimmer and May School — have in fact done this, to good account). However, a school within a school inevitably creates tensions among the faculty, between the "ins" and the "outs," or, as several teachers in a particularly volatile school savagely put it, between the "essential school" and the "superfluous school."

The student-as-worker principle has been another likely point of entry, because it can be addressed even within a traditional structure. Teachers can readily talk less and stimulate more, become coaches and questioners more often than lecturers. As they do so, their professional talk changes in promising ways, according to a 1988 Essential Schools evaluation report. Each faculty knows that it must craft its own best approach to the commonsense student-as-worker principle — rather than applying a detailed "method" that had been delivered unto them in a workshop — and this responsibility appears to be a source of energy. The faculty is itself in charge, in a fundamental way.

The student-as-worker idea has other ramifications. Teachers find that they need larger blocks of time; the daily schedules have changed at many Essential Schools. They often find the curriculum rigid, cast in terms of delivery by teachers rather than activity by students. One often sees Essential School teachers in a mad dash to create new, appropriate materials. If the students have to do the work, and master it thoroughly, the pace of the courses slows down. The student-as-worker mode, thus, tends to emphasize the importance of other matters, such as the allocation of time, the development of the curriculum, and the scope and expectations of tests.

Students in Essential Schools where they have increasingly become the workers have done well on standardized tests, even if these tests (paradoxically) included matters not covered in conventional ways. This can be seen in the record of, for example, Walbrook High School in Baltimore and Westbury High School in Houston.

Exhibitions are a third point of entry, the one pursued by Horace's committee. If we are reasonably clear, the members said, as to where the students should be to deserve a diploma, we can better set priorities for helping them get there. Evidence to date shows the process to be a difficult one. Casting a course of study in terms of rich, genuine, and compelling results is unfamiliar business. And even as a committee of teachers works at it, the school rushes on in its traditional ways, ones which too often value superficial coverage and mere display. To switch abruptly is exceedingly difficult. Schools moving in this direction have needed substantial outside help with the process.

Another popular point of entry into Essential School work — and recommended by Horace's committee — revolves around personalization. Schools usually move in two ways simultaneously, creating a formal advisory system and establishing small units within the larger school, called Houses or clusters or teams. These units typically involve 90 to 120 students and 3 to 5 teachers; their activities usually span the core of the school's curriculum (generally mathematics, science, English, and social studies). The effectiveness of these policies has been substantial and measurable, particularly for schools previously suffering from unacceptable truancy and drop-out rates, such as Pasadena High School in California and Hope High School in Providence, Rhode Island.

Essential Schools have demonstrated how important leadership is in the process of substantial reform and how political the process is. Essential Schools with rapid turnover of principals or the departure of key "senators" (people like Patches, the veteran, the mathematics teacher, and Coach on Horace's committee) suffer deeply. Changes in superintendencies also slow down movement. Schools with stable and sensitive leadership have moved ahead effectively, even in the face of sometimes daunting outside pressures.*

Coalition work has also highlighted the importance of helpers from the outside, critical friends like the visitor. Good schools are, paradoxically, often myopic: the close attention paid to students and their progress tends to limit perspective. An outsider can give broader perspective, can ask all those obvious questions which no one inside has the courage to ask again, and, in a time when bold changes are desired, can bring the ideas and research from other places into the discussion. The coalition and Re:Learning, with the generous help of Citibank and the Danforth Foundation, have created the National Re:Learning Faculty, a large team of able leaders experienced in Essential Schools and their districts and states who serve as critical friends on a sustained basis to schools, districts, and states early in the process. These veterans bring not only wisdom and experience; they are viewed well by even skeptical school people simply because they are themselves in the middle of consequential reform. Horace's committee recommends that such people routinely be available as state and district employees.

In many schools the first conflict is between frustration and satisfaction, between thinly veiled anger at the compromises forced on school people and a view that "if it's not broke, don't fix it." There is tension created here, conflict otherwise masked from view — as amply demonstrated in the deliberations of Horace's committee. Evidence is emerging that the conflict is not just between the Horace Smiths and the outspoken defenders of the status quo; the fence sitters, the teach-

---

*The story of New Hampshire's Thayer High School and its principal, Dennis Littky, has been told by Susan Kammeraad-Campbell in *DOC: The Story of Dennis Littky and His Fight for a Better School* (Chicago: Contemporary Books, 1989). The paper edition is titled *Teacher*.

ers, even principals, and others who do not take sides, who simply to go about their traditional business, have a profoundly negative influence. The burden carried by the apostles of change is heavy.

Incentives are everything in the process of change. The role of political leaders in Re:Learning states is notable; schools there move forward with greater ease than was experienced by the earliest schools in the coalition. Money helps, from the state or from private sources, as seen in Horace's committee. Ultimately incentives are power; these grants and signals from political pulpits are the beginning of a change in power relationships. Re:Learning is not old enough yet to see how this will play out, but the initial incentives appear consequential.

Re:Learning and the Coalition of Essential Schools are asking people in the schools and in the educational system to think in new ways about schooling and learning, and to act upon them. Principals and teachers from several Essential Schools have been at the task of redesign long enough to see some results in the lives of their students. They are properly encouraged. Despite the drag of tradition and the thinness of public resolve to insist on serious schools that foster the deepest and most optimistic values of the American tradition, students are "doing what they were unsupposed to do." The evidence is spotty; there are differences among schools; the search for ways to teach students serious intellectual habits, and to assess their progress, is only started. We remain hopeful.

Information on the Coalition of Essential Schools and Re:Learning is available at the Coalition of Essential Schools, Box 1969, Brown University, Providence, Rhode Island 02912, and at the Education Commission of the States, 707 Seventeenth Street, Suite 2700, Denver, Colorado 80202–3427. The coalition's newsletter, *Horace,* provides comment on progress. The first major documentation of the coalition, of its first years, is being prepared by two anthropologists, Donna Muncey and Patrick McQuillan, and will be published in 1993.

Comments on specific Essential Schools and their leaders have recently appeared in several books. In addition to the Kammeraad-Campbell portrait of Dennis Littky, see Edward B. Fiske, *Smart Schools, Smart Kids: Why Do Some Schools Work?* (New York: Simon and Schuster, 1991), pp. 62–77, for a portrait of Fairdale (Kentucky) High School's social studies teacher Jim Streible; and Thomas Toch, *In the Name of Excellence: The Struggle to Reform the Nation's Schools, Why It's Failing, and What Should Be Done* (New York: Oxford, 1991),

APPENDIX A

p. 260 et seq., on Central Park East Secondary School, New York City.

As of August 1991, the following schools were partners in the Coalition of Essential Schools–Re:Learning effort. These schools have completed the coalition's membership process and are implementing new practices based on the nine common principles of Essential Schools.

Member Schools

Bishop Carroll High School, Calgary, Alberta (Canada)

Sheridan Junior High School, Sheridan, Arkansas

Springdale High School, Springdale, Arkansas

Rancho San Joaquin Middle School, Irvine, California

Mid-Peninsula High School, Palo Alto, California

Pasadena High School, Pasadena, California

Lincoln Middle School, Santa Monica, California

Avon High School, Avon, Connecticut

Watkinson School, Hartford, Connecticut

Weaver High School, Hartford, Connecticut

Middletown High School, Middletown, Delaware

Hodgson Vo-Tech High School, Newark, Delaware

Nova Blanche Forman School, Davie, Florida

Nova Eisenhower School, Davie, Florida

Nova High School, Fort Lauderdale, Florida

Nova Middle School, Fort Lauderdale, Florida

University School of Nova University, Fort Lauderdale, Florida

Anna Jonesboro High School, Anna, Illinois

Carpentersville Middle School, Carpentersville, Illinois

Calumet High School, Chicago, Illinois

Chicago Vocational High School, Chicago, Illinois

Du Sable High School, Chicago, Illinois

Englewood High School, Chicago, Illinois

Flower Vocational High School, Chicago, Illinois

Lindblom Technical High School, Chicago, Illinois

Mather High School, Chicago, Illinois

Paul Robeson High School, Chicago, Illinois

Steinmetz High School, Chicago, Illinois

Sullivan High School, Chicago, Illinois

Wendell Phillips High School, Chicago, Illinois

Elmwood Community School, Elmwood, Illinois

North Middle School, Godfrey, Illinois

Malta Junior-Senior High School, Malta, Illinois

Broadmoor Junior High School, Pekin, Illinois

Roosevelt School, River Forest, Illinois

Lake Park High School, Roselle, Illinois

Sparta High School, Sparta, Illinois

Metro High School, Cedar Rapids, Iowa

Ballard High School, Louisville, Kentucky

Brown School, Louisville, Kentucky

Doss High School, Louisville, Kentucky

Eastern High School, Louisville, Kentucky

Fairdale High School, Louisville, Kentucky

Iroquois High School, Louisville, Kentucky

Seneca High School, Louisville, Kentucky

Western High School, Louisville, Kentucky

Pleasure Ridge Park High School, Pleasure Ridge Park, Kentucky

Mayme S. Waggener High School, St. Matthews, Kentucky

Valley High School, Valley Station, Kentucky

Bryn Mawr School, Baltimore, Maryland

Park Heights Street Academy, Baltimore, Maryland

Walbrook High School, Baltimore, Maryland

Portland High School, Portland, Maine

Andover High School, Andover, Massachusetts

Boston English High School, Boston, Massachusetts

Fenway Middle College High School, Boston, Massachusetts

Brimmer and May School, Chestnut Hill, Massachusetts

Parkway South High School, Manchester, Missouri

Whitfield School, St. Louis, Missouri

Thayer High School, Winchester, New Hampshire

Capital High School, Santa Fe, New Mexico

Capshaw Middle School, Santa Fe, New Mexico

Sweeney Elementary School, Santa Fe, New Mexico

Fox Lane High School, Bedford, New York

The Bronx New School, Bronx, New York

Bronxville High School, Bronxville, New York

Adelphi Academy, Brooklyn, New York

The Brooklyn New School, Brooklyn, New York

The New Program, Brooklyn, New York

Croton-Harmon High School, Croton-on-Hudson, New York

Alternative Community School, Ithaca, New York

John Jay High School, Katonah, New York

Central Park East I, New York, New York

Central Park East II, New York, New York

Central Park East Secondary School, New York, New York

Crossroads School, New York, New York

P.S. 234, New York, New York

River East, New York, New York

Satellite Academy–Forsyth, New York, New York

University Heights High School, New York, New York

Urban Academy, New York, New York

School Without Walls, Rochester, New York

Scarsdale Alternative School, Scarsdale, New York

Elizabethtown Area High School, Elizabethtown, Pennsylvania

Alternative for the Middle Years, Philadelphia, Pennsylvania

The Crefeld School, Philadelphia, Pennsylvania

Central Falls Junior-Senior High School, Central Falls, Rhode Island

St. Xavier Academy, Coventry, Rhode Island

The Gordon School, East Providence, Rhode Island

Narragansett Elementary School, Narragansett, Rhode Island

Narragansett Pier School, Narragansett, Rhode Island

Narragansett Senior High School, Narragansett, Rhode Island

Hope High School, Providence, Rhode Island

School One, Providence, Rhode Island

Mary V. Quirk Junior High School, Warren, Rhode Island

Heathwood Hall, Columbia, South Carolina

Hixson High School, Chattanooga, Tennessee

St. Andrews-Sewanee School, St. Andrews, Tennessee

Paschal High School, Fort Worth, Texas

Westbury High School, Houston, Texas

The Judson Montessori School, San Antonio, Texas

The Putney School, Putney, Vermont

Finn Hill Junior High School, Kirkland, Washington

Jemtegaard Middle School, Washougal, Washington

Lincoln High School, Manitowoc, Wisconsin

Walden III, Racine, Wisconsin

These schools are in an active planning stage as they prepare for change based on Essential School principles.

Networking Schools

Bald Knob Junior High School, Bald Knob, Arkansas

Woodland Junior High School, Fayetteville, Arkansas

Flippin High School, Flippin, Arkansas

Perryville High School, Perryville, Arkansas

Sacred Heart High School, Waterbury, Connecticut

Wilmington High School, Wilmington, Delaware

El Dorado Elementary School, Santa Fe, New Mexico

Santa Fe Technical High School, Santa Fe, New Mexico

Dowa Yalanne Elementary, Zuni, New Mexico

Twin Buttes High School, Zuni, New Mexico

Zuni High School, Zuni, New Mexico

Zuni Middle School, Zuni, New Mexico

Bellefonte High School, Bellefonte, Pennsylvania

Central Bucks High School East, Buckingham, Pennsylvania

Central Bucks High School West, Doylestown, Pennsylvania

Lenape Junior High School, Doylestown, Pennsylvania

Rhode Island School for the Deaf, Providence, Rhode Island

The International School, Bellevue, Washington

These schools are researching and discussing Essential School principles.

Exploring Schools

Fayetteville High School East, Fayetteville, Arkansas

Heber Springs Elementary School, Heber Springs, Arkansas

Central High School, Little Rock, Arkansas

Lonoke Junior High School, Lonoke, Arkansas

Siloam Springs High School, Siloam Springs, Arkansas

Central High School, West Helena, Arkansas

Akron High School, Akron, Colorado

APPENDIX A

Aspen Elementary School,
Aspen, Colorado

Aspen High School, Aspen,
Colorado

Hinkley High School, Aurora,
Colorado

Basalt High School, Basalt,
Colorado

Burbank Junior High School,
Boulder, Colorado

Fairview High School, Boulder,
Colorado

Horizon High School, Boulder,
Colorado

Martin Park Elementary School,
Boulder, Colorado

Roaring Fork High School,
Carbondale, Colorado

Castle Rock Junior High School,
Castle Rock, Colorado

Douglas County High School,
Castle Rock, Colorado

Adams Elementary School,
Colorado Springs, Colorado

Coronado High School,
Colorado Springs, Colorado

East Junior High School,
Colorado Springs, Colorado

Queen Palmer Elementary
School, Colorado Springs,
Colorado

Wasson High School, Colorado
Springs, Colorado

Edgewater Elementary School,
Denver, Colorado

High School Redirection,
Denver, Colorado

Lincoln High School, Denver,
Colorado

Jefferson High School,
Edgewater, Colorado

Lumberg Elementary School,
Edgewater, Colorado

Evergreen High School,
Evergreen, Colorado

Fort Lupton High School, Fort
Lupton, Colorado

Fort Lupton Middle School,
Fort Lupton, Colorado

Twombley Primary School, Fort
Lupton, Colorado

Orchard Mesa Middle School,
Grand Junction, Colorado

Thunder Mountain Elementary
School, Grand Junction,
Colorado

University High School,
Greeley, Colorado

Molhom Elementary School,
Lakewood, Colorado

Lamar Middle School, Lamar,
Colorado

Larkspur Elementary School,
Larkspur, Colorado

Lake County Elementary
School, Leadville, Colorado

Lake County High School,
Leadville, Colorado

Lake County Intermediate
School, Leadville, Colorado

Chatfield High School, Littleton,
Colorado

Skyline High School, Longmont,
Colorado

Centennial Junior High School,
Montrose, Colorado

Columbine Middle School,
Montrose, Colorado

Montrose High School,
Montrose, Colorado

Northside Elementary School,
Montrose, Colorado

Riverside-Woodgate Elementary School, Montrose, Colorado

Olathe Elementary School, Olathe, Colorado

Olathe Middle-High School, Olathe, Colorado

Pagosa Springs Elementary School, Pagosa Springs, Colorado

Pagosa Springs High School, Pagosa Springs, Colorado

Pagosa Springs Junior High School, Pagosa Springs, Colorado

Park View Elementary School, Pueblo, Colorado

Pueblo County High School, Pueblo, Colorado

Risley Middle School, Pueblo, Colorado

Riverdale Elementary School, Thornton, Colorado

Skyview Elementary School, Thornton, Colorado

Skyview High School, Thornton, Colorado

Cotton Creek Elementary School, Westminster, Colorado

Martensen Elementary School, Wheat Ridge, Colorado

Stevens Elementary School, Wheat Ridge, Colorado

Wheat Ridge High School, Wheat Ridge, Colorado

Wheat Ridge Junior High School, Wheat Ridge, Colorado

The Rippowam Center, Stamford, Connecticut

Caesar Rodney Junior High School, Camden-Wyoming, Delaware

Central Middle School, Dover, Delaware

William Henry Middle School, Dover, Delaware

Sussex Central Senior High School, Georgetown, Delaware

Laurel Central Middle School, Laurel, Delaware

Redding Middle School, Middletown, Delaware

John G. Leach School, New Castle, Delaware

Wallace Wallin School, New Castle, Delaware

Brookside Elementary School, Newark, Delaware

Christiana High School, Newark, Delaware

George V. Kirk Middle School, Newark, Delaware

Seaford Middle School, Seaford, Delaware

Coral Springs Middle School, Coral Springs, Florida

Westchester Elementary School, Coral Springs, Florida

Silver Ridge Elementary School, Davie, Florida

Cape Elizabeth High School, Cape Elizabeth, Maine

Cleveland Middle School, Albuquerque, New Mexico

Emerson Elementary School, Albuquerque, New Mexico

Manzano High School, Albuquerque, New Mexico

West Mesa High School,
Albuquerque, New Mexico
Algodones Elementary School,
Algodones, New Mexico
Gil Sanchez Elementary School,
Belen, New Mexico
Jaramillo Elementary School,
Belen, New Mexico
Bernalillo High School,
Bernalillo, New Mexico
Bernalillo Middle School,
Bernalillo, New Mexico
Bloomfield High School,
Bloomfield, New Mexico
Mesa Alta Junior High School,
Bloomfield, New Mexico
Rio Vista Elementary School,
Bloomfield, New Mexico
Estancia Middle School, Des
Moines, New Mexico
Jemez Mountain Schools,
Gallina, New Mexico
Jefferson Elementary School,
Gallup, New Mexico
John F. Kennedy Middle School,
Gallup, New Mexico
Hagerman Elementary School,
Hagerman, New Mexico
Hermosa Heights Elementary
School, Las Cruces, New
Mexico
Tombaugh Elementary School,
Las Cruces, New Mexico
Vista Middle School, Las
Cruces, New Mexico
Memorial Middle School, Las
Vegas, New Mexico
Los Alamos High School, Los
Alamos, New Mexico
Loving Middle School, Loving,
New Mexico

Melrose Municipal Schools,
Melrose, New Mexico
Placitas Elementary School,
Placitas, New Mexico
Alameda Junior High School,
Santa Fe, New Mexico
Alvord Elementary School,
Santa Fe, New Mexico
Pojoaque Senior High School,
Santa Fe, New Mexico
Santa Fe High School, Santa Fe,
New Mexico
Cliff Schools, Silver City, New
Mexico
Harrison Schmitt School, Silver
City, New Mexico
La Plata Middle School, Silver
City, New Mexico
Silver High School, Silver City,
New Mexico
Hot Springs High School, Truth
or Consequences, New
Mexico
A. Montoya Elementary School,
Tijeras, New Mexico
Roosevelt Middle School,
Tijeras, New Mexico
Tucumcari Junior High School,
Tucumcari, New Mexico
Tularosa Elementary School,
Tularosa, New Mexico
Conestoga Senior High School,
Berwyn, Pennsylvania
McGuffey High School,
Claysville, Pennsylvania
Freeland High School, Freeland,
Pennsylvania
Halifax Area Senior/Junior High
School, Halifax, Pennsylvania
Hazleton Senior High School,
Hazleton, Pennsylvania

Honesdale High School,
Honesdale, Pennsylvania
Lower Dauphin Junior-Senior
High School, Hummelstown,
Pennsylvania
McCaskey High School,
Lancaster, Pennsylvania
Garden Spot Senior/Junior High
School, New Holland,
Pennsylvania
New Hope-Solebury Junior-
Senior High School, New
Hope, Pennsylvania
Parkway West Area Vocational
Technical School, Oakdale,
Pennsylvania
Furness High School,
Philadelphia, Pennsylvania

Simon Gratz High School,
Philadelphia, Pennsylvania
Strawberry Mansion High
School, Philadelphia,
Pennsylvania
Keystone Oaks High School,
Pittsburgh, Pennsylvania
Tyrone Area Junior-Senior High
School, Tyrone, Pennsylvania
William Tennent High School,
Warminster, Pennsylvania
West Hazleton High School,
West Hazleton, Pennsylvania
William Penn Senior High
School, York, Pennsylvania

Appendix B

A Budget and Schedule for Franklin High School*

How should Horace's committee respond to the visitor's query: "How can the school's human resources be redistributed so that no teacher has responsibility for more than eighty students?" How can Franklin High School best deploy its other limited resources, given the number of hours in the school day?

The committee put the following highest on its list of priorities:

- Teacher-to-student loads should be no more than 1 to 80. Personalization is crucial for individual success, and its efficiency contributes to the overall productivity of the school.
- The large numbers of staff and students should be divided into more manageable units, or Houses.
- Groups of students should be heterogeneously divided among Houses and teams.
- Among all of the teachers, these areas should be covered: mathematics-science, the arts, history-philosophy, languages other than English, the skills of expression, the techniques of inquiry, and study habits.
- Franklin's budget should remain as it is, or should increase no more than 10 percent.

---

*This budget and schedule were designed by Rick Lear and Jill Davidson, with advice from Joe McDonald. The text comes largely from the hand of Jill Davidson. This work draws from earlier budget and schedule studies of the Coalition of Essential Schools' Mythos project, led by Susan Follett Lusi, Joseph McCarthy, and John Watkins. See *Horace*: "Mythos High School: A Case Study" (September 1987); "The Eleventh Commandment" (April/May 1988); "Affording the Essential School" (November 1988); "Scheduling the Essential School" (May 1989).

APPENDIX B

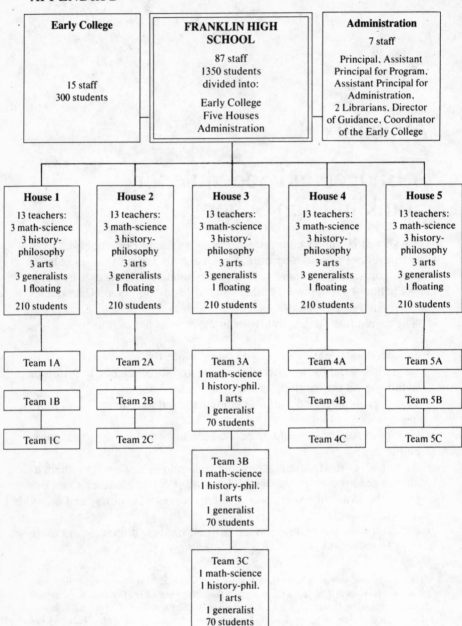

Early College	FRANKLIN HIGH SCHOOL	Administration
15 staff 300 students	87 staff 1350 students divided into: Early College Five Houses Administration	7 staff Principal, Assistant Principal for Program, Assistant Principal for Administration, 2 Librarians, Director of Guidance, Coordinator of the Early College

House 1	House 2	House 3	House 4	House 5
13 teachers: 3 math-science 3 history-philosophy 3 arts 3 generalists 1 floating 210 students	13 teachers: 3 math-science 3 history-philosophy 3 arts 3 generalists 1 floating 210 students	13 teachers: 3 math-science 3 history-philosophy 3 arts 3 generalists 1 floating 210 students	13 teachers: 3 math-science 3 history-philosophy 3 arts 3 generalists 1 floating 210 students	13 teachers: 3 math-science 3 history-philosophy 3 arts 3 generalists 1 floating 210 students

Team 1A — Team 2A — Team 3A (1 math-science, 1 history-phil., 1 arts, 1 generalist, 70 students) — Team 4A — Team 5A

Team 1B — Team 2B — Team 3B (1 math-science, 1 history-phil., 1 arts, 1 generalist, 70 students) — Team 4B — Team 5B

Team 1C — Team 2C — Team 3C (1 math-science, 1 history-phil., 1 arts, 1 generalist, 70 students) — Team 4C — Team 5C

224

The chart on the facing page is one cut at expressing these priorities. It is assumed that nonpersonnel expenditures will remain constant, from the "old" Franklin to the "new," but that the eighty-seven existing professional staff might be redeployed in new ways. The plan here addresses the high school alone; a comparable model can serve the middle school.

The large box at the top shows the resources Franklin High School has at its disposal. In the Early College, the staff-to-student ratio is somewhat higher than that of the rest of the school, as those older students will engage in more independent work and will benefit from contact with faculty members from local colleges and technical schools and from having other adults in the community as mentors.

Fifteen teams within a House are the basic units where students and teachers work from day to day. Each team has four teachers — math-science, history-philosophy, arts, and a generalist — and seventy students. In addition to each team's four constant members, each House has a "floating" teacher who spends part of her day with each of the House's three teams. Between them, the floating teacher and the generalist will be in charge of inquiry and expression and foreign language study.

How to schedule a high school with such a configuration? At Franklin High School, the central priorities are time in class, time for community service, and time for teachers to plan individually and to work with colleagues, within their disciplines and on their team, on curricular, pedagogical, assessment, and advisory tasks, talk with parents, and so on. One possible schedule appears on the next page.

This schedule demonstrates the way House 1's Team A spends its time. Periods One, Two, and Six are each one hour and forty-five minutes. Periods Three, Four, and Five share two hours, which are used for lunch and advisory and tutorial activities; thirty minutes are reserved for lunch (see below), while the remainder of the time may be divided among advisory and tutorial activities as team members decide. Period One has a ten-minute passing period built in; all others include five-minute passing periods. In the example, the classes rotate through the long periods (One, Three, and Six) to provide the opportunity for teachers and students to meet at different times of the day and to even out the time available for teachers to prepare classes during the four-day scheduling cycle. A weekly rotation could serve the same purpose, although one teacher would have a shorter preparation period for a week at a time.

The special hours, before and after the academic day, and the team meeting at the end of the day are schoolwide activities, occurring

House 1, Team A–Master Schedule

TIME	MONDAY	TUESDAY	WEDNESDAY	THURSDAY	FRIDAY
7:00 Special #1	Band, choir, other activities	Band, choir, other activities	Band, choir, other activities	Band, choir, other activities	Band, choir, other activities
8:00 Period One	Math-Science History-Philosophy *Arts* (Generalist has prep time)	*History-Philosophy* Arts *Generalist* (Math-Science has prep time)	*Math-Science* Arts Generalist (History-Philosophy has prep time)	Math-Science *History-Philosophy* *Generalist* (Arts has prep time)	The schedule is a four-day rotation. The Monday schedule would start again here.
9:55 Period Two	Math-Science History-Philosophy Generalist (Arts has prep time)	Math-Science History-Philosophy Arts (Generalist has prep time)	History-Philosophy Arts Generalist (Math-Science has prep time)	Math-Science Arts Generalist (History-Philosophy has prep time)	
11:45 Periods Three, Four, and Five	Lunch Advisory Tutorial: History-Philosophy Arts/Generalist (Math-Science prep)	Lunch Advisory Tutorial: Math-Science Arts/Generalist (History-Phil. prep)	Lunch Advisory Tutorial: Math-Science History-Phil./Gener. (Arts prep)	Lunch Advisory Tutorial: Math-Science/Arts History-Philosophy (Generalist prep)	
1:45 Period Six	Math-Science Arts Generalist (History-Philosophy has prep time)	Math-Science History-Philosophy Generalist (Arts has prep time)	Math-Science History-Philosophy Arts (Generalist has prep time)	History-Philosophy Arts Generalist (Math-Science has prep time)	
3:30	Team Meeting for staff	Team Meeting for staff	Team Meeting for staff	Team Meeting for staff	Team Meeting for staff
4:00 Special #2 6:00	Band, choir, other activities	Band, choir, other activities	Band, choir, other activities	Band, choir, other activities	Band, choir, other activities

across each of the five Houses. Three lunch periods are built into the schedule: two Houses, including A, have lunch at 11:45, two others at 12:15, and the fifth at 12:45. (Early College students are scheduled to eat at 12:45 whenever possible to balance out the demand on the cafeteria.) Other than those fixed points, each House and the teams within each House are "descheduled" from the rest of the school and are free to allocate time as the staff determines.

In the example provided, students in each team are divided into three groups of twenty-three students which rotate together through Periods One, Two, and Six; these groups may be reorganized as frequently as the team determines. They also rotate through four courses: history-philosophy, math-science, arts, and a general period, which could be devoted to language, special emphasis on inquiry and expression, or some other topic agreed on by the staff. Rotating three groups of students through four courses allows each teacher an individual preparation period every day.

Each House has one staff position in addition to those shown above, available to use as the House decides. In the example, the additional person "floats" across all teams in the House; she will spend Period One with Team A, Period Two with Team B, and Period Six with Team C. The italicized letters indicate the groups of students this floating teacher may spend time with during one cycle of the schedule. In the above example, the floating teacher may, with Team A on Monday, spend half of Period One with the math-science group and the other half of that period with the arts group. The floating teacher would also have half her time available to coordinate community service activities for the students in her house. This person would be used in ways that complement the generalist on each team; effective use of this person's time and talent will require careful thought within each House.

Each team has thirty minutes daily to spend together built into the schedule. While this is insufficient time for substantive planning, it is ample for daily discussion of students, something that virtually all teams will want and need.

Each team within a given House could — perhaps should — schedule its rotation of classes so that all three math-science teachers would have the same planning time one day, the history-philosophy another, the arts a third, and the generalists another to allow for cross-team planning within a discipline. Such common planning time would be particularly valuable in the early years, when teachers are learning to work in newly defined disciplines. Multi-House common planning could be done in the same fashion from time to time.

APPENDIX B

Common planning time for each team can be created by setting aside a half day of each student's week for community service. During this time, the seventy students on a team would be engaged in community service both within the school and in the community. Simultaneously, the teachers on that team would have a three-hour block in which to do team planning.

Scheduling three overlapping blocks of time for community service would result in a community service schedule like the following. (House One, Team A is 1A, etc.):

	Monday	Tuesday	Wednesday	Thursday	Friday
8:00–11:00	1A	2A	3A	4A	5A
10:00–1:30*	5B	1B	2B	3B	4B
12:30–3:30	4C	5C	1C	2C	3C

Because the community service schedule is weekly, and the course schedule is on a four-day cycle, students would miss the same class only once in four weeks. Each team of students would have community service the same time of day and same day of the week for a third of the year, then shift both time and day of the week.

When lunch, advisory, and passing time in the hallways is deducted from Franklin's six-period day, each student has six hours of class time daily, or thirty hours a week. In most secondary schools today, students are in class twenty-three to twenty-five hours per week.

*The middle community service time slot includes an additional thirty minutes for lunch.

228

Acknowledgments

IN WRITING THIS BOOK, I have incurred a debt to a legion of friends. Much of what I have learned over the past seven years about Essential Schools and how they emerge is from watching and listening to an extraordinary group of school people, able risk takers of a remarkable sort.

I have room to mention here only a token group, some of the pioneers, the friends with whom I started on this trek toward different kinds of schools. Dennis Littky of Thayer High School in Winchester, New Hampshire, was the first. Clint Vickers of Adelphi Academy in Brooklyn, New York, followed a few weeks later. Deborah Meier telephoned from Manhattan; she wanted to start a school and she believed that we agreed on the important things about adolescent schooling. The result of her quest is the remarkable Central Park East Secondary School in East Harlem. Paul Gounaris came from Providence's Hope High School down the street from Brown University; he was soon joined by Albin Moser, the architect of the Hope Essential High School. Barbara Anderson came from Portland High School, Portland, Maine. Radford Gregg and Larry Barnes came from Paschal Senior High School in Fort Worth, Texas, and Tom Davis from Westbury High School in Houston. Judy Codding of Bronxville High School in Westchester County, New York, joined the conversa-

Acknowledgments

tion, as did Tom Jones of Brighton High School in Rochester, New York. Sister Terry Foley of St. Xavier Academy in Coventry, Rhode Island, and Charlie Como of United Day School of Laredo, Texas, brought in two additional nonpublic schools. Sam Billups and Marian Finney of Walbrook High School and Irving Hamer from the Park Heights Street Academy added Baltimore, Maryland, to our conversation.

These were the people at the start, and they brought with them a strong company of colleagues. As in all things, some of their schools prospered and some have struggled, but I have learned lessons from all. Since the forming of this first mid-1980s group, scores of additional friends have joined our coalition, and I have gained much from them and their schools.

At Brown, I have been blessed by two presidents, Howard Swearer and Vartan Gregorian, two provosts, Maurice Glicksman and Frank Rothman, and a department chairman, William Damon, who have encouraged the Coalition of Essential Schools from the start. From immediate coalition staff and Education Department colleagues, many of whom worked over my manuscript, I have learned and continue to learn much: Holly Houston, Grant Wiggins, Susan Follett Lusi, Amy Gerstein, Amy Berfield, Beth Hakola, and Molly Schen; Ed Campbell, Paula Evans, Bob McCarthy, Rick Lear, Pat Wasley, Joe McDonald, David Niguidula, Gene Thompson, Pat Smith, Beverly Simpson, Carolyn Wyatt, Myra Cline, Tom Wilson, Lisa Lasky, Nonie O'Farrell, Susan Fisher, Sharon Clark, Fayneese Miller, Thomas James, David Kobrin, Grace Taylor, Liliana Costa, Julia Nisbet; and associates in the ethnography project, Donna Muncey and Patrick McQuillan. My views on the arts were influenced by an informal seminar in 1989 involving John Chamberlain and Karen Lee from the Rhode Island School of Design and Brian Keaney and Julie Henderson of Brown. I have been helped by colleagues who are on the coalition roster but work away from Rhode Island: Joan Carney in New York; Maggie Szabo, David Marsh, Steve Jubb, and Tom Wilson in California; Rob Fried in New Hampshire, and a growing host of Re:Learning colleagues, both in Denver at the Education Commission of the States and in the states themselves. In Denver, Frank Newman and Beverly An-

230

derson have been my special mentors. In Providence, four colleagues have especially and devotedly submerged themselves in
the details of producing *Horace's School*: Kathy Hardie, Jill
Davidson, Susan Fisher, and Lily Carter.

New and old friends generously read the manuscript. Betsy
Lerner, my editor at Houghton Mifflin, has advised and encouraged me throughout. Frances Apt once again gave superb edito-
rial advice. Four friends gave repeated close readings to the text:
Nancy Sizer, Arthur Powell, Robert Hampel, and Philip Zaeder.
The hours that these four expended in what must have been an
enervating struggle with my ideas and my prose are beyond
counting. Rick Lear generously spent hours on key details of
Horace's School. My Providence coalition colleagues and Beverly Anderson and Judy Bray at ECS read much and often; their
counsel was critical. Deborah Meier gave wonderful counsel, as
did Alice Sizer Warner and Crystal Campbell.

Horace's School depended on a base at Brown, colleagues at the
Education Commission of the States in Denver, and on reforming
schools; all required financial and political backing. Four foundations started us off in 1984 — the Carnegie Corporation of New
York, the Charles E. Culpeper Foundation, the Exxon Education
Foundation, and the Danforth Foundation — and since that time
many others, some anonymously, have stepped forward with aid
for us at Brown, for ECS in Denver, and directly to our many colleague schools. I took much time especially of Ray Handlan, Alden
Dunham, and Scott Miller. I warmly acknowledge below the support to the coalition and to Re:Learning of a group of remarkable
philanthropies that have made possible a project which embodies
as much risk as promise, which trusts teachers in a project,
where no one is any one else's paid consultant, where the conversation is about children and learning rather than contracts.

Our effort in this Essential School and Re:Learning effort is to
encourage a conversation about growing up and learning, about
ideas for better schools, a conversation that now involves several
thousand people, from governors to teachers, from principals to
legislators. To them all I owe a great debt.

As before and always, my profoundest debt is to my closest
professional colleague, who is also my wife, Nancy Faust Sizer.

Acknowledgments

As a deeply involved high school teacher, she keeps me honest.
As a person who believes unflinchingly in the human spirit and
in its inherent decency and rationality, she insists that I raise my
eye to a distance worthy of our calling as teachers.

Supporting Corporations: Citibank, N.A.; Southwestern Bell
Foundation; Exxon Education Foundation; International Busi-
ness Machines Corporation; Aetna Institute for Corporate
Education; Aetna Life and Casualty Foundation, Inc.; ARCO
Foundation; the Chase Manhattan Bank, N.A.; Circuit City
Foundation; the Coca-Cola Foundation; Emerson Electric Co.;
Kraft General Foods Foundation; Monsanto Fund; Pacific
Telesis Foundation; RJR Nabisco Foundation; the UPS Founda-
tion, Inc.; the Xerox Foundation.

Supporting Foundations: John D. and Catherine T. MacArthur
Foundation; DeWitt Wallace–Reader's Digest Fund; Carnegie
Corporation of New York; the Danforth Foundation; the Ahman-
son Foundation; George I. Alden Trust; Cabot Family Charitable
Trust; the Champlin Foundations; Charles E. Culpeper Founda-
tion, Inc.; the Aaron Diamond Foundation, Inc.; Joseph Drown
Foundation; the Ford Foundation; Gates Foundation; Morris
Goldseker Foundation of Maryland, Inc.; the Edward W. Hazen
Foundation, Inc.; William Randolph Hearst Foundation; the Wil-
liam and Flora Hewlett Foundation; W. Alton Jones Foundation;
the Joyce Foundation; the Esther A. and Joseph Klingenstein
Fund, Inc.; the Andrew W. Mellon Foundation; Edward John
Noble Foundation, Inc.; the David and Lucile Packard Founda-
tion; the Pew Charitable Trusts; Rockefeller Brothers Fund;
Rockefeller Family Fund, Inc.; the San Francisco Foundation;
Anne Burnett and Charles D. Tandy Foundation.

Notes

Chapter One

1. The "treaties" metaphor is used by Arthur Powell in Chapter 2 of Arthur G. Powell, Eleanor Farrar, and David K. Cohen, *The Shopping Mall High School: Winners and Losers in the Educational Marketplace* (Boston: Houghton Mifflin, 1985).
2. The visiting consultant could very well have been Grant Wiggins. See Wiggins's "Eleven Suggestions for Reform That Are Radical — But Shouldn't Be," *Horace* (October 1987), p. 1.
3. This argument about Horace and his conundrum reflects my earlier accounting: *Horace's Compromise: The Dilemma of the American High School* (Boston: Houghton Mifflin, 1984, 1985).

Chapter Two

1. Thomas Toch and Edward B. Fiske have summarized the reform record of the 1980s well: Toch, *In the Name of Excellence: The Struggle to Reform the Nation's Schools, Why It's Failing, and What Should Be Done* (New York: Oxford, 1991), and Fiske, *Smart Schools, Smart Kids: Why Do Some Schools Work?* (New York: Simon and Schuster, 1991). See also Chester E. Finn, Jr., *We Must Take Charge: Our Schools and Our Future* (New York: Free Press, 1991).

Chapter Three

1. In my consideration of Exhibitions, I am especially indebted to Arthur Powell, Grant Wiggins, Richard Lear, Joseph McDonald, Mary Hibert, Grace Taylor, Jill Davidson, and Howard Gardner and his colleagues at Harvard University's Project Zero. The Exhibitions in this book are not meant to cover fully the range of areas and topics that constitute a sound

secondary education. They serve as examples and stimuli. For an earlier argument for Exhibitions, see my *Horace's Compromise: The Dilemma of the American High School* (Boston: Houghton Mifflin, 1984, 1985), ch. 5. See also Arthur G. Powell, "Exhibitions of Mastery: Some Preliminary Considerations," unpublished manuscript, Coalition of Essential Schools, Brown University, 1986; Fred M. Newmann and D. Archbald, *Beyond Standardized Testing: Assessing Authentic Academic Achievement in the Secondary School* (Reston, VA: National Association of Secondary School Principals, 1988); Grant Wiggins, "Teaching to the (Authentic) Test," *Educational Leadership* (April 1989), p. 41; Grant Wiggins, "Rational Numbers: Toward Grading and Scoring That Help Rather Than Harm Learning," *American Educator* (Winter 1988), p. 20; Joseph P. McDonald, "Authentic Assessment from a School's Perspective," paper delivered at the American Educational Research Association, April 1991; and Kathleen Cushman, "Performances and Exhibitions: The Demonstration of Mastery," *Horace* (March 1990).

Chapter Four

1. The literature on individual differences is vast. Of most provocative recent interest are Howard Gardner, *Frames of Mind: The Theory of Multiple Intelligences* (New York: Basic Books, 1983); and Howard Gardner and Thomas Hatch, "Multiple Intelligences Go to School: Educational Implications of the Theory of Multiple Intelligences," *Educational Researcher* (November 1989), p. 4. On the topic of "learning styles," a useful summary of evidence is in Lynn Curry, "Learning Styles in Secondary Schools: A Review of Instruments and Implications for Their Use," unpublished manuscript, National Center on Effective Secondary Schools, University of Wisconsin, Madison, 1990. See also work at the National Association of Secondary School Principals, summarized in "Learning Styles: Key to Improving Schools and Student Achievement," NASSP Curriculum Report (January 1989).

2. See Howard Chudakoff, *How Old Are You? Age Consciousness in American Culture* (Princeton: Princeton University Press, 1989).

3. The literature on tracking is very large. Most important is Jeannie Oakes, *Keeping Track: How Schools Structure Inequality* (New Haven: Yale University Press, 1985). My argument here also draws from Arthur G. Powell, Eleanor Farrar, and David K. Cohen, *The Shopping Mall High School: Winners and Losers in the Educational Marketplace* (Boston: Houghton Mifflin, 1985), chs. 1, 4.

4. I am indebted to Debby Zuberbueler of San Antonio, Texas, for this anecdote.

5. Nancy Sizer has equipped me with this pedagogically useful historical anecdote. See her *Making Decisions: Cases for Moral Discussion* (Wellesley Hills, MA: Independent School Press, 1984), p. 157; and her *China: Tradition and Change* (New York and London: Longmans, 1991), p. 40.

6. Several school systems have honestly confronted tracking. See the Background Papers for the Panel on Tracking and Retention of the Boston Public Schools (1990–91).

7. Meaningful generalized pupil-to-teacher ratios for high schools are difficult to evolve, given the varied "loads" staff are expected to carry in different subject areas. Further, there are very large differences from school to school. On a rough average, however, the National Center for Educational Statistics projections in 1980 — about 16 to 1 — seem reasonable. See *The Condition of Education: 1980* (Washington, DC: U.S. Government Printing Office, 1980), p. 71.

Chapter Five

1. I have earlier sorted out "sense of agency" in my *Places for Learning, Places for Joy: Speculations on American School Reform* (Cambridge: Harvard University Press, 1972), Part II.
2. Foxfire is the program started over twenty-five years ago by Eliot Wigginton in Rabun Gap, Georgia. See his (and his students') *Foxfire: 25 Years* (New York: Doubleday, 1991).

Chapter Six

1. The importance of habits has been effectively pressed on me at the Coalition of Essential Schools by Grant Wiggins and by Deborah Meier and her colleagues at New York City's Central Park East Secondary School. John Dewey's writing undergirds much of our thinking: *Human Nature and Conduct* (New York: Random House, 1922), Part I.
2. Dewey, p. 42.
3. See Rexford Brown, *Schools of Thought: How the Politics of Literacy Shape Thinking in the Classroom* (San Francisco: Jossey-Bass, 1991).

Chapter Seven

1. See John Goodlad, *A Place Called School* (New York: McGraw-Hill, 1983) ch. 4.
2. Apprenticeship is getting a fresh look from cognitive scientists. See Howard Gardner, *The Unschooled Mind: How Children Think and How Schools Should Teach* (New York: Basic Books, 1991), ch. 12.
3. See several articles by Fred M. Newmann: "Higher Order Thinking in Teaching Social Studies: A Rationale for the Assessment of Classroom Thoughtfulness," *Journal of Curriculum Studies* (Jan.–Feb. 1990), pp. 41–56; "Qualities of Thoughtful Social Studies Classes: An Empirical Profile," *Journal of Curriculum Studies* (May–June 1990), pp. 253–275; "Promoting Higher Order Thinking in Social Studies: Overview of a Study of Sixteen High School Departments," in *Theory and Research in Social Education* (in press); and "The Prospects for Classroom Thoughtfulness in High School Social Studies," in *Building the Quality of Thinking in and out of Our Schools in the Twenty-First Century,* edited by C. Collins and J. N. Mangieri (Hillsdale, NJ: Lawrence Erlbaum Associates, in press).
4. Fred M. Newmann, "Linking Restructuring to Authentic Student Achievement," *Phi Delta Kappan* (Feb. 1991), pp. 458–463.
5. There is a growing and encouraging literature on "collaborative educa-

tion," much dependent on the research of Robert E. Slavin. Two of his early articles have been especially influential: "When Does Cooperative Learning Increase Student Achievement?" *Psychological Bulletin* 2 (1983), p. 429 et seq.; and "Cooperative Learning and the Cooperative School," *Educational Leadership* (Nov. 1987), pp. 7–13. Edward B. Fiske in *Smart Schools, Smart Kids: Why Do Some Schools Work?* (New York: Simon and Schuster, 1991), pp. 81–86, summarizes much of the current argument and highlights the important research of Roger and David Johnson of the University of Minnesota. See also Fred M. Newmann and Judith A. Thompson, "Effects of Cooperative Learning on Achievement in Secondary Schools: A Summary of Research," unpublished manuscript, National Center on Effective Secondary Schools, University of Wisconsin, Madison, 1987.

6. See Mortimer Adler, *The Paideia Proposal: An Educational Manifesto* (New York: Macmillan, 1982).

7. On assessment of Essential Schools and related matters of evaluation, see Kathleen Cushman, *Horace* (September 1991).

Chapter Eight

1. See Arthur G. Powell, Eleanor Farrar, and David K. Cohen, *The Shopping Mall High School: Winners and Losers in the Educational Marketplace* (Boston: Houghton Mifflin, 1985), ch. 5.

2. For example, see Chester E. Finn, Jr., *We Must Take Charge: Our Schools and Our Future* (New York: Free Press, 1991), Part I.

3. The 1991 (unpublished) proposal for a National Examination System of the National Center on Education and the Economy in Rochester, New York, is notable.

4. The literature criticizing many conventional tests is large and growing. Some of it is contemptuous (for example, David Owen, *None of the Above: Behind the Myth of Scholastic Aptitude* [Boston: Houghton Mifflin, 1985]); some is technical (for example, three articles in the June–July 1991 issue of *Educational Researcher* [pp. 2–20]: Thomas Haladyna, Susan Bobbitt Nolan, and Nancy S. Haas, "Raising Standardized Achievement Test Scores and the Origins of Test Score Pollution"; Mary Lee Smith, "Put to the Test: The Effects of External Testing on Teachers"; and Scott G. Paris et al., "A Developmental Perspective on Standardized Achievement Testing"). On how increased testing has played out in school policy and practice during the 1980s, see Thomas Toch, *In the Name of Excellence: The Struggle to Reform the Nation's Schools, Why It's Failing and What Should Be Done* (New York: Oxford, 1991), ch. 6; and Edward B. Fiske, *Smart Schools, Smart Kids: Why Do Some Schools Work?* (New York: Simon and Schuster, 1991), ch. 5.

5. See George Madaus and Thomas Kellaghan, "Student Examination Systems in the European Community: Lessons for the United States," report submitted to the Office of Technology Assessment, U.S. Congress, June 1991.

6. See Baird W. Whitlock, *Don't Hold Them Back* (New York: College Entrance Examination Board, 1978); and National Center on Education and

the Economy, "America's Choice: High Skills or Low Wages?" June 1990. I have been much influenced by personal experience with VI Form studies in Australia and " Sixth Form Colleges" in the British system generally.

Chapter Nine

1. Chester E. Finn, Jr., *We Must Take Charge: Our Schools and Our Future* (New York: Free Press, 1991), p. 27.

Chapter Ten

1. American Association for the Advancement of Science (AAAS), *Science for All Americans* (Washington, DC, AAAS, 1989), p. 20.
2. National Research Council (NRC), *Everybody Counts: A Report on the Future of Mathematics Education* (Washington: National Academy Press, 1989), *Summary,* p. 15.
3. National Assessment of Educational Progress (NAEP), *Accelerating Academic Achievement* (Princeton: Educational Testing Service, 1990), p. 72.
4. NAEP, 73.
5. National Science Teachers Association (NSTA), "Scope, Sequence, and Coordination of Secondary Science: A Rationale," unpublished manuscript, May 10, 1990, p. 2.
6. NSTA, 1.
7. AAAS, 4, 5.
8. Committee on High-School Biology Education (CHSBE), *Fulfilling the Promise: Biology Education in the Nation's Schools* (Washington, DC: National Academy Press, 1990), p. 105.
9. CHSBE, 83; AAAS, 3; Bradley Commission on History in Schools (Washington, DC: Educational Excellence Network, 1988), pp. 7, 10–11; National Commission on Social Studies in the Schools (NCSSS), "Charting a Course: Social Studies for the 21st Century" (Washington, DC: NCSSS, 1989), ix.
10. AAAS, Part II.
11. Philip Phenix, *Realms of Meaning: A Philosophy of the Curriculum for General Education* (New York: McGraw-Hill, 1964), chs. 1, 12, 13, 14, 15; Howard Gardner, *Frames of Mind: The Theory of Multiple Intelligences* (New York: Basic Books, 1983), ch. 1.
12. College Entrance Examination Board, "Academic Preparation in the Arts: Teaching for Transition from High School to College" (New York: CEEB, 1985), Part III.
13. Elliot W. Eisner, "Why Art in Education and Why Art Education," in *The Place of Art in America's Schools* (Los Angeles: The Getty Center for Education in the Arts, 1985), pp. 68–69.
14. Ibid., p. 65.
15. NCSSS, 6 et seq.
16. NCSSS, 7 et seq.
17. See Stephen F. Hamilton, *Apprenticeship for Adulthood: Preparing Youth for the Future* (New York: Free Press, 1990), chs. 7, 8.
18. See Appendix B.

Notes

19. See Appendix B.
20. A vigorous case for a longer school year has been made by Michael J. Barrett, "The Case for More School Days," *The Atlantic* (November 1990), p. 78.

Chapter Eleven

1. On these matters of policy, I am grateful for the counsel of Frank Newman, President of the Education Commission of the States. I have also been continually but constructively discomforted by the counsel of Seymour B. Sarason. See his *The Predictable Failure of Educational Reform* (San Francisco: Jossey-Bass, 1990).
2. Many states fail to provide for equitable — or overall sufficient — funding. See Jonathan Kozol, *Savage Inequalities: Children in America's Schools* (New York: Crown, 1991).
3. Beverly Anderson of Education Commission of the States, private communication.
4. See, for example, John E. Chubb and Terry M. Moe, *Politics, Markets and America's Schools* (Washington, DC: The Brookings Institution, 1990).
5. Arthur G. Powell, Eleanor Farrar, and David K. Cohen, *The Shopping Mall High School: Winners and Losers in the Educational Marketplace* (Boston: Houghton Mifflin, 1985), ch. 3.
6. See Peter L. Berger and Richard John Neuhaus, *To Empower People: The Role of Mediating Structures in Public Policy* (Washington, DC: American Enterprise Institute, 1977); David S. Seeley, *Education Through Partnership: Mediating Structures and Education* (Cambridge, MA: Ballinger, 1981); and my chapter, "Public Literacy: Puzzlements of a High School Watcher," in *The Right to Literacy,* edited by Andrea A. Lunsford, Helene Moglen, and James Slevin (New York: Modern Language Association, 1990), pp. 9–12.

Chapter Twelve

1. The idea for a free-standing qualification for high school graduation is not new. Millions have taken the GED (General Educational Development) tests, offered since the late 1940s by the American Council on Education. All ultimately depends, of course, on the sensitivity and rigor of the Exhibitions. See my "Changing Schools and Testing: An Uneasy Proposal," paper presented at the ETS Invitational Conference, October 26, 1985; reprinted by ETS, 1985.
2. One such entrepreneur — Christopher Whittle — has already launched his ambitious Edison Project of newly designed schools. Whittle sees two hundred of his for-profit schools functioning by the mid-1990s.